I0031757

Greening the Black Urban Regime

GREAT LAKES BOOKS

A complete listing of the books in this series can be found online at
wsupress.wayne.edu

Editor

Thomas Klug
Sterling Heights, Michigan

Greening the Black Urban Regime

The Culture and Commerce of Sustainability in Detroit

Alesia Montgomery

WAYNE STATE UNIVERSITY PRESS
DETROIT

© 2020 by Alesia Montgomery. All rights reserved. No part of this book may be reproduced without formal permission.

ISBN 978-0-8143-4651-8 (paperback)
ISBN 978-0-8143-4650-1 (hardcover)
ISBN 978-0-8143-4652-5 (e-book)

Library of Congress Control Number: 2020933976

Wayne State University Press
Leonard N. Simons Building
4809 Woodward Avenue
Detroit, Michigan 48201-1309

Visit us online at wsupress.wayne.edu

In memory of my parents, Minnie Louise and Carl Lee Montgomery, and their generation of dreamers, strivers, and fighters, to whom we owe everything

Contents

Acknowledgments

FIRST AND FOREMOST, I am grateful to Cheryl Danley, Lionel Williams, and Ileana Cortez—my guides into the "interior architecture" of Detroit. Their research assistance in the early stages of my project made this book possible. Cheryl, a scholar who has worked on health and agriculture issues in the U.S. and South Africa, taught me about the food justice movement in Detroit and introduced me to key players in that movement. She also helped me to do oral histories and to familiarize myself with the streets of Detroit. Many thanks for your help, Cheryl—I enormously benefited from your knowledge and expertise. Lionel and Ileana were my students at MSU, but I was their student in Detroit. Lionel, thank you for your hard work doing interviews and for your insights about Detroit's black neighborhoods. Ileana, thank you for gathering interviews and information about immigrant communities and radical movements in Detroit. You bluntly told me that Detroit had been a victim of "drive-by research" and that I needed to move to the city if I wanted to understand its streets. I am glad that I took your advice and overcame my fear of snowy commutes. Yes, Californians *can* learn to drive in Michigan winters!

I also am grateful to the Detroit groups who invited me to discuss my research. I shared my preliminary findings at a meeting of the Detroit Food Justice Task Force at Cass Corridor Commons; a gathering of neighborhood groups organized by Building Movement at Central United Methodist Church; a panel at the People's Platform Convention at Marygrove College; a meeting of Catholic religious women and men's communities at the Samaritan Center; and a panel at the Arts in a Changing America conference at the Charles H. Wright Museum of African American History. These gatherings gave me encouragement and critique that helped me to push on, revise some of my conclusions, and complete the manuscript.

I appreciate everyone at Wayne State Press who helped me to bring this book into being. I particularly thank Annie Martin, the editor-in-chief who championed my project and gave great advice; Carrie Teefey, the senior production editor who listened to my requests and skillfully moved my project forward; and Dawn Hall, the copy editor whose attention to detail was much appreciated. My thanks also to the anonymous reviewers of the manuscript, who gave me excellent suggestions. I also am indebted to the journal editors and peer reviewers who gave feedback on earlier versions of my work. Some chapters include excerpts of my articles in the *International Journal of Urban and Regional Research*, *Antipode*, *Ethnography*, and the *Michigan Quarterly Review*.

A special note of thanks to Donna Snowden, who gave permission for me to use art by her sister, the late Gilda Snowden, for the book cover. Born and raised in Detroit, Gilda Snowden was an African American abstract painter whose *Flora Urbana* series was inspired by the community gardens of Detroit. I became familiar with her work while researching the history of the Corridor; she had been part of the Corridor art scene during the 1970s and 1980s. Snowden served as a professor in the Department of Fine Arts at the College for Creative Studies in Detroit, where she influenced generations of artists. Coincidentally, Tracy Cox, the designer that Wayne State Press hired to craft the cover, was one of her former students. I sought Snowden's art for the cover because her abstraction of gardens, open to multiple interpretations, provokes reflection. I do not seek to have the final word about ecological urbanism. I want *Greening the Black Urban Regime* to stir thought and debate about the future of cities.

Last but not least, I thank my family: my brothers Ronald, Bucky, and BB; Cousin Patty (the keeper of our family recipes who also serves up food for thought); Mrs. Moore (my mother's best friend and my "other mother"); the children and partners and buddies and dogs with whom we share our lives; and the spirits of our parents and all the ancestors who warm our hearts. Your brilliance is my North Star.

TABLE 1. **Greening timeline**

Date	Detroit	United States	Global
1980s	Gardening Angels transform vacant lots under Mayor Coleman Young's Farm-A-Lot program	Reagan-Bush years	Landless Workers Movement (MST) founded in Brazil
	Greening of Detroit founded	Whole Foods Market founded	1987 Brundtland Report warns of climate change
1990	**Population: 1,027,974** *(down from 2 million in 1950)*		
	Marie Farrell-Donaldson, city ombudsman, proposes "mothballing" high vacancy areas	National People of Color Environmental Leadership Summit writes "Principles of Environmental Justice"	1992 UN "Earth Summit" urges cities to consider threats to ecosystems and vulnerable groups (Rio de Janeiro, Brazil)
	Mayor Coleman Young retires	Congress for New Urbanism advocates mixed use, walkable neighborhoods	
	Dennis Archer becomes mayor	Bill Clinton becomes president (1993)	
	Midtown Detroit Incorporated (MDI) develops plan to revitalize "Eds and Meds" hub near downtown	Trend of downtown gentrification in US central cities	

(continued)

TABLE 1. **Greening timeline** *(continued)*

Date	Detroit	United States	Global
2000	**Population: 951,270**	George W. Bush becomes president (2001)	2002 UN World Summit on Sustainable Development (Johannesburg, South Africa)
	Archer negotiates Compuware move to downtown, agreeing to renovate Campus Martius as anchor for mixed-use enclave	Hurricane Katrina hits New Orleans (2005)	Abahlali baseMjondolo (Shack Dwellers) movement begins in Durban, South Africa
		Great Recession begins (2007)	
	Kwame Kilpatrick becomes mayor in 2002; approves a risky Wall Street deal that proves disastrous for city when Great Recession hits; resigns in 2008 amid sex and bribery scandal	Barack Obama becomes president (2009); signs American Recovery and Reinvestment Act, funding green projects	*Reaja ou Será Morto* (React or Die) issues manifesto against police violence in Brazil
	Detroit Black Community Food Security Network (DBCFSN) & D-Town Farm founded	Harvard Graduate School of Design holds conference and publishes edited volume on "ecological urbanism" (2009)	

Date	Detroit	United States	Global
2010	**Population: 713,777**		
	Dave Bing finishes mayoral term of Kilpatrick then elected to full term as mayor, which begins in 2010		2012 UN World Summit on Sustainable Development (Rio de Janeiro, Brazil)
	Billionaire Dan Gilbert moves Rock Ventures headquarters downtown and begins buying buildings; downtown gentrifies		
	US Social Forum (USSF) 2010 held downtown		
	Detroit Works Project (2010–2012)	Obama Administration forms federal-local partnership with Detroit (2011–2016)	
	Emergency manager appointed (March 2013); city declares bankruptcy (July 2013)	Black Lives Matter organizing begins after acquittal in Trayvon Martin case	*Reaja ou Será Morto* (React or Die) holds March Against Genocide of Black People in Salvador, Brazil
	Detroit Future City opens implementation office		
	Mike Duggan becomes first white mayor in 40 years (2014)	Flint water crisis begins	

(continued)

TABLE 1. Greening timeline *(continued)*

Date	Detroit	United States	Global
	Emergency manager approves DWSD mass water shutoffs for non-payment		
	Street protests against water shutoffs; UN reps visit Detroit stating that cutting off water to poor violates human rights		
	End of Detroit bankruptcy, with "Grand Bargain" (2014)		
	Great Lakes Water Authority (GLWA) established, regionalizing water control	Trump becomes president; rolls back environmental protections (2017)	
	Fight for Community Benefits Agreements (CBA)	Amazon acquires Whole Foods Market	
	DBCFSN announces plan to open Food Cooperative in North End	Newly elected progressives in US Congress call for a Green New Deal	Jair Bolsonaro, the far right newly elected president of Brazil, calls for end to protection of indigenous land in Amazon rainforest

I

Empire and the Garden

Why Doesn't Black Political Power Save Black Lives?

A THIN BLACK woman clutched a coat that hung off her shoulder. She walked up to me before daylight at the corner of Woodward and State Street: "Sista, can you help me out with a quarter?" She said that she had not eaten in days. An engine stalled in the dark, perhaps around the corner on Griswold where the strip club—with its light box sign of naked silhouettes—had not yet been evicted by a suspicious fire and the Thai café and the Botox clinic had not yet come and the homeless still slept outside abandoned buildings. Griswold was the past; Woodward bore signs of the future. I asked the woman if she wanted to go to a store on Woodward that was open at this hour; it had begun to stock sandwiches and fruit as entrepreneurs and engineers, including black geeks, moved into downtown Detroit. I was walking to the store before I drove to teach my urban studies class in East Lansing. A year earlier, when I had moved here in 2010, the store had little food other than chips and candy. There had been little foot traffic. An African American baker whose beautiful cakes sat unsold had closed her shop on my block.

Then organic food shops opened—promoted via social media to young suburbanites—and a buzz began that Detroit was "coming back." Like the downtowns of majority black cities such as Baltimore and Cleveland, downtown Detroit is gentrifying. Across these places, the culture and commerce of sustainability draw newcomers. Boosters strive to rebrand these once prosperous industrial hubs—stigmatized for years as "black ghettos"—as green cities. This book describes the struggle to shape green redevelopment in Detroit as its rule by an unbroken line of black mayors comes to an end and the return of capital and the middle class unfolds. The history of race and class in the United States influences how Detroiters see and take sides in this struggle. The decades of hostility between the black and white residents of the region shape the main narrative, yet indigenous, Asian, Arab, and Latinx people who live here—and members of global design firms and the transnational green movement who pass through—add to the conflict and how it is framed. Opposing sides express environmental concern and use *justice-speak* (talk of justice) to legitimate their aims; they do not mean the same thing. As activists defend democracy and fight for a Green New Deal nationwide, the greening of Detroit holds lessons.

In the 1950s, Detroit auto executives and their gloved wives brushed shoulders on downtown streets with women and men who built cars at Dodge Main and River Rouge. Those auto workers—the aristocracy of labor—shopping in elegant stores with marble floors and elevator operators, included perhaps the grandparents of the woman who asked me for a quarter. On those long-ago streets, black auto workers faced discrimination, but some of them earned enough to buy a taste of the American dream. The dream faded as industry left and vacant storefronts spread: the baker had run her shop in a corner of the shell that was once the grand Kresge department store. As capital returned to the central business district in the 2000s, the grandchildren of the auto executives and the workers walked on remade streets; upscale lofts opened and billionaire Dan Gilbert relocated his umbrella of firms here. In 2010, the mayor announced the Detroit Works Project—a public-private alliance with a dream team of international consultants—to redesign the city. The project was led by Toni Griffin, a black architect who headed the J. Max Bond Center on Design for the Just City at City College of New York. The center was named after a legendary black architect who—battling racism that limited life chances in black neighborhoods and his own career—advocated community control of planning in Harlem during the 1960s. In 2013, Detroit Works released a plan, paid for largely by a foundation set up in the 1920s by Sebastian Kresge, the founder of Kresge department store. The foundation had grown to hold $3.1 billion in assets. Kresge—once synonymous with the shopping pleasures of industrial Detroit, now a key player in urban greening—has funded Notre Dame's Global Adaptation Institute, which evaluates vulnerabilities to climate disasters, and Kresge also has supported the Georgetown Climate Center, which maintains a database to help cities adapt to climate change. The Detroit Works plan calls for an (ecologically, financially) green future city that revives the entrepreneurial spirit of old Detroit without its social and environmental ills. Praised for its innovations and outreach, the plan has won awards from the Michigan chapters of the American Planning Association and the American Society of Landscape Architects. Even before the plan, an urban garden and new cafés appeared downtown. A vacant building—the M@dison—became a space for tech firms. Twitter opened offices there. The streets were still empty on weekends when the commuters were gone, but young white people began to stop me outside my building, asking about vacancies—the staff started a waiting list. One late afternoon, as a warm summer rain started to fall, a young man with a mass of black curls (white, black, biracial?) in a dinner jacket played a saxophone on a corner. Hopeful headlines buried bad news. As the governor appointed an emergency manager to run Detroit and the city fell into bankruptcy, the central business district boomed—speedboats carved the Detroit River under blue skies.

But hunger was still here. In the store, the woman told me that she had "prayed to God" for food so that she wouldn't have to "go with the rapists." To get food and a place to stay, she had to "go with" men, and once she had to jump out of a window to get away. As we left the store, the woman pressed her cheek against mine as though we were sista friends leaving a church picnic or house party, sure to see each other again. I watched her disappear into the darkness. As gentrification and policing intensified in the central business district, I saw fewer street people downtown, but statistics showed that roughly 35 percent of Detroiters—including almost half of children—lived below the official poverty line.[1] On these pages I describe the challenges of black Detroiters who live in poverty, but this is not another book about greenwashing or gentrification or eviction or harsh policing. I want to understand the root causes of these dangers, which requires studying the ability of different classes of African Americans to shape urban futures. Since the 1968 Kerner Report, commissioned by President Lyndon Johnson to explain the fiery rebellions in Detroit and other cities, problems in low-income black neighborhoods have been the topics of countless books. Yet government support has faded for the reforms urged in these works, even in cities with black mayors.

At the headquarters of an environmental justice group, the activist Charity Hicks told me about the lives of the jobless and the working poor in Detroit. She said that developers and planners (including the old guard black elite) treated these people as "dredges." Hicks—a dark, powerfully built woman in

Comparison of the intersection of Woodward and State Street in 2012 and 2018 (*facing north*). In 2012, there was little foot traffic, but young entrepreneurs and professionals had begun to move in. By 2018, new shops opened and foot traffic increased.

A view of Woodward and State Street (*facing south*). In 2012, faint letters were visible on a defunct restaurant. The empty building next to it on the corner was the old Kresge store, which developer Dan Gilbert bought in 2012. Before his purchase, small shops—including a bakery and a handbag store—constantly opened and then vanished from the first floor. By 2018, Under Armour, a chain store, came to the Kresge site. Across the street, in another building bought by Gilbert, Avalon—an organic bakery—opened a branch.

a blue African headwrap and dress—reminded me of street art in Cuba and Brazil of *Yemoja*, the mother spirit of oceans and rivers. She had served on the advisory board for Detroit Works, but she began to criticize the project for being undemocratic and for failing to prioritize the needs of low-income people. The project promoted itself as inclusive but it was, she argued, "running a game on the people." Born in Detroit, she said that she had faced hard times in her own life. Then she lifted her chin and spoke about the power of people who are called "dredges" to transform the world. Hicks saw the African diaspora as coming out of a history of struggle in which we used our power, generation after generation, to bring about a "culture shift." For us to activate this power, Hicks said that we must invest in one another, and we must see ourselves as agents of change and reimagine the earth. Giving food (as I did) is inadequate to build the relations of respect and co-creation that we need to save one another. The threats to life on our streets cannot be solved by representing black bodies as the problem and handouts as the solution (the message of "poverty porn"). Hicks's work included serving on the Detroit Food Policy Council, the Detroit Black Community Food Security Network, and D-Town urban farm. She viewed food and water insecurity as outcomes of violent (mental | material) systems that break down the social and ecological relations needed for life.[2] Hicks had traveled to Brazil—the country with the largest black population outside the African continent—to talk with organizers of the Landless Workers Movement (*Movimento dos Trabalhadores Rurais Sem Terra*): "I slept on the floor in Brazil . . . hang[ing] out with rural Brazilian women . . . who rush to São Paulo . . . or . . . Rio . . . and they were living in those *favelas* [informal settlements] . . . they have no infrastructure, they don't own the land . . . all these wealth-ass white Brazilians own fucking two-thirds of all the land."[3] The battles differed in Detroit and São Paulo, but there was the same centuries-old struggle of the African diaspora for *spatial agency*: the ability to be in, act on, and exert control over the built-and-natural environment and its temporalities—the land use plan, the daily round, the remembrance and re-vision of place. Across places, Hicks spoke in down-to-earth terms about environmental justice and climate change. She said, "Climate in Detroit is rooted in the lived experience of our people. It's not tree-hugging or kayaking. . . . Did your pipes just burst? Climate is the hundreds of people whose pipes burst because of the polar vortex. . . . [W]hen someone has a heart attack and dies shoveling snow, that's climate. It goes from city services to our individual quality of life."[4] Hicks urged us to hold government officials accountable: "If you are afraid to go to an elected servant and say, 'This is what we demand,' you're already defeated."[5] She was known as a "water warrior," battling water shutoffs in low-income neighborhoods of Detroit. This work led to her arrest in 2014:

> Think of Charity Hicks as the Rosa Parks of the Detroit Water Struggle. She was arrested in Detroit early on May 16 for resisting the shut off of her own water [and that of her neighbors] . . . she went door to door rousing people to say: "He's coming; fill your tub, fill pots and pans!"[6]

Hicks died weeks later—struck by a hit-and-run driver in New York as she waited at a bus stop to go to the Left Forum, where she was scheduled to be on a panel. Her life inspires artists, clergy, and street scholars who organize to end food and water insecurity. These cultural workers also fight climate change, warning that it poses threats to all and that the *climate gap* across races and classes in climate change impacts worsens the dangers black and low-income Detroiters face.[7] If steps to reduce these impacts are not taken, the severity of summer heat and winter storms in Detroit will increase weather-related deaths, interacting with the normalized crises of militarized policing; disparate exposure to toxic hazards; and unequal access to water, food, housing, and transportation.[8] To build movement, cultural workers craft spaces with pleasures (poetry, music, murals, gardens) that feed not only hunger for bread but also longings for communion—beautiful spaces of laughter and song and work and elders and babies and youths that recall the real-and-imagined community before the industrial city.

I hear gentrifiers of all races (drawn to the street art and the gardens but steering clear of the social critique and the radical action) say that talk of food problems in Detroit is wrong, as—blind to their narcissism—they rattle off tasty meals that *they've* eaten as proof.[9] It *is* a myth that all of Detroit is a "food desert," but suggesting the entire city is a food oasis is equally misleading— sweet talk by gentrifiers who frame themselves as defenders of the new Detroit and its image. Stories of their goodness, their enterprise, and their pleasures— read as signs that Detroit is "coming back"—are changing the city's bad press.

Forbes hails "Detroit 2.0"—the rise of a new downtown with high-tech firms.[10] The *New York Times* raves: "As capitalism returns to Detroit's downtown in all its feverish forms, you can see the city materialize before your eyes. It's like watching hot lava cool."[11] *Saveur* salutes Detroit's "revved-up food scene"[12]— *Reuters* declares it a "food revolution"[13]—flavored by urban farms, farmers markets, and organic restaurateurs. On spring mornings, as the sun rises on the river, the aromas of baking bread, scrambled eggs, sizzling bacon, and hot coffee pull newcomers into new cafés. The same aromas drifted from cafés during Detroit's heyday, but menus now list bread as "organic," eggs "cage-free," bacon "locally butchered," and coffee "fair trade." On winter nights— when Arctic winds, sweeping down from Canada, freeze the streets to black ice—free hot cider draws newcomers into shops that hawk warm coats and snow boots. Timeless gear, but the brands now boast "recycled" and "cruelty free" materials. Mindfulness is cultivated at studios that offer guided meditation and breath work. These practices (often satirized) are not the problem; self-care and kindness help to sustain social movements. The problem is that when these practices take place on streets cleansed of the appearance but not the reality of trouble, the inward gaze—(re)imagining the self in nostalgic relation to the pristine wilderness or the family farm—can become alienated from the here-and-now relations among self, others, and the earth. Boosters tout the eco-friendliness of the new downtown, with its light rail and bike share stations, but its livability differs at the intersection of race, class, and gender. At the start of green redevelopment, perhaps on a night that the smiling staff of my upscale loft offered hot cocoa to residents, a sixty-year-old homeless woman froze to death in a doorway around the corner.[14] The environmental modernization of old industrial cities appears to create a new moral order, yet its blind spot is deadly.

I question the social awareness of today's urban greening, but I do not deny the need for earth conscious redevelopment. Daily routines distract from news of the growing threat: wildfires devour homes in Los Angeles, floods fill subways in New York, boats rescue families in Houston, and hospitals go dark as winds rip power lines in San Juan.[15] The National Centers for Environmental Information estimates that, in 2017 alone, there were sixteen weather and climate disaster events in the United States that each had losses over $1 billion.[16]

MoGo Bike Share Station at Grand Circus Park—a sign of the new, eco-friendly Detroit. Launched in 2017, MoGo—a nonprofit affiliate of the Downtown Detroit Partnership (DDP)—collaborates with the City of Detroit Department of Transportation.

This estimate does not take into account that the burden of these crises falls disproportionately on impoverished and stigmatized individuals for whom life had been a struggle (materially, psychologically) before the "natural" disaster hit. Detroit has less exposure to climate change impacts than cities at risk of hurricanes and wildfires. For its gentrifiers, it is a relatively safe place to be. However, Detroit's high poverty rates make many residents particularly vulnerable to severe weather. Everyone is put at risk by environmental degradation, but oppressive structures of race, gender, class, sexuality, and immigrant status increase risk.

As Detroit "comes back," efforts by race-class groups to reduce their environmental risks and realize their ecological visions must contend with trends in income and wealth distribution. Since the mid-twentieth century—the days when auto executives and workers brushed shoulders at downtown department stores in Detroit—the power of organized labor has declined and income inequality has increased. The return of capital to the urban core reduces physical but not social distances between race-class groups. Between 1979 and 2007, the top earning 1 percent of US households enjoyed an average 275 percent increase in their incomes (after federal taxes), while middle- and low-income households saw much smaller increases (roughly 40 percent and 18 percent, respectively).[17] Changes in the global economy, state and local government employment, and federal and corporate policies drive these inequalities. Tax cuts have benefited top executives while their employees—especially those in working-class jobs—have suffered from the reduced bargaining power of labor. Black workers, disproportionately concentrated in the most vulnerable public- and private-sector jobs, have been particularly harmed. Beyond contending with structural changes in the economy, African Americans face persistent job discrimination: audit experiments in Milwaukee and New York during the 2000s revealed that black men with no criminal records fared no better in getting job callbacks than white men fresh out of prison even when they had the same qualifications.[18] Yet the civil rights struggles of the 1960s—the decade in which the architect Max Bond fought for Harlem—have helped some African Americans (including the black planners and architects on the Detroit Works team) to enter high-paying professions. In 2016, African Americans in the top 10 percent of the income distribution earned 9.8 times more than African Americans in the bottom 10 percent.[19] Compared to the income gap among African Americans, the income gap among whites (7.8) was smaller but still substantial. Wealth disparities are even more striking: in 2013, 1 percent of US households owned 37 percent of the wealth.[20] African Americans tend to have much less wealth than whites; the history of housing and job discrimination limits the transfer of intergenerational assets.[21] Thus, compared with their white peers, even top-earning black professionals tend to have less capital for entrepreneurial ventures and to buffer hard times. In 2007, Detroit had a higher percentage of black-owned businesses (64 percent) than other large US cities, but their profitability was hindered by their limited capital and their segregated locations, which limited their revenues and their ability to withstand the Great Recession (recall the baker on my block who went out of business just before the return of professionals increased moneyed foot traffic).[22] The Great Recession hit hard in Detroit, reducing black wealth and tax revenues in the city as families lost jobs and homes.[23] Detroit's fiscal crisis intensified as the state eased its own fiscal troubles by reducing revenue sharing with the city.[24] The disparities in and across race-class groups—compounded by the Great Recession—shape a complex political dynamic as the white middle and upper classes return to the financial core of central cities, interacting with whites (some destitute) who never left these cities and African Americans of all classes (including black gentrifiers and an affluent old guard with long-established enclaves).

In Detroit, political and economic elites harness technical experts (planners, engineers, architects) and cultural workers (artists, clergy, street scholars). Cultural workers are used (1) to legitimate the green strategies of technical experts by framing them in justice-speak and (2) to engage people in green redevelopment through the crafting of spaces, narratives, and networks that captivate the senses and the heart and thus move people to action. The production of symbols by cultural workers—their transformation of bread into communion—adds value to urban markets even as it incites resistance to commodification. This cultural work increases the ability of low-income black Detroiters to creatively implement green plans, but decisions about the city's future remain top-down. During outreach for Detroit Works (the public-private partnership to redesign Detroit), Detroiters had opportunities to see expert presentations and to say their opinions, but there was no process for democratic decision-making. The mayor served as spokesperson, but private foundations led the project. Detroit Works is not a government agency, and it did not produce an official plan; it is the "tip of an iceberg" of the maneuvers of business, financial, and philanthropic interests that preceded public outreach and proceeded after it ended. Redevelopment began before the Detroit Works redevelopment plan. Detroit Works is a vantage from which to glimpse the vast power reshaping Detroit and other central cities; it is not the base of that power.

I write this book as calls to revive the US economy—locked and loaded with a weaponized nostalgia ("Make America Great Again")—legitimate voter suppression, climate change denial, and racist attacks. Like Detroit's central business district, Wall Street has rebounded. This revival is a mirage. Reckless policy masquerades as fiscal conservatism, ignoring social and environmental degradations for which we must eventually pay.[25] Green rebranding in Michigan holds lessons; it is at once a primer on "alternative facts," a grammar on co-optation, and a testament to what Ralph Ellison's Invisible Man called the *boomerang* of history (a.k.a. progress as the return of the past). Years before the billionaire Manhattan developer, Donald Trump, became president by whipping up crowds with "alternative facts," the billionaire Detroit developer, Dan Gilbert, rebuilt downtown to counter bad press and make Detroit (appear) great again. Detroit is great, but its greatness does not reside in nice places for gentrifiers to eat and shop. It endures in the work of artists and engineers and labor leaders and community organizers who expand the possibilities for urban life. Misrepresentation begins by manipulating impressions: downtown embellishment makes lies about the city seem plausible. The undermining of democracy did not begin with Trump. Before the voice of untruth became violent and vulgar, it spoke in sweet tones in Michigan. Rick Snyder—the governor who appointed emergency managers to run Detroit and Flint—said as he left office that the "greatest threat to our country is our lack of civility."[26] Lack of civility is the greatest threat? During his administration, state officials had said that nothing was wrong when Flint residents had told them that their water (switched to the Flint River without proper treatment by a state-appointed emergency manager) was making them sick.

The shock of the Trump presidency makes peddlers of sugary civility seem defenders of truth and justice. But their gaslighting is not an antidote to Trump's lies. The indifference of elites is a bitter lesson, but it is even harder to admit co-optation of the grass roots. For decades, some Detroit activists have advocated community gardens and cooperative economics to increase collective well-being, strengthen community power, and create a new moral order. This advocacy has parallels from Harlem to Durban to São Paulo. The vision of these projects, prioritizing direct action over electoral politics, has been stolen and in some cases bought to serve a patronizing plan for uneven development that treats the black urban poor as children who can choose seed packets but cannot decide their future. Studying this co-optation leads to insight about the boomerang: even "new" ideas can reproduce past harms. Old (mental | material) structures reappear at the sites where they were torn down.

I am a middle-aged black woman, an ethnographer with one foot in the social sciences the other in the storytelling craft of the griot. For me, science is not divorced from critique, which is not stripped of toasts. My home is California, but as a black woman, I blended into life in Detroit. A Detroiter would have written a different book, enriched by her intimate knowledge of its streets. For a view from insiders, listen to Pearl Cleage[27] talk about her childhood or reflect on Maureen Taylor and Marian Kramer's words[28] about the history of struggle or study Monica White's writings[29] about black urban farmers or see Gilda Snowden's paintings[30] or think about Halima Cassells's creations[31] or watch dream hampton's films[32] or read Tawana Petty's[33] poetry or explore Maya Stovall's dissertation on "liquor store theatre."[34] My perspective is that of a familiar stranger. Similar to others in the diaspora who have passed through Detroit since the Underground Railroad, I am in search of freedom. My research emerges from that search.

I lived in and studied Detroit from 2010 to 2013, a pivotal time in the city's history. During this period, a citywide planning process began and ended, plans for the greater downtown were developed, pockets of greater downtown began to gentrify, and a battle to stop state takeover of the city was defeated. Before moving to Detroit in 2010, I had spent a few years collecting oral histories and getting to know the streets of Detroit. After leaving Detroit in 2013, I continued to visit and track developments, combining my case study with a comparison of the city plans of thirty-two US cities, including Detroit and the fourteen other cities that are *historical black urban regimes* (HBURs).[35] Modifying a term coined by Adolph Reed, I define an HBUR as a US city that by 1990 (1) had elected its first black mayor, (2) had roughly 40 percent or more black residents—a percentage large enough to sway local elections, and (3) had a total population over one hundred thousand. During the rise of HBURs in the 1970s and 1980s, black neighborhoods such as Harlem and South Central in majority white cities also elected black politicians and fought for community control, but they lacked the voting power to dominate city government. If the spatial agency of African Americans exists anywhere, one would expect to find it in the HBURs. The fifteen HBURs consist of historically important US cities: Atlanta, Baltimore, Birmingham, Chicago, Cleveland, Detroit, Gary, Hartford, New Orleans, Newark, Oakland, Philadelphia, Portsmouth, Richmond, and Washington, DC. The environmental struggles of African Americans in these cities go beyond fads for green lifestyles. By framing these cities as a set, we can learn from their struggles.

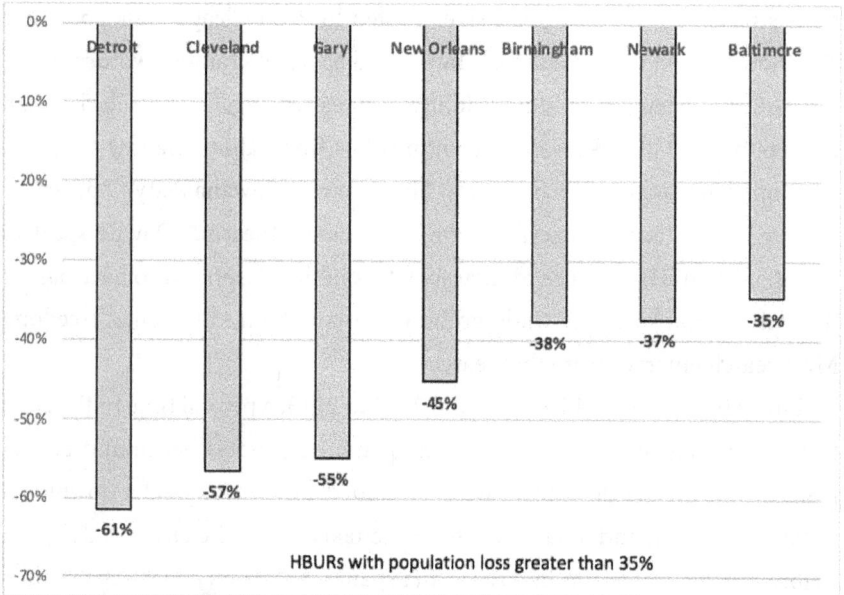

Graphic 1a. Historical Black Urban Regimes: % Population Loss Since Peak (2010). Source: US Census Bureau.

The fifteen HBURs differ in their economies, yet African Americans in these cities share common challenges. Oakland (my current home) is a major port and tech hub; Atlanta is an economic engine that connects the Deep South to global commerce; Chicago is a global city that serves as the headquarters for international corporations and financial and professional services firms; and Washington, DC, is the hub of the US government and its lobbyists. Gentrification and green city plans are further along in these four HBURs than in HBURs such as Detroit (synonymous with the auto industry) and Gary (dependent on steel), which suffered as shifts in the global economy hurt their key industry. Given that African Americans and political liberals are more likely to express concern about social equity, local hazards, and global climate change than do white/non-Hispanic individuals and political conservatives in the United States, one might expect that black political power, which supports liberal causes, forces the inclusion of environmental and equity goals in HBUR city plans.[36] However, quantitative research on this topic provides no evidence that the size of the local black population matters.[37] One might suppose that HBURs at least pay lip

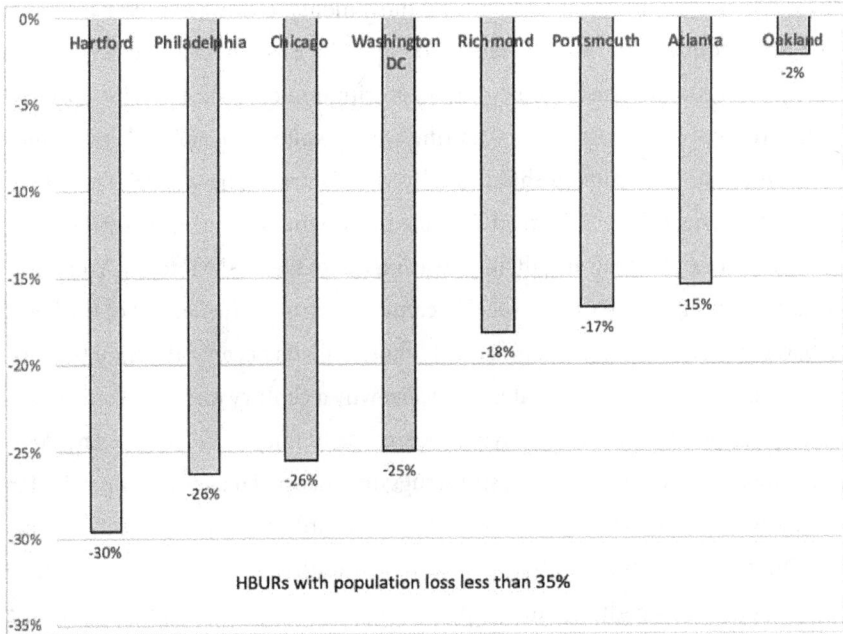

Graphic 1b. Historical Black Urban Regimes: % Population Loss Since Peak (2010). Source: US Census Bureau.

service to the concerns of their black residents, even when they do not outline goals to address these concerns. One would assume that black elected officials and technical experts feel pressure to use justice-speak. In my qualitative comparison of city plans, I examined whether the framing of goals—not the goals themselves—differs between HBURs and non-HBURs. I found that severely depopulated HBURs (losses over 35 percent) such as Detroit use more justice-speak. In contrast, the green discourse of HBURs such as Atlanta with population losses *under* 35 percent is like that of the whitest and the most politically conservative US cities. Oakland has a unique "earth friendly" lingo that advocates cultural change, but like Atlanta, it avoids justice-speak. The more gentrified HBURs draw selectively on the language of cultural workers: their planners associate greening with commerce, pleasure, and charity but not justice. As Detroit and other severely depopulated HBURs follow the path of more gentrified HBURs, their justice-speak—which supports political demands—may vanish.

For centuries, African diasporic movements have connected the cities that would become HBURs. Detroit—a station on the Underground Railroad—linked black abolitionists in the United States and Canada, and it remains at the heart of black political and cultural movements. During the 1960s, Broadside Press, founded in Detroit, helped to ignite the Black Arts Movement, while Motown—the most celebrated cultural contribution of black Detroit—fostered a shared lifeworld across cities. Chatting with a waiter at a café in a small midwestern town, I mentioned that I had lived in Detroit. The waiter's face lit up. He said, "I was raised 'n Detroit!" I asked him what part of the city. He said, "Oh no, I grew up in Savannah, but I was *raised on* Detroit! Motown! You know what I'm talking 'bout! Oooh weee!" I came to Detroit—the fiercest of the black urban regimes, a city much vilified yet whose ballads became the Soul of communities across the United States—to learn why a century and a half since slavery, five decades since black mayors took office in major US cities, many African Americans remain in crisis, still struggling for spatial agency. In particular, I want to understand how the recent move toward urban greening influences possibilities for agency. Other scholars have outlined the historical context: when black urban regimes came to power in the 1970s, African Americans, long denied civil rights, saw them as the "fulfillment of grand democratic ideals."[38] However, these victories coincided with global shifts in industry, which made it hard for black mayors to meet the demands of residents for jobs and services. Their challenges increased as white religious conservatives in the South and white economic conservatives in the North forged a coalition. Pandering to racists did not begin with the Trump administration. For decades, this coalition has demonized the black urban poor to justify *neoliberal* restructuring. By "neoliberal," I mean the return of the freewheeling capitalism—investing and disinvesting around the world with little regulation or taxes—that enriched nineteenth-century robber barons such as John D. Rockefeller, the oil magnate, and J. P. Morgan, the financier, during the Gilded Age. Social Darwinism—the belief (corrupted from Darwin's theory of natural selection) that some individuals, races, and nations are more "fit" to survive—interlocked with a market ideology to justify crimes against humanity. Neoliberal scholars tidy up this history. In a 1972 lecture, economist Milton Friedman states that capitalism integrates diverse people: "The market is color blind. No one who goes to the market to buy bread knows or cares whether the wheat was grown by a Jew, Catholic, Protestant, Muslim, or atheist; by whites or blacks."[39] Thus, the market is said to foster "peace" as people who "may even hate one another" exchange on the basis of self-interest. Neoliberal scholars also argue that private property promotes good environmental management: when no one owns a plot of land, the cost of using it is zero, which can lead to dumping and overexploitation.[40] These scholars concede that "a taste for discrimination" exists in the market and that the market imperfectly addresses pollution, yet they suggest that the market is a better remedy than the state for societal problems.[41] They see "no inconsistency between a free market system . . . and compassion," asserting that entrepreneurs lift living standards and enrich private charity.[42]

In this new Gilded Age, the geographer Jamie Peck and his colleagues call for studies of "actually existing neoliberalism" that "illuminate the complex, contested ways in which neoliberal restructuring strategies interact with pre-existing uses of space, institutional configurations, and constellations of sociopolitical power."[43] As climate change worsens, there is growing research on the interaction of the neoliberal order with the natural histories of cities. However, the interaction of the neoliberal order and the urban ecology with race-making histories is still (oddly) undertheorized, even though the market, race, and nature intertwine in cities. Various cities in the Americas were sited to further settler-colonialism and the slave trade. Brian Dunnigan, a curator of maps, concludes that the early Detroit's location was chosen (in part) because its high riverbank enabled a defensible fort.[44] Carl Anthony, an architect who cofounded Urban Habitat—an early environmental justice group—connects the rise of today's metropolises in the Americas to settler-colonialism, the plantation system, and ecological exploitation. The production of racial geographies to serve the market for furs, lumber, and cash crops sped the loss of biodiversity:

> The plantation served as a kind of open-air factory that consumed people and laid to waste the natural environment. . . . Whether it was cotton, rice, or sugar, its production involved a rudimentary form of industrial agriculture. Africans were thought of as beasts and treated accordingly. . . . Although their work was essential to creating the infrastructure that supported the emergence of city life, blacks were not allowed to share in the wealth they helped create . . . slave labor and the wealth generated from the crops produced by slaves provided the wherewithal to expand . . . the surrounding village and town economies . . . [and] the burgeoning international economy in the port cities along the Atlantic shorelines.[45]

Cities in the Americas predate European conquest.[46] Since the slave trade and colonial empires, cities in the Americas have been shaped by *racial capitalism*, with its militarization of space, its uneven development of communities, its demonization of the racialized, and its intensive exploitation of nature, which have combined to create categories of disposable life. I borrow the term "racial capitalism" from historian Cedric Robinson, who notes that, since the rise of the modern world system, the "development, organization, and expansion of capitalist society pursued essentially racial directions, so too did social ideology."[47] A free market that liberates people from racism is a beautiful utopian dream; for the African diaspora, it has not been historical reality. Consider the triangular trade of Europe, Africa, and the Americas in the eighteenth and nineteenth centuries: no one who went to the market to buy sugar cared that the sugar cane was grown by enslaved Africans (to recast Milton Friedman's dictum).[48] Subjected to floggings, rapes, and disease, packed together with little air, food, and water, an estimated two million Africans died crossing the Atlantic.[49] In the gamesmanship of financial speculation, some of the victims were "unloaded" as spoiled cargo:

On 6 September 1781 the [*Zong*], a [merchant ship] purchased by a Liverpool consortium, set sail from . . . the coast of West Africa with approximately 470 African slaves and seventeen whites on board. It was bound for the lucrative slave-markets of Jamaica. By 27 November, the ship had neared the island, when for an unclear reason, Captain Collingwood steered the ship to leeward. Two days later, realizing that he had missed Jamaica, that his supplies of water and food were running low, and that many of the Africans were dangerously ill, it appears that Collingwood made a cold calculation. The only way he would be able to guarantee a profit to himself, and for the Liverpool merchants for whom he was acting, was to jettison all the ship's sick Africans who were threatening the healthy by consuming the remaining supplies. The loss would be recovered by claiming them against the Zong's marine insurance policy. Over a period of days, Collingwood ordered 133 Africans thrown overboard.[50]

The women, men, and children of the *Zong*, thrown into the ocean day after day on the basis of cold calculation, reappear as hyperspeculation reassembles in our time to drive triage politics in cities. Then and now, the "reasonable" plan in crises is deadly; those placed in danger have no say—racialized as disposable, they are cast aside so that resources can be concentrated on those with market potential (the precariously fortunate). The "free" market could not impose this vicious order alone; for centuries, capitalists have petitioned the state to enforce this triage.

As HBURs replaced white supremacist urban regimes, racial hostilities sped up the out-migration of employers who had already begun to leave central cities in search of cheap land and a docile workforce. Racially motivated out-migration drove sprawl and its ecological damage. Seven of the fifteen HBURs are severely depopulated, having lost 35 percent or more of their residents. By 2010, Detroit had lost over half of its 1950 peak population of almost two million residents. Depopulated HBURs find it hard to maintain basic services in high poverty, high vacancy areas. Faced with fiscal challenges, black mayors have conceded power to corporations and foundations that fund urban projects.

Across cities, talk of *urban greening*—revitalizing old industrial cities with eco-friendly infrastructure, industries, and amenities—is popular. Green amenities, appealing to the eye, the taste buds, and the heart, reduce the "discursive redlining" of majority black areas.[51] Not all supporters of the new Detroit are white gentrifiers; there are new and longtime black residents who—tired of the decades of scorn that Detroit has suffered—embrace the change. A black fashion designer's downtown shop, serving environmentally and socially conscious consumers, proudly states on its window: "Détroit Is The New Black." To explain why some black Detroiters support the new regime, one must admit that developers and foundations have brought some beneficial changes to Detroit's streetscape. Market-driven green redevelopment makes steps toward climate change mitigation and adaptation, increases foot traffic in depressed commercial areas, and expands opportunities for some black professionals, entrepreneurs, and artists. Some middle-income residents enjoy better places to shop, and some low-income residents get fresh produce from new charities. However, deadly disparities persist. Boosters argue that the revival will eventually increase good jobs and housing for all and that the expanded tax base will be used to reduce inequities. Determining the truth of this argument—and intervening if it is false—requires a virtuous feedback loop, which some call democracy. It assumes that experts will analyze pertinent data, which will be reported by a free press. If problems exist, citizens will demand action from city officials, who will heed their concerns and join with them in problem solving.

This is not how things work. The US Environmental Protection Agency (EPA) defines sustainability as a balance of the "three Es"—economy, environment, and equity. However, equity typically gets scant mention in US city plans.[52] Cities with greater numbers of sustainability policies tend to be in the western United States (especially California) and to have higher resident incomes. Downtown Detroit aspires to the green amenities, high tech firms, and escalating rents of gentrified enclaves in the San Francisco Bay Area, where the affluent buy green, vote green, and fund green projects, and they speak much about being mindful of self, the other, and the earth. Nevertheless, low-income people (disproportionately people of color) in the Bay Area face not only toxic hazards but also housing and food insecurity.[53] Here in Oakland, I see housing costs drive black families out of the city, and I see black people living in tents, cars, and RVs along the freeways. According to the US Census Bureau, by 2010,

A new black-owned shop in downtown Detroit (2018).

the black population had dropped to 28 percent in Oakland (from a high of 47 percent in 1980). A 2017 study reports that roughly 70 percent of the homeless here are African American.[54] One might assume that the homeless are addicts or the mentally ill, but that is not always the case; some people simply can't pay rising rents. Even middle income folks—teachers, postal workers—find it hard to afford Oakland rent.[55] As people move to cheaper rents in the Bay Area far from the cities where they work, they must contend with pay-by-distance fares on public transit. Community gardens, organic cafés, and farmers markets add beauty and fresh food to low-income areas, but they cannot solve structural injustices and can do unintended harm; as low-income areas go "green," they attract the affluent, which can drive up rents and displace longtime residents.[56] Mindfulness has been captured by the market. The growing inequality does not foster empathy. On the contrary, even some "liberal" professionals in the Bay Area call for punitive policies that will push the unhoused out of sight and out of mind. These professionals have benefited from rising incomes in their job sectors, but they find themselves increasingly unable to enjoy their expensive homes and their daily rounds because of the misery on the street. Planners in eco-friendly cities acknowledge that global human activity has led to climate change, but they find it hard to address the ways that the global order and local policies cause environmental injustices.

As green redevelopment unfolds, why doesn't black political power safeguard black lives? It is widely assumed that black folks in the "hood" do not care about the environment. Low-income African Americans may not sound like middle-class white environmentalists when they talk about environmental risks, yet studies show that they recognize their vulnerability.[57] We must ask whether the city plans that black mayors endorse reflect the environmental concerns of residents. Interurban competition for investment—combined with their own political ambitions—push black mayors to cater to corporate interests. At any rate, the control of black mayors over urban projects is limited, and the power of the black vote has been suppressed. In March 2014, Detroit Water and Sewerage (DWSD) announced mass water shutoffs in high poverty areas of the city.[58] An hour's drive away in Flint, a different health crisis began in April of the same year as the water supply was switched without proper treatment from the Detroit system to the cheaper, corrosive Flint River, which leached lead from old pipes into the water.[59] Before their water crises, both cities got great press for their revived downtowns and their new green city plans made by public-private partnerships. These plans had fine features, but they did not make green redevelopment mean decision-making power and environmental justice for black and low-income residents. Water protests in Detroit and Flint, which drew statements of concern from the United Nations Commission for Sustainable Development and the United Nations Human Rights Office, blamed the water problems on the suspension of local democracy.[60] Emergency managers—appointed by the governor under a Michigan law for cities in fiscal crisis—approved the water shutoffs in Detroit and the water supply switch in Flint. Mayors have regained formal control, but as of the date of this writing, mass shutoffs continue in Detroit, lead exposure has not been adequately addressed in Flint, and the underlying challenge of long-term planning for equitable infrastructure in southeastern Michigan—including universal access to clean, affordable water—has not been resolved. For old industrial cities in fiscal crisis, the pursuit of local democracy may seem less important than economic growth. However, open, inclusive decision-making is critical in these cities, which face risks to health and well-being as elites devise strategies to balance the books. Sustainability offices and food policy councils, which have spread across the United States, institutionalize engagement between local governments and community groups on climate change concerns and food and water security.[61] Unfortunately, city governments often lack the resources and the will to heed their reports. Public-private partnerships develop city plans, maintain parks, manage storm water, and coordinate urban agriculture, street reforestation, and waterfront beautification. These partnerships seek local input, but inclusion of the voices of low-income residents during outreach often obscures their distancing from decision-making.

A few years before the start of Detroit Works, Laura Reese—the director of Michigan State University's Global Urban Studies Program and a planning consultant—had suggested that effective responses to urban crises are more likely after natural disasters than economic ruin because of political differences:

> It is true that disasters on the scale of [the] New Orleans [hurricane] and East Grand Forks [flood] provide the opportunity for sweeping clearance (or urban renewal for the more cynical). . . . In a city such as Detroit, with vast numbers of vacant parcels . . . scattered throughout the city and a relatively dispersed population for a large city, it would enable clearing and clustering redevelopment, creating fewer, more densely populated neighborhoods and providing services only to those concentrated areas. Such radical solutions may be necessary but are deemed politically and logistically infeasible by most officials and observers.[62]

Reese argued that this *rightsizing*—relocating residents from depopulated areas into dense neighborhoods to cut service costs—required collaboration among public, private, and philanthropic entities to achieve economic development, but years of hostility and mistrust had hampered cooperation. She also suggested that Detroit needed the media attention that Hurricane Katrina got to create a sense of national urgency: "Sustained media attention to the chronic economic distress of central cities . . . even with its likely sensationalism . . . might contribute to the public attention, understanding, and commitment necessary to effect long-range solutions." In addition, she stated that Detroit needed a "visioning process" that would help residents to realize that the city would never be the same but—with their input and support—it could become something better. After Dave Bing became mayor of Detroit in 2010, in line with prevailing views, he sought cross-sector collaboration, national media attention, and a local visioning process. Given Detroit's fiscal crisis, the city relied on the Kresge Foundation and other donors to fund the Detroit Works Project. To bring national attention to Detroit's plight and its revitalization efforts, the Bing administration engaged in talks with Time Inc. executives to produce a series of stories about the reinvention of Detroit. For one year, journalists from Time Inc. publications—including its business and real estate magazines—occupied a house (dubbed the "D-Shack" by rapper Kid Rock) in a Detroit neighborhood, writing stories about Detroit for a national audience. In February 2011, supported by the Ford Foundation, Mayor Bing led a Detroit delegation that visited New Orleans to engage in a "Detroit-NOLA Learning Exchange." During the trip, Bing and his staff met with Mayor Mitch Landrieu and various nonprofit and philanthropic groups to discuss urban revitalization issues. Mayor Landrieu put out a press release that drew parallels between New Orleans and Detroit, stating that the two cities could "create the road map for urban revitalization in America."

However, some scholars view the media coverage and the redevelopment of New Orleans as a neoliberal effort to reclaim the city for affluent whites. Henry Giroux notes that exaggerated reports of looting, rape, and murder after Hurricane Katrina fueled a racist narrative.[63] As gentrification proceeds in HBURs such as New Orleans and Detroit, nightmarish portrayals give way to upbeat coverage, exemplified by Time Inc's promotion of Detroit as a "beautiful wasteland" (in the words of scholar Rebecca Kinney)—a wild yet rich frontier that is being (re)settled by whites.[64] This "good news" frame obscures the politics of the return. John Arena states that activists in New Orleans have been co-opted into a nonprofit complex in which they soften their demands to obtain funds.[65] Darwin BondGraham argues that philanthropy in New Orleans has become a parallel government.[66] Across cities, puff pieces about redevelopment appear in financially struggling newspapers that have slashed their staff and cut back on investigative journalism.[67] Meanwhile, critical analysis of redevelopment appears in scholarly journals that hide behind pay-for-view firewalls. Thus, the market stifles critique.

The HBURs differ in the risks that they face from severe weather, yet they share common political and cultural threats. The greatest threat to environmental justice is not a bad policy decision; rather, it is a bad decision-making process, shaped by a politics, economy, and culture that value some lives more than others. The most alarming thing about the greening of Detroit is the absence of open, inclusive decision-making—a structural malevolence that requires a change of heart but cannot be fixed solely by reforming individuals. Some pundits describe gentrification as a cure for urban ills; the return of monied whiteness is seen as the restoration of ingenuity, civility, charity, and progress. In short, it is the return of Man.

Yet environmentalists warn that the Anthropocene—the Age of Man—has (paradoxically) harmed the possibilities for human life by altering the atmosphere, polluting the oceans, and causing mass extinctions.[68] After the last glacial period, humans wiped out many large mammal species and reduced the great forests through overhunting and farming, but these impacts on the earth were minimal in comparison with what was to come. Since the rise of the "modern" world system, the Anthropocene has been bound to white supremacy and the market, which have combined to violently suppress other ways of being on the earth. The Anthropocene has imposed hierarchical relations not only between humans and other species but also among humans. Climate change proceeds from centuries of abuse of habitats *and* cultures. The fires set by ranchers in the Amazon rain forest, threatening indigenous ways of life and the ecosystem, exemplify this abuse. Sylvia Wynter, a cultural theorist, argues that the subordination of the earth to Man—a projection of the Western bourgeoisie, which represents itself as the measure of the human—has provoked "struggles with respect to race, class, gender, sexual orientation, ethnicity, global warming."[69] Beneath the gloss of technological and moral progress, lives that neither mirror nor profit Man are treated as expendable. Overwhelmed activists move from crisis to crisis, reacting to police brutality and housing evictions and poisoned water and hurricane-flattened homes. This horror is anesthetized by market-driven greening. Progressives who might be mobilized into political action are instead enticed into consuming green lifestyles that feel morally and physically good. This good feeling lulls them into thinking that progress is being made. Wynter states that "the struggle of the new millennium" will be "securing the well-being, and therefore the full cognitive and behavioral autonomy of the human species" from its overrepresentation as Man. The "rainbow coalition" of the twentieth century did not achieve this liberation. Instead, white supremacy and the market began to interlock with a *rainbow of domination* by elites of diverse countries and races who prosper from oppressive systems and ideologies with origins in and beyond the West. These elites collaborate as a class yet appeal to race or nation to silence protest. I do not argue that only class matters, and I do not claim that elites are simply self-seeking: at times elites fight each other to advance their visions of the good society. Yet their battles do little to undermine racial capitalism. As the Combahee River Collective understood decades ago, the struggle for black lives must become a fight for (mental | material) freedom from Man *and* this deceptive rainbow.[70] If the past is any guide (New Orleans after Hurricane Katrina comes to mind), harsh policing and surveillance, legitimated by demonization of the racialized, the impoverished, and the uprooted, will be used by elites of all races to suppress panic, anger, and disorder as (un)natural disasters multiply.[71] Reflecting on Hurricane Katrina, the poet Jayne Cortez draws us into a critical reading of disaster. As she describes a flood victim, Cortez questions not only the rose-colored glasses of those who celebrate US democracy ("Is this freedom?") but also sterile science ("is this global warming?") that fails to frame the social production of isolation and dislocation.[72] Urban greening must address the interplay between climate change and social death. After Hurricane Katrina, LGBT evacuees reported being discriminated against by faith-based relief groups, jail inmates told of banging on their cells as their jailers fled, low-income evacuees at the Superdome protested being defamed as monsters.[73] To save lives, it is not enough to reduce carbon; we also must end threats to dignity and freedom.

Detroit—the largest majority black US city—has much to teach about black agency. As you enter Detroit from the darkness of the Lodge Freeway tunnel, as the silver towers of General Motors pull your eyes to the right, a giant black fist swings into view on your left, closing in on your driver's side window. Suspended by a pyramid frame, the disembodied fist of boxer Joe Louis guards city hall, which bears the name of a long-buried black mayor, whose mention con-jures the angry past. But a serene Jefferson Avenue, gleaming along the Detroit River, welcomes you; the latest reinvestment scheme (not to be confused with the 1970s Renaissance that built the towers) has revived the central business district for the middle and upper classes.[74] Years ago, some researchers had ar-gued that the gentrification that one sees in global cities such as New York and Chicago would not occur in cities such as Detroit and Saint Louis because they lack global connections.[75] Yet pockets of Detroit and Saint Louis have begun to undergo gentrification, albeit not on the same scale. Even before the latest revival, the isolation of Detroit from its region and the world was overstated. There is much residential segregation: in 2010, almost 80 percent of whites in the Detroit metropolitan area would have had to move to get an even mix of whites and blacks across tracts.[76] But whites never completely abandoned the city: out-migration has been *selective flight*. General Motors and other big cor-porations are headquartered here, and the city has important arts, educational, and medical institutions. Further, Detroit's location on the US-Canada border makes it a hub for international trade. For decades, the city has drawn com-muters. In 2010, commuters held 70 percent of the jobs in Detroit.[77] Planners and developers strive to convert these commuters into residents.

In its heyday, Detroit—the birthplace of the auto industry—shipped cars and the American dream. Detroit factories gave a middle-class lifestyle to many workers and served as the "arsenal of democracy" during World War II. Yet the auto industry also had violent conflicts and harmful ecological im-pacts. Before World War II, Henry Ford's anti-Semitic rants pleased Hitler so much that he awarded him the Grand Cross of the Supreme Order of the German Eagle.[78] Fears about climate change, merging with a longing for com-munity, pull people from the Fordist dream to the vision of a green city. How-ever, as this vision pulls idealistic young whites to Detroit, developers harness engineers and artists to develop green amenities that many longtime black residents cannot afford.

If you turn past Joe Louis's fist onto Woodward Avenue—the main street that runs from the river through rich and poor black neighborhoods to the Eight Mile demarcation line and beyond to the white suburbs—you will see Campus Martius, the hub of the revived financial core. A privatized park,

Campus Martius draws young professionals, who enjoy its jazz concerts and French bistro. Its fountain has water jets that flare a hundred feet, in synchronized bursts, with hisses and booms like fireworks. Steps away, a cross once blazed in the night, lit by the Detroit branch of the Ku Klux Klan.[79] But that nightmare was long ago, during another boom, when Art Deco skyscrapers rose downtown, as white couples danced to jazz bands on white nights at the Graystone Ballroom and the Purple Gang (allegedly) kept the booze flowing at Little Harry's, before the stock market crashed and the police and private guards shot four white workers dead as they marched to the River Rouge auto plant in the Ford Hunger March of 1932. Joe York, Coleman Leny, Joe DeBlasio, and Joe Bussell (a wavy-haired newsboy, just sixteen) died that day.[80] A fifth marcher, Curtis Williams—an African American—is said to have died later from his wounds.[81] The cemetery reportedly refused to bury him with his comrades. Some say that the workers—defying segregation—hired a plane to scatter his black ashes over the cemetery. Others say that the plane dropped his ashes on Ford's Rouge. Worker solidarity had its moments, but race trumped class: in 1935, Silas Coleman—an African American laborer— was shot to death in a marsh near Detroit by the Black Legion, a white hate group.[82] A ringleader said that he wanted to know how it felt to kill a black man.

The new Detroit is promoted as inclusive, safe, and benevolent. Near Campus Martius, Lafayette Greens—a corporate garden donated to a nonprofit—has fruit trees, vegetable beds, bioswales, and yoga classes, pervaded by the calming scent of lavender. The garden donates its produce to charities. New shops and lofts line this stretch of Woodward, clustering around firms that have opened offices here as the central business district reconnects (yet again after a world financial crisis) to regional and global markets. The alleged Little Harry's is now a tame Tommy's—a tourist pub—as downtown is secured by surveillance cameras, guards, and police patrols. City planning has merged with the downtown placemaking of a billionaire developer who moved his headquarters here in 2010. Two years earlier, the stock market had crashed (again) and people had lost homes and jobs. Protesters had (again) filled the streets. Their actions included disrupting the redevelopment meetings of the Detroit Works public-private partnership that had begun in 2010, charging that it furthered land grabs, corporate welfare, and a takeover of democracy. Cultural workers urged people at community gardens, block parties, churches, and schools to reimagine and rebuild Detroit as a green city. Then the planners and developers increased their use of cultural workers: they hired artists, put clergy on their boards, consulted with street scholars. Boosters tout the Future City; the memory of racial and class warfare—and protests about today's problems—are said to block progress. At a talk to business leaders in New Orleans, the head of a Detroit business group described downtown place-making as a public relations strategy: "Detroit has had significant negative headlines. . . . Those of you outside of our city and our region are starting to hear the change. . . . The headlines are entirely different. We're starting to have a much more positive reaction, and a lot of that is focused on this public space."[83] The downtown streetscape, using nature (the river, the park, the garden) as a lure, showcases urban greening. Meanwhile, red trucks move through low-income neighborhoods beyond downtown, cutting off water.

Yet the struggle for collective freedom and well-being persists. Below your line of vision as you enter Detroit, signaled only by seagulls, the Detroit River flows on your right. If you park and walk to the river's edge—past the new carousel with its saddled menagerie of river life (a sturgeon, the river monster, a chariot of swans), beyond the concession stands and the tour boat—you will see the gray statues of black adults and children in head scarves and battered hats, clutching sacks with their few belongings as they stride from the darkness of the nineteenth century. They gaze across the river toward Canada. The boy lags behind them, beckoning to someone unseen. The Gateway to Freedom memorial of black people fleeing slavery, crafted by the black sculptor Edward Dwight (a US Air Force test pilot who became an astronaut trainee), calls to future generations to continue on the path toward liberation. Before Detroit became synonymous with the auto industry, its financial core was a last stop on the Underground Railroad. Black radicalism here can be traced at least as far back as 1833, when black Detroiters strategized at night meetings to rescue a married couple who were being held for transport back to slavery in Kentucky.[84] In solidarity with the centuries-old movement to make black lives matter, two black women freed the wife from jail through a clever ruse: while visiting the wife, one of the women—Caroline French—exchanged clothes with her, which enabled the wife to escape in disguise with her face covered in a pretense of weeping. The jailer did not realize the switch until the next morning. The *Detroit Courier* reported: "By a contrivance that demonstrates that Negroes are not wholly wanting in shrewdness, the female was rescued from jail on Sunday evening and made her escape to Canada where she is now." Later, black women and men, together with their white allies, gathered at the jailhouse to forcibly free the husband. They put him on a boat, and he joined his wife in Canada. After the ensuing race riot (the first in Detroit), new laws made it hard for African Americans to remain in Detroit. Undeterred, some of the liberators founded Second Baptist, a black church that doubled as a station on the Underground Railroad. Benjamin Willough-by—a black real estate speculator and lumberyard owner who had helped to organize the 1833 rescue—sat in the pews at Second Baptist. The black capitalist and the black worker, as former slaves in a hostile city, saw freedom as dependent on their unity.

The challenge today is to forge alliances that can free the green city from its domination by Man and the deceptive multiracial rainbow of elite alliances. The dependence of wealthy developers on cultural workers—their partners and rivals in placemaking—is their Achilles heel. The call for social and environmental justice resonates among cultural workers across the United States and the world. "Get woke and stay woke," the woman on the radio warns. Winona LaDuke—the cofounder of the Indigenous Women's Network—echoes a mantra of Black Lives Matter activists.[85] Miles from the Michigan radio station, Alicia Garza—a cofounder of the Black Lives Matter organizing project—speaks at a gathering in California: "We believe that we could build political space for folks to start to understand to get woke . . . if we want to live in a time where race doesn't matter, then you have to dismantle systems."[86] LaDuke warns of ecological dangers; Garza protests urban injustices. "We need a movement of movements," LaDuke says. Garza states: "our task in this moment is not to split ourselves into smaller and smaller categories and then do oppression olympics . . . what we can do is learn each other's histories and how we got here . . . if it's just my movement we're not going to get anywhere."

Defining "Sustainability" and "Just Sustainability"

SINCE THE WILDERNESS preservation movement and the early climate science of the nineteenth century, environmentalism has evolved into a scientifically informed understanding of the ecological limits to industrial production and economic growth.[1] This New Environmental Paradigm (NEP) has influenced urban planners.[2] In the 1980s, sustainability planning began to spread around the world. Copenhagen has cleaned its harbor, expanded bicycle use, reduced waste, and replaced fossil fuel with renewable energy, toward the goal of becoming carbon neutral by 2025. Kitakyūshū, once a polluted steel town, is now an "eco-city" with green infrastructure and industries. Lagos, a megacity, participates in a statewide project that has reportedly planted over six million trees to capture carbon. Quito has an urban agriculture program to increase food security. Key documents that inspire these projects include:

- the 1987 Brundtland Report by the United Nations, which warns of climate change and defines sustainable development as "meet[ing] the needs of the present without compromising the ability of future generations to meet their own needs"[3]
- the 1991 Principles of Environmental Justice, composed at the National People of Color Environmental Leadership Summit in Washington, DC, which describes environmental destruction as a product of "500 years of colonization and oppression"[4]
- the 1992 Rio Declaration and Agenda 21 that urge cities to consider threats to ecosystems and vulnerable groups—these documents were conceived at the United Nations "Earth Summit" in Rio de Janeiro[5]
- the 1993 Charter of the Congress for New Urbanism, which advocates mixed use, mixed income, walkable neighborhoods to enhance sociality, the environment, and prosperity[6]

These approaches for defining and designing the green city are sometimes framed in opposition. New Urbanism, for example, has been criticized for violating principles of environmental justice by fostering gentrification. In old industrial cities, sustainability planning intersects with perennial land use strategies such as community gardens that bloom in hard times. This moment is unique for US cities because (1) greening is a revitalization strategy, not a subsistence plan, (2) it is wed to austerity, and (3) its network of developers, foundations, and nonprofits take on government functions.

Revolutionaries and reformers have long voiced concern about the crowded, polluted streets of the industrial city, while poets and painters have expressed nostalgia for the lost wilderness and the family farm. In the nineteenth century, Friedrich Engels[7] denounced the degrading, unhealthy conditions in which workers lived, and Ebenezer Howard[8] proposed small "garden cities" with cooperatively managed land that brought industry and agriculture into harmony. In the 1940s—inspired by Howard's vision—the United Auto Workers (UAW) tried unsuccessfully to get Detroit to construct satellite cities with greenbelts held in trust for recreation or agriculture to control sprawl.[9] In her 1969 song "Had, Took, Misled," Bernice Johnson Reagon warned of ecological degradation ("the west world done messed up the weather") in terms that foreshadow today's protests against climate change, and she mourned the loss of food sovereignty in terms that would be echoed years later by black urban farmers.[10] Marvin Gaye's song "Mercy Mercy Me (The Ecology)"—protesting environmental destruction—came out on his 1971 Motown album that also decried poverty, racism, and war. In the 1970s, Nathan Hare, a founder of black studies, hailed the "concept of ecology" as useful for the "liberation of black people," but he criticized environmentalists for ignoring urban conditions.[11]

Dorceta Taylor, a sociologist, traces the rise of the environmental justice paradigm (EJP): black activists expanded their agenda to include protests against toxic hazards and to reframe their concerns about living conditions (inequitable access to jobs, housing, transit, parks) in environmental justice terms, describing sprawling, segregated metropolitan areas not simply as a social problem but also as an environmental threat.[12] These activists included Hazel Johnson, who began organizing in the 1970s against a "toxic donut" of environmental hazards on the south side of Chicago, and Dana Alston, who co-organized the National People of Color Environmental Leadership Summit in 1991. The frame bridging of these activists was strategic: it helped to build coalitions among civil rights, labor, and environmental movements during the Reagan-Bush era when these movements were under attack. Scholars and activists in Michigan had key roles in the rise of the environmental justice movement: in 1990, Paul Mohai and Bunyan Bryant—professors at the University of Michigan—began a study of environmental inequities in the Detroit metropolitan area and held a historic conference on race and environmental hazards. As scientific studies began to support the claims of activists and artists, the EJP won recognition by the US government and the mainstream environmental movement. However, tensions linger between environmental justice activists who pursue multiple agendas and environmentalists who focus on ecological preservation.

Julian Agyeman and his colleagues frame the Just Sustainability Paradigm (JSP) as a bridge between the NEP and the EJP.[13] They define "just sustainability" as an integrated strategy "to ensure a better quality of life for all, now and into the future, in a just and equitable manner, whilst living within the limits of supporting ecosystems."[14] Agyeman and his colleagues argue that environmental justice requires environmental protection at regional and planetary scales—most notably, steps to address climate change—and environmental protection requires ending the world-historical injustices that have caused ecological destruction.

To make cities sustainable, the United Nations advises the "integration of four pillars: social development, economic development, environmental management, and urban governance."[15] When urban governance lacks integrity, the other pillars collapse. How and why do some cities fail at planning for just sustainability? The problem is not simply that mayors ignore scientists' warnings or that they lack managerial, technical, and financial capacities.[16] Racial capitalism rots the integrity of urban governance. I distinguish between city plans that refer only to sustainability (which is often made to mean green capitalism) and those that underscore *just* sustainability.

Yet we should not equate *justice-speak* (talk of justice) with the social good. By using this Orwellian-sounding term, I do not imply that talk of justice is always bad or deceitful. I use the term to describe the language of people whom I admire as well as folks whom I regard as venal. In a debate on Dutch television in 1971, Michel Foucault—a self-described "historian of systems of thought"—frames the danger:

> These notions of human nature, of justice . . . are all notions and concepts which have been formed within our civilization, within our type of knowledge and our form of philosophy, and that as a result form part of our class system; and one can't, however regrettable it may be, put forward these notions to describe or justify a fight which should . . . overthrow the very fundaments of our society.[17]

To make the quote relevant to the fight for environmental justice, one need only substitute "environment" for "human nature." If civil rights were not the language of the courts—a language that we must use to win remedies—perhaps we would not speak of "environmental justice." "Environmental" frames nature as a container for—rather than a web that includes—humans. "Justice" typically measures the goodness of this container by the legal yardstick of equality: a means to protect people from being *disproportionately* poisoned or drowned or made destitute. What type of system would we build—what would freedom mean—if we could move beyond reactionary demands and name the beauty that we want to see and feel in the world? Unlike Foucault, I regard demands for justice as necessary in our time. To a greater extent than Foucault, I see concepts as equivocal and emergent—always on the verge of meaning something else (for better or worse). Yet I heed his warning: there is a fierce undertow of talk of justice toward domination. We must be alert to the use of justice-speak, operating within racial capitalism, to limit our vision and to produce the deadly conditions that the discourse appears to combat. It is not simply a question of whether elites are hypocritical when they speak of justice. We also must ask about a greater danger: the possibility that there are moments when the discourse of justice unites races and classes in producing threats to life and freedom. Green lingo—wedding pleasure and morality—can be made to further neoliberal privatization and voluntarism as the government disinvests in low-income black areas. Wealthy philanthropists give poor people a hoe to grow tomatoes and trees when they demand jobs, housing, and services; green romanticism distracts attention from cuts to social welfare. Urban agriculture and forestry can help communities, but by themselves green practices do not further the beloved community. There is a mystical belief that healing Mother Earth will bring about an egalitarian society. This belief lacks historical support. Feudal life in Europe had vast inequalities in status and wealth, but it generated a small ecological footprint. Compared to the impacts of today's struggles for distinction, neither the hungry peasant child clothed in rough wool nor the well-fed little lord with a velvet cap had much effect on the earth. Global capitalism and its culture industries, constituted by new technologies and a racist logic, expand the social and ecological devastation of hierarchies.

Power Constellations, Practice Theory, and "Getting Woke"

THE BLACK ELDERS who got their downtown apartments when rents were cheap worried as they saw their streetscape change. William, a black musician in his sixties, said that he liked going to concerts at Campus Martius. He felt that the renovated park and new businesses were "good," but he could not afford the shops and he was concerned about displacement. He said that there was a need for "natural integration that flows from brotherly love." William's mild words contrasted with the blunt outrage of James, a municipal retiree. He said that white developers were fixing up the park and riverfront for whites. "In ten or twenty years, *we're* [blacks] not going to be here. *They* [whites] like to live near water, and they're going to push us out." He felt betrayed by black city officials: "Where are our black leaders?"

As the central business district gentrified, the elders feared that they would lose control of their place in the world. The geographer Ruth Gilmore notes that the struggle for freedom in the civil rights movement of the mid-twentieth century focused on spatial agency:

> The freedom riders and much of the civil rights movement targeted, of all things, infrastructure for desegregation. They targeted schools, they targeted highways, they targeted mass transportation. Their focus . . . sought to put into the landscape, the land around us, something new: the capacity for us to determine for ourselves protections from calamity and opportunities for advancement . . . inspired by a long-term vision to shift the foundations for the struggle for freedom. . . . so that freedom wouldn't turn into . . . simply the absence of cuffs . . . or being in a cage.[1]

The black elders questioned whether redevelopment would improve their capacity to determine protections and opportunities.

In the mid-twentieth century, battles over urban renewal (protested as "Negro removal") in the United States led to studies of local power structures. In *Who Governs?*—a classic study of urban renewal in New Haven, Connecticut—Robert Dahl suggests that a plurality of interests shapes local policy making; the government mediates between interests who have strengths and weaknesses that balance each other (the upper classes have economic power but lack voting power; the lower classes have voting power but lack economic power).[2] In *Who Really Rules?*, William Domhoff disputes Dahl's conclusion, arguing that a "power elite" dominates through policy networks of corporations, foundations, universities, think tanks, and law firms.[3] Since the 1980s, scholars have developed more nuanced theories. Logan and Molotch argue that "growth machines"—local power structures with booster ideologies—foster land use intensification that maximizes *exchange values* (rent from land and buildings) for real estate interests at the expense of *use values* (quality of community life and the natural environment) for residents.[4] Real estate interests forge coalitions with government and business leaders to drive growth. This coalition of *growth elites* promises jobs to win the favor of working-class residents, yet the new jobs go to college-educated newcomers. In contrast to Logan and Molotch, "urban regime" theorists such as Clarence Stone posit that a power structure in which business elites are hegemonic is just one possible outcome.[5] The strategic resources of groups must be combined to get things done. Group resources determine inclusion in coalitions. Perhaps grassroots groups can become part of these coalitions, using their (material | symbolic) resources to push for just sustainability. Yet inclusion can lead to co-optation.

What types of alliances enable democratic urban futures (and how should we define democracy)? Representative democracy is the dominant political model in the United States. Black voting power, mobilized by local activism, enabled the rise of Detroit's black urban regime. However, Coleman Young and his successors found it necessary to make corporate concessions to gain resources. Black urban regimes tempered their demands to maintain the good will of wealthy whites. Some cultural workers became disillusioned and began to advocate alternative forms of democratic practice. Some activists strive for direct democracy through community empowerment; local residents participate in and act on collective decision-making without (co-opted) intermediaries. Yet community groups often find themselves in the same bind as their elected officials. As these groups seek resources, they become open to co-optation. Complicating matters, technological and natural entities operate as *agents*. By "agent," I mean someone or something that exerts power. Most models of political action assume alliances among human agents. Emergent and green democracy differ from these models in that they frame webs of human and nonhuman agents. Emergent democracy posits that technology—for example, social media—influences political outcomes.[6] Green democracy affirms that all people, species, and future generations must be respected—not every life form can vote, but each life form has rights and a life-sustaining power.[7] Advocates of emergent and green democracy overlap in Detroit, forming an important strand of its grassroots movements. Critics of emergent and green democracy argue that their assumptions about technology and the earth are utopian. Perhaps some advocates are naive. However, theorizing power as a union of the human and nonhuman is not inherently utopian or even normative; it is the recognition that power combines forces of dissimilar materialities.[8] The concept of *urban metabolism*, which has roots in Marxist theory and engineering models, frames the interaction of social, natural, and technological systems in a city.[9] Similar to a living organism, a city takes in energy and pushes out waste. Advocates of green and emergent democracy go beyond this metaphor, describing technology and nature as inseparable from the space of political action across cities and nations.

To visualize the possibilities for bringing about just sustainability, we must imagine shifting power constellations of human and nonhuman agents. The nature of the green city and the black urban regime emerge in cross-place coalitions that span cities and institutions—intergovernmental entities, multinational corporations, government agencies, nonprofits, foundations, universities, engineering firms, art collectives. These constellations have internal conflicts—comprising variable races, genders, classes, nations—with different connections to technologies and the land. Given the neoliberal takeover of urban governance, we must address these constellations that operate beneath the surface of urban life, reshaping cities. Growth elites, technical experts, and cultural workers—operating in power constellations that span the globe—hold the key roles. I define growth elites as leaders of real estate, government, business,

TABLE 2. Alternative models of democracy*

	Community Empowerment/ Pluralist Commonwealth	Emergent/Absolute Democracy	Green Democracy
Process	Projects to increase community wealth through new institutions/relations Cultivate sense of community Develop community-based enterprises	Distributed problem solving and assembly (e.g., Occupy Movement) Use of new technologies (e.g., social media)	Care for the needs of all species and future generations Earth-centered worldview and practices
Type of Agent	Human Pragmatic	Human and Nonhuman Swarm intelligence	Human and Nonhuman Multifold Intelligences
Space	Institutions (collective space)	Common (networked space)	Commons (evolving earth)
Outcome	Collective well-being	Equality and innovation	Eco-Justice

* Note: Each category has internal disputes, and its advocates overlap.

finance, philanthropy, and nonprofit sectors who unite to increase land values. They include the black officials whom James—the retiree quoted earlier in this section—said had betrayed people like him. Technical experts are the planners, architects, and engineers who design urban space. Cultural workers are the artists, clergy, and intellectuals who craft the *interior architecture*—what people feel and dream on city streets. Growth elites are recognized as political players, while technical experts and cultural workers are often seen as apolitical. This is not the case.

Power constellations are more than social and material networks; they are always also webs of memories and dreams. Urban residents—including growth elites, technical experts, and cultural workers—are not the rational agents imagined in some models of democracy. I combine *practice theory* with the social psychological insights of African and African diasporic writers to frame how power constellations form. Practice theory is a family of social science approaches that are used to explain the interaction of social structure, embodied histories, and material conditions in shaping strategic action.[10] Theorists in this tradition include Pierre Bourdieu, Laurent Thévenot, and Ann Swidler. The approaches under this broad umbrella differ, yet they share the argument that neither rational choice nor social norms determine action. We are not free from the past, yet we are not robots; we can be creative in how we work with the resources of the past that are inscribed in our bodies, our minds, our tools, our institutions, and the built-and-natural environment. We improvise at home and work, but it is hard to resist the social order because we tend to remake the world that we have the dispositions, know-how, networks, and resources to make: a world that is second nature. Freedom struggles strive for another world, yet they are embedded in (mental | material) structures, regulated by the state and capital, that compose the existing order. Reassemblages repeat qualities that threaten the status quo, yet they also iterate features that shut down inquiry, reinforce hierarchies, and limit our understanding of the possible.

Practice theorists, underscoring domination by the state and capital, tend to undertheorize how folk narratives stir the dark sea of the self into motion. A strand of practice theory describes stories as part of "cultural tool kits," but this strand does not articulate a theory of power.[11] Ntozake Shange ("a moon in her mouth") invites us to recall the tidal force of the ancestors' tales.[12] We humans do not react directly to this or that event—we are captured by stories and the sound of stories. Magical realism—animating the work of Toni Morrison, Ralph Ellison, Octavia Butler, Ben Okri—alerts us to the power of submerged stories (recurrent dreams) that have resonance in particular bodies, at times and places that hold significance. The challenge is this: how do we "get woke" as the past that we echo is made to revive deadly constellations?

Technical and cultural work are harnessed in downtown Detroit to bring back past glory. Amid fresh landscaping, gentrifiers relax with green tea lattes and organic sugar scrub pedicures. The tropical crops that stimulated world trade at the rise of colonial empires, shades of the southern pastoral and the island paradise, reappear to revive commerce in the financial core of this old port city. In their second life, they still signify an indulgent class. Nature also reappears on the market with the aura of the Garden: if you continue driving down Woodward Avenue, you will pass the artist enclaves near downtown, where shops tout their eco-friendly, Detroit-grown produce that is said to heal the body and the commons. These shops thrive on dollars from gentrifiers and banks in the globalizing business district, yet they have roots in dreams of self-sufficient communities with sweat equity in the land. These centuries-old dreams motivated the Stapleton Colony in England and the Life and Labor Commune in Russia. They led Black Panthers to organize community gardens in Oakland, and they moved the Nation of Islam to establish a farm in Georgia. In Detroit, the Shrine of the Black Madonna raised money to buy Beulah Land—a southern farm—and the Boggs Center shared visions of Adamah—an agricultural community imagined for the lower east side. Dreams of the Garden, which bloomed in radical agrarian and maroon communities of the early modern age, recur among the alienated and the oppressed. These dreams, even when they embrace no deity, invoke *spirit*; the return to nature is genesis, the (re)creation of harmonic union. Mystical writings that use nature—water, wind, sun, soil—to symbolize spiritual union almost seem written by the same hand. A verse of the ancient *Katha Upanishad*[13] ("As pure water poured into pure water remains the same, thus O Gautama, is the self of a thinker who knows") echoes in the *Conference of the Birds* by Farid ud-Din Attar,[14] the twelfth-century Sufi mystic ("A pure object dropped into the ocean will lose its specific existence and will participate in the ocean and in its movement") that resonates in the *Interior Castle* of Teresa de Avila,[15] the sixteenth-century nun ("Spiritual marriage is like rain falling from heaven into a river or stream, becoming one and the same liquid"). Listening to nature arouses a sense of mystical union that inspires submergence of the self. Nature's message to the soul seems beyond race and nation, thus it appears ultimate truth. Yet the communication of land with spirit is not free from particularisms. When Nazis[16] or the Afrikaner Broederbond[17] go to the river, it whispers to them about racial purity and the Fatherland. Fascism, racism, and conservation have entwined roots.[18] Fervor for the landscapes of Africa, Asia, Europe, the Americas, and Oceania have inspired deadly regimes. Even movements for justice can become brutal, interpreting the natural in ways that enforce conformity and silence dissent: justice-speak can mutate into the language of murder. The Khmer Rouge began with the vision of a socialist agrarian paradise.

The moral truth of the Garden—that right relations among humans, the earth, and spirit bring freedom and peace—is not the same as the material reality of the past. The Garden seems the antithesis of Empire, yet time and again, Empire and the Garden have declared a truce (think of the Emperor Constantine and early Christianity). Empire finds use in the hold of the Garden on people's hearts, and the Garden seeks security and status from Empire. Empire has lost its scepter, but it still wields fear. The seventeenth-century philosopher Thomas Hobbes, fleeing England in fear for his life at the brink of the English Civil War, proselytized for Leviathan—a sovereign with god-like power who enforces security by threatening death.[19] Scholars today reframe Leviathan as the cause of insecurity. Theorists Hardt and Negri assert that a "new Leviathan"—a global network that they call Empire—acts as a global police force as it caricatures those whom it crushes as security threats.[20] Sociologist Loïc Wacquant notes that the "neoliberal Leviathan" defends mass incarceration (for black men) and reduced social welfare (for black women and children) by demonizing the black poor.[21] Yet Empire does not simply condemn; as it advances, it uses the Garden to cultivate, beautify, and beguile.

An international literature, urging decolonization of the imagination, celebrates creative forces that practice direct democracy as they build humane, ecologically conscious spaces. This literature tends not to address the sustainability of these spaces. In Henri Lefebvre's heuristic of spatial production, *conceived space* consists of abstractions (for example, city plans) that are tools of domination.[22] Planners, architects, and engineers devise these tools for capitalists and the government to commodify and regulate space. *Perceived space* is the observable reality of city streets. *Lived space* is everyday experience, mediated by symbols and images. Represented by artists, it serves as a base to critique capitalist space and to demand a "right to the city." The geographer David Harvey, building on Lefebvre's frame, calls for a "dialectical utopianism" in which the right to the city is realized over time through collective spatial projects that are continuously critiqued and transformed.[23] In a photo essay about community gardens and street art in Detroit, the architect Andrew Herscher uses the term "unreal estate" to signify land that, devalued by global capital, has been made valuable in cultural systems outside the market.[24] Katherine McKittrick writes about the potential of "demonic grounds"—the haunting presence of disappeared black women—to unsettle landscapes where black women and their memories and visions of place uneasily rest "deep within the crevices of power."[25] Harvey, Herscher, and McKittrick offer brilliant insights into placemaking that unsettles racial capitalism; there is an urgent need to build on this work and ask how these spaces can be maintained. The market and the state have a history of resettling "unreal estate" by appropriating its symbols; controlling its finances and infrastructure; and co-opting, jailing, or killing its organizers. To advance a strategic theorization of black spatial agency in cities, the critical task is neither to condemn gentrified parks nor to praise community gardens but rather to explain how urban space emerges, with all its contradictions, from race-class struggles. The businessman who supports a garden today may insist on more profitable uses of the land tomorrow when land values rise. Spatial agency is not simply being able to plant a garden; it is also the ability to control the future of land use.

If you visit the gardens, natural food shops, tree farm, art collectives, and maker spaces—the craft beer brewery, the guitar pedal manufactory—that are hailed by planners in Detroit, you will see the groundwork for the Future City. Yet as Carlos Fuentes reminds us, a city has many layers. Like the Aztec city of Tenochtitlán that haunts Mexico City, like the ancient ruins that possess the spirit of Rome, the past persists in Detroit. If you drive to Detroit's southwest border and step out, you will see the tower for a mineshaft. Under your feet, a hundred miles of underground roads, left from the mining of salt in the early twentieth century, stretch out into the suburbs. Millions of years ago, the salt deposits formed as a warm sea evaporated over the land. The advance and retreat of ice, repeated in vast cycles, carved the green hills and valleys of Michigan. Thousands of years ago, the freezing wind and silence of a glacial advance ended when the Laurentide ice sheet cracked and the Great Lakes took their present form. This climate change, so different from our own, gave life to plants and animals that nourished human communities in the Great Lakes watershed for generations—caribou, moose, deer, sturgeon, salmon, berries, nuts, wild rice, sweet maple sap. The Anishinaabe recall this creation as the bringing into being of a vision:

Kitche Manitou (The Great Spirit) beheld a vision. In this dream he saw a vast sky filled with stars, sun, moon, and earth. . . . Kitche Manitou heard songs, wailings, stories. He touched wind and rain. He felt love and hate, fear and courage, joy and sadness. Kitche Manitou meditated to understand his vision. In his wisdom Kitche Manitou understood that his vision had to be fulfilled. Kitche Manitou was to bring into being and existence what he had seen, heard, and felt. . . . Last of all he made man. Though . . . weakest in bodily powers, man had the greatest gift—the power to dream.[26]

This power endures, yet what is the vision? When Antoine Laumet de Lamothe Cadillac, a French soldier and trader, arrived at Waawiyaataanong (At the Curved Shores) and named his post Fort Pontchartrain du Détroit in 1701, he chained the land that would become today's central business district to the new world order of racial capitalism. Cadillac shared his vision in a letter to the King of France:

This country, so temperate, so fertile, and so beautiful that it may justly be called the earthly paradise of North America, deserves all the care of the King to keep it up and to attract inhabitants to it, so that a solid settlement may be formed there which shall not be liable to the usual vicissitudes of the other posts in which only a mere garrison is placed.[27]

The conquest of the "earthly paradise" and indigenous resistance to settler-colonialism have been fossilized in hierarchical commodity forms as the mythic past: Cadillac became a luxury vehicle, while Pontiac—an Odawa who led an attack on Fort Detroit—became an economy car. Kyle Mays, an indigenous urban historian, makes us aware of this fossilization and reminds us that the Anishinaabe are still in Detroit; their erasure in accounts of the city's present perpetuates settler colonialism.[28] At the dawn of the modern world system, other worlds of capitalism existed, most notably in the Ming dynasty. These worlds withered: the capitalism that would spread across the seas espoused white supremacy, sugarcoated by the Garden. Thomas Jefferson, the slaveholding founding father who penned the Declaration of Independence, idealized the private ownership of land that, he argued, would liberate small farmers from control by kings, bankers, and industrialists. In his celebration of individual liberty, Jefferson sidestepped the reality that the early republic and his own fortune depended on land grabs and slave labor, which enriched kings, bankers, industrialists, and his own planter class. His Monticello plantation merged Empire and the Garden: his mansion of white columns and rounded dome, distanced from his fields and the enslaved Africans who plowed them, was a tribute to ancient Rome. Hostile to a strong federal government, Jefferson nevertheless wed his ideal of the yeoman farmer to US expansionism, which supposedly would extend freedom ("The Empire of Liberty") to the world.[29] This empire rose from the blood of the millions who perished in the Middle Passage and those who died from brutal slave regimes in the Americas and from fire and lynching after the "peculiar institution" ended.

Some community organizers see opportunity in capital flight from cities—a chance to reimagine the human.[30] Yet resistance to Man must battle not only white racists but also elements of the beloved community and the self; the Jeffersonian ideal has colonized the dreams of the diaspora. In Barack Obama's 2008 Yes We Can campaign speech—a redux of Manifest Destiny turned into a multiracial music video by the Black-Eyed Peas—Obama (con)fused "the pioneers [settler-colonialists] who pushed westward" with "a King [civil rights movement] who took us to the mountaintop" in the same message of hope about the march of progress.[31] Compromise with Empire is not new. Indigenous people sometimes traded black runaways to whites for guns and other goods; in Detroit, desperate black men fleeing slavery agreed to load their guns to defend Detroit against the Anishinaabe, in exchange for their own freedom.[32] The devil's bargain reappears. Lester Spence, a political theorist, argues that black artists, professionals, and entrepreneurs devise "self-help" projects that shift costly services from the state to low-income black communities.[33] They conform to the neoliberal order not only because its logic has colonized their imagination, but also because, as government help shrinks, their projects rely on the patronage of neoliberal elites. Western Marxists have long argued that capitalists suppress revolt by dividing workers and dominating their consciousness.[34] Getting people to rebel is not the biggest hurdle; the challenge is to transform ways of seeing and being in the world. Too often, resistance to Empire and its deceptive Garden is driven by a longing for the Garden of a lost Empire. The greatness of precolonial Africa is rendered in tales about the majesty of its kings—even those kings who captured and sold farmers, fishermen, cattle herders, metalworkers, storytellers, mothers, fathers, children whose greatness is not recalled. This is not simply a problem for the African diaspora; diverse peoples take pride in their (imagined) histories of Empire without recollecting how Empire debased their ancestors. Slavery is an enduring worldwide problem that began long before the Middle Passage. As Empire and the Garden align in urban greening, as Leviathan rebuilds, what are the possibilities for (mental | material) freedom?

About Me and the Study

BORN AND RAISED in South Los Angeles, I come from work-and-fuss-and-holler-and-pray-and-try-to-do-until-you-fall-down-dead-and-they-stick-you-in-the-ground folk, whom scholars categorize as the working class and the lower middle class. Most African Americans are work-and-fuss folk. Our history of struggle places us in an ambivalent relation to Empire and the Garden. I recall the day (or perhaps it was a host of days that memory has telescoped) that my third grade teacher—a young woman with red hair and a fringed purse who was less strict than the nuns—read to us about Jonathan Livingston Seagull, and showed us how to make butter by shaking cream in a jar, and let us feel raw cotton. We oohed and aaahed. These were back-to-nature, hippie days, and she said she wanted us city kids to see where things came from. Then one morning a student's father came in a business suit. He took the teacher aside and told her in a low growl that he had sworn his son would never touch cotton. He said that he didn't work night and day to pay tuition for this Catholic school so that his son could learn how to churn butter—he could buy it for him at the store. His son needed to learn reading, writing, and math for his future—he didn't need to know where things came from. The teacher stood there, turning as red as her hair. It made me very aware that the teacher was white and most of us kids (except the Irish kid and the few Mexican kids) were black. I didn't know why the father was so mad, but I guessed it had to do with "Down Home"—the rich soil of the South that grew the sweetest peaches and the most flavorful greens, the land of pine woods with creeks and berries and wild turkeys and small towns where our kin had lived for generations and hunted and fished and swam and built homes and churches and celebrated birthdays and buried our dead. Down Home was the place that the grown folks spoke of with love, yet—terrorized—they had fled. Grown folks called each other "country" as an insult, but they cherished the pecan pies and homemade quilts and fresh-picked turnip greens that relatives visiting California would bring from Down Home. They gave us soul food and black dolls and inspirational stories (the mandatory copy of *Great Negroes:*

Past and Present), but they hid their pain. This legacy left us kids distanced from yet drawn to nature and the past.

My parents' generation of work-and-fuss folk struggled so that mine would be "judged by the content of our character." Much has changed. Black mayors won office in large US cities, and a member of my generation made it to the White House. However, racial capitalism, with its *Zong* ship logic, persists. Urban researchers hope that the rigor of their work will convince elected officials to adopt their policy recommendations. Research should be rigorous, but rigor is insufficient for political action. In my parents' generation, the civil rights and black power movements drove reform by producing compelling narratives and building coalitions. In the absence of movements to effectively frame problems and mobilize support, data on racial disparities may be used as proof of racial pathologies. W. E. B. Du Bois criticized the white scholars of his day for focusing on lurid aspects of black life and ignoring how contexts shape black "strivings." Today's researchers pay more attention to opportunity structures and success stories but still neglect analysis of black people's strivings. As crises intensify, we do not need flattering portraits—we need strategic theorizing. Possibilities for saving black lives cannot be understood without listening to the views and analyzing the practices of black people, in all our complexity.

"Giving voice to the oppressed" and *listening* to black people are not the same. Years ago, a fellow grad student—a white ally—took on the burden of speaking for me. I would quote a black scholar in class, and my ally would translate it into a reference to a white theorist: "I think what Alesia means is that . . ." This appropriation, or as Wynter would say, this *overrepresentation*, made my peer into my proxy—no, more than that, into my guardian. With gentle care, he scrubbed my words clean of their original sense and their genealogy. The other students spoke to him about what I meant, not to me. This is crazy, I thought. I finally told him and the class: "Alesia said what Alesia meant to say." The translations stopped, but I do not know if I was heard. It is useful to relate black scholars to other scholars, yet our work offers unique insights that demand citation/engagement/debate, emerging from dialogues with the self, others, and the earth that confront—but cannot be reduced to—the history of racial violence. These dialogues include the untold millions who have disappeared into our faces and our bones, my Alabama grandmother shaking crumbs from her apron out the backdoor of our South Los Angeles home at dawn, sighing, "*Always feed the birds . . .*" At night my grandmother—a tall silent woman with a hawk face—would stand in our garden of snap beans and vine tomatoes and collard greens and yellow squash, near the fragrant mint beneath our windows and the peach tree and the lemon tree that she plucked for pies, and read the blood moons and thunder clouds that had been predicted in her bible and farmer's almanac. A paragon to me, she had none of the softness of TV grandmothers. Sitting on her lap was like climbing onto the limbs of a high tree where I was safe yet alone. At six, seven, eight years old, I was always at her elbow but did not understand her, learned Catholic dogma at my school but breathed in her sorrow songs (*Swing low sweet chariot . . .*) and unnerving morning prayers (*Thank you that my bed was not my cooling board nor my blanket my winding sheet . . .*). She made me French toast and eggs for breakfast—like on TV—while she ate fried fish and hoecake and drank coffee from a thick mug. It was the TV that told me about the bus burning in Anniston, her hometown. It showed me the black smoke, the flames. How long ago was that, I asked. Who were the Freedom Riders? Who were the Ku Klux Klan? She pretended not to hear. When I cornered her, pointing to Anniston in the world atlas that her daughter—my mother—had bought for me, she said that maybe it wasn't the same Anniston where she had lived, this place on TV and the map. Her denial confused me. I felt the truth in her rumblings (*Stay in your books so you won't ever have to work in no white man's kitchen*) and in her silences.

I stayed in my books, spending Saturdays in the shadowy back aisle of a second-hand store, where old mysteries lay scattered on the floor. For a quarter, I could buy a Nancy Drew or Agatha Christie story from the blue-haired old white woman who owned the store. As the book pile in the store shrank, my library at home grew. I loved owning the books almost as much as reading them, loved the copyright dates (1931, 1933 . . .) because it felt magical to touch the past and because I imagined the vintage books—first editions in mint condition—might be worth a pile of money one day. I was careful not to break their spines. But it troubled me that these books reduced my grandmother's generation to a joke or a menace or a mule—they were the porters, the maids, the cooks who served the clever detectives; they were the sinister masks and the jovial clowns. I tried to ignore old racial terms such as "negress" until one day I turned a page and Ned Nickerson (Nancy's boyfriend) said he had seen a "darky." I put the book down. I got my #2 pencil and a sheet of brown penmanship paper, copied the copyright date, and calculated that men like Ned would be dead or dead soon by the time my generation came to power (I overheard the adults talking about our rise). I folded the sheet and slipped it within the pages—it became my bookmark—and went back to the story: the past could not harm my future.

My calculating generation of upwardly mobile African Americans (the precariously comfortable, the temporarily safe) has followed the trajectory that our parents and grandparents plotted. There was no error in our figures, but we did not arrive at the place we thought. From our earliest years, we were trained to outrun the past, but the past ran with us. The problem is not simply the longevity of white racists; my generation's habits of thought and action—at once enabling our escape and capture—betrayed us. We have been miseducated not so much by lies as by the evils that we have learned to ignore (which we correctly surmise as the price of the ticket). We unsettled the racial order, but Empire absorbed us into its power constellations, undermining the communities whose struggles enabled our rise. This sad truth is not cause for despair; social change requires continuous recalibration. Given human and ecological crises, we must rethink our strategies for realizing freedom. Using the greening of Detroit as a pivot to analyze processes that span HBURs, I focus on four questions that address the political and cultural struggle to shape green redevelopment:

(1) When capital abandons a city, how do people interpret their world—do their minds become emancipated from or more dominated by Man?

(2) How and why is green redevelopment on the agendas of growth elites, technical experts, and cultural workers in HBURs?

(3) How do growth elites, technical experts, and cultural workers—whose interests do not always align—mobilize (symbolic, social, material) resources for shaping perceptions and agendas in HBURs?

(4) How can these frames and agendas be made to support the spatial agency *and* the freedom (forms of power that overlap but are not one and the same) of low-income African Americans?

My definition of cultural workers overlaps with Gramsci's *organic intellectuals*—individuals who (claim to) express the interests of a social group. All community organizers are cultural workers, but the inverse is not true: I am a cultural worker but not a community organizer. I do not assume that we cultural workers always serve our communities; we have our own interests. As a cultural worker, I cannot control whether I am heard, but I can choose what I represent. The inescapable past frames ancillary concerns: how and why do Empire and the Garden reappear in the physical design and the interior architecture of streets? How does freedom, variously defined (individual liberty, group power, right relations), emerge in this psycho-social and structural dynamic? What constellations of power in and across cities does this dynamic make possible?

As I address these questions, I critique the social order, but I do not dwell on condemning this or that person. One day, while I spoke with an activist in a Detroit coffee shop, the activist greeted a man who came in. The man shook my hand and chatted a bit. After the man was out of earshot, the activist asked me if I recognized the man's name—he was tied to a corruption scandal. The activist, seeing my frown, laughed and said, "I would have introduced you to Jesus, but it wasn't Jesus who walked in." In Detroit, I learned to listen to all who "walked in." Some "bad" people speak frankly and some "good" people are evasive about the redevelopment of Detroit. Perhaps the latter group sidestep the truth for reasons that they feel are good; maybe they are right and I am wrong. I have no way of knowing anyone's heart, and it is more useful to identify the agendas, strengths, and vulnerabilities of social formations. My aim is to inform the strategizing of social movements. I do not strive to (directly) "inform policy makers"—the rote line of scholars who fail to recognize the import of their own findings about the capture of the state by business and financial interests. Only powerful movements can make policy makers listen. My goal is to further social change, but I do not seek to advance a glorious future or to reclaim a paradisiacal past. I come from work-and-fuss folk, and I can imagine no greater heaven than us—with our songs and our stories and our gardens and our work boots and even our sorrows—but our lives no longer chained to the market. Free.

My four research questions mingle in the sections of this book. In Section II ("Paradise Lost"), I begin to address my first and second research questions:

when capital abandons a city, how do people interpret their world—do their minds become emancipated from or more dominated by Man? How and why is green redevelopment on the agendas of growth elites, technical experts, and cultural workers in HBURs? Any analysis of urban politics in the age of MAGA and the Garden must deal with the mythic past. Before moving to Detroit in 2010, I had spent a couple of years collecting oral histories from Detroit residents and those who fled to the suburbs. These oral histories tend to follow a moralizing template, which I call "the narrative of the fall": the Fall mourns the loss of an Eden that is thought to have once woven life-sustaining connections among humans and the built-and-natural world. This narrative affirms an image of the communal past—a Moral We—that has been used to win support for neoliberal agendas. Yet it has liberatory potentials. Section III ("Redemption") continues this exploration and starts to address my third research question: how do growth elites, technical experts, and cultural workers mobilize (symbolic, social, material) resources? In greater downtown and the neighborhoods beyond it, the cultural workers of Detroit have woven the narrative of the fall into a *narrative of redemption*—a vision of a city in which the practice of social and environmental justice by the Moral We brings pleasure and meaning to everyday life. The placemaking of cultural workers with this vision feeds (literally and metaphorically) a hunger for the idealized past. The ability of this placemaking to win support from gentrifiers and longtime residents draws the attention of growth elites, who merge their own revival of the commercial past with cultural workers' vision of an earthly (and spiritual) paradise. Competing groups use the *parade/march*, the *tour*, the *mission*, and the *forum* to shape perceptions of Detroit and to gain resources for their agendas. In Section IV ("The Forum"), I deepen my analysis by examining public outreach for the Detroit Works Project. Its outreach had the semblance of democratic practices (multicultural interaction, community engagement), yet it did not in fact allow residents to deliberate on and make decisions about the future of the city. Rather, it harnessed the networks woven by cultural workers, and it exploited their grand narrative of redemption. Section V ("Consilium Principis") continues my analysis of cultural and technical workers to address my fourth question: how can the frames and agendas of green redevelopment be made to support the spatial agency and the freedom of low-income African Americans? I examine the ties and practices of cultural and technical workers. I also compare city plans across cities, exploring the generalizability of my findings about Detroit. In Section VI ("Naming the Baby"), I discuss changes in Detroit since I left six years ago, and then I summarize and reflect on my findings. My conclusions are bleak, yet I note possibilities for community organizers to subvert power constellations. The appendix details my methods.

Some readers may wish that I had provided an in-depth structural critique of racial capitalism. My work here is limited. I offer insights for a stage in the larger struggle—the equivalent of a holler to throw the emergency brake when the regular brake fails. This type of intervention has perils; the ideal is to build societies that do not require risky maneuvers to avert disaster. Others may wish for an inspiring narrative that shows all races and classes working together in love to rebuild Detroit. I seek the good, but I must report the good and the bad that I find. In the words of one of my favorite poets, Countee Cullen, "loved have I much, but I have not been blind."[1] Yet my vision is partial; my social position shapes my interests and limits my worldview, and I am not as unbossed as I hope to be. No doubt my analysis has errors and omissions. I encourage you to check and build on my work, in the spirit of a dialogue that furthers freedom.

II

Paradise Lost

Sankofa and the Angel of History

THE RETURN OF the white and black middle classes to the central cities that have long been black urban regimes reawakens old fears, sorrows, longings, and resentments. Historian Jason Stanley warns that fascist politics use tales of a glorious mythic past to justify brutal attacks on racialized scapegoats who are blamed for political corruption, economic decline, and cultural decay.[1] He notes that in fascist ideology, longings for lost empire combine with nostalgia for the family farm, which is framed as the source of the nation's values and vigor—the backbone that enables it to go forth and once more conquer the world. Stanley focuses on how fascist leaders manipulate stories about the past, yet we also should attend to narratives that exceed their grasp.

A white suburbanite told me that she had heard that, night and day, addicts wait in the bushes above the Lodge Freeway, the artery into downtown Detroit. Whenever a car stalled, they would scramble down, murder the driver, and strip the car. Decades ago, the woman had raised her children in a working-class neighborhood of Detroit, and she had enjoyed shopping downtown at Hudson department store. Now she was afraid to visit the city, and she warned her friends not to visit the new downtown shops. Violence is real in Detroit, but her story is surreal. No doubt crime happens on freeways, yet what makes a horde of murderers—lying in wait on the Lodge Freeway—seem plausible?

A black Detroiter walked me outside her palatial home near a golf course. The enclave once housed white auto executives. It had become an African American fortress with a private security force. I asked about the high poverty area nearby. She told me: "I don't want to see it. I try not to think about it." She folded her arms as if chilled. The woman recalled the fun that she had, as a child, exploring the streets of her working-class neighborhood and going downtown to shop at Hudson's. She told me: "Those were the days when I was a queen." She waved in the direction of the vacant homes and stores a short drive away. "I try to block it out of my mind. It makes me so depressed. So much is gone." Why did this woman who lived in a palace recall her working-class childhood as the days when she was a queen?

In the days before skyscrapers rose along the Detroit River, long before the rise and fall (and rise again) of a consumer culture here, the stories that people told about Michigan alternated between tales of a paradise and a hell. Some said that the only way to cleanse the paradise of "swamps and beasts and dangers" was to drive out the "savage."[2] Others spoke of the sadness of being driven out; still others told of the pain of being made invisible. Centuries past the "Indian Wars" but before Detroit Works began—at a moment again of fear and melancholia—I began collecting oral histories from current and former Detroiters. The violence that drives some of them to flee even the *thought* of the city's streets cannot be reduced to street crime. Walter Benjamin, the early twentieth-century philosopher who critiqued the modern city, noted that planners had to demolish not only the medieval city but also the remembrance of its oppressed past.[3] His focus was Paris, which he described as "the capital of the 19th century." The creation of splendid shops and boulevards, serviced by a new water and sewer system, made Paris into a beautiful and clean city for the upper classes. Yet this seemingly beneficial modernization masked the displacement of the poor, which involved not only their bodily removal but also the eviction of the memory of their presence. Time and again, the oppressed have built community in perilous spaces, only to have those spaces destroyed. From the vantage of the "angel of history" (a figure in a different fragment of Benjamin's work), the cleansed streets are wreckage, smashed by "homogeneous, empty time." The angel "would like to stay, make whole what has been smashed" but the wind of progress arrests moral agency:

> [A] storm is blowing from Paradise; it has got caught in his wings with such violence that the angel can no longer close them. The storm irresistibly propels him into the future to which his back is turned. . . .
> This storm is what we call progress.[4]

For some cities in the West, the era of rich spectacles has passed. Does ruin unmask, in the words of Benjamin, "the inhuman character of the metropolis"? When progress stops, do possibilities for other temporalities—other daily rounds, other city plans, other recollections and re-visions of humans and nature—emerge? When Empire abandons a place, does consciousness become emancipated from Man or desperate to make concessions?

Detroit—the backwater outpost of France that became the capital of the twentieth century—is a good place to ask these questions. Unlike nineteenth-century Paris, which drove its poor beyond its borders into the Red Belt, an area that would become a communist stronghold, Detroit drew its working classes into the consumer paradise of its financial core. Even if one could not afford the lifestyle modeled by the mannequins in bright store windows, one could work and hope and dream. The dream secured a measure of labor peace. Then the market shifted, and like a conjurer's trick, this consumer paradise—which had paved over the earthly paradise that had enchanted the French soldier-trader Cadillac—vanished. As capital left in the mid-twentieth century, the white middle class left too. In black neighborhoods, rumors began that a white cabal (the phantom counterpart to the Monsters-on-the-Lodge) were waiting and watching from the suburbs, plotting their return to crush the black regime. Black solidarity against this cabal held for many years, but by the century's close, much of the black middle class had fled Detroit too.

Planners say that between twenty-five to forty of Detroit's roughly 140 square miles is vacant land. But these miles are not empty: people, plants, and animals still live in, work on, and move through these areas, bearing the beauty and troubles of the past. Detroit is built on the boulders, sand, clay, and organic matter (the remains of terrestrial and aquatic life) deposited by retreating glacial ice. The indigenous past that began before the arrival of Europeans, the colonial past that began with Cadillac, and the industrial past also left traces. This past impacts the richness of species, the qualities of soil and water, and the configuration of water and sewer pipes, gas and electric lines, street lights and utility poles. The aging infrastructure, built for a larger population, is costly to maintain. Resident teams mow grass on the lots of neighbors who have gone—reclaimed spaces where ground beetles scurry through garden rows, honeybees feed on wildflowers, and birds sing near boarded-up homes under blue skies as far as the eye can see. Seasonal rains nurture this life, but storm water that hits the miles of pavement cannot seep into the ground. Storms (which will become more severe with climate change) flood abandoned factory lots once busy with workers, before being swallowed by gutters and carried to the river. Mixed with ground contaminants and sewage overflows, this runoff pollutes the river, which poses risks for people who fish. As bulldozers demolish old factories and homes, the industrial past leaves poisons on the land that must be remediated before anything can safely grow here. Thousands of properties have detected or potential contaminants. The aging housing stock places families at risk: in 2016, an estimated 8.8 percent of children under six in Detroit had elevated lead levels, which is linked to living in an old house with lead paint or near a demolished house with lead paint.[5] The United States did not outlaw lead house paint until 1978. For decades, the paint industry had suppressed studies that showed the dangers of lead for children.[6] Michigan reportedly has a large difference between people of color versus whites living near hazardous waste facilities.[7] For years—until it closed in 2019—Detroit's incinerator burned trash from suburbs that exported the bad smells and health risks. The most toxic zip code in Michigan is in southwest Detroit, polluted by oil refining and coal plants and by heavy truck traffic.

The past influences possibilities for future (material | symbolic) constructions. For decades, efforts to revive commerce in Detroit failed. The Renaissance Center, built in the 1970s, shadowed vacant buildings; the new monorail ran nearly empty cars in a circle around downtown. Then the global financial crisis of 2008 hit. Chakravartty and Ferreira da Silva argue that the crisis caused by predatory lending has been "recast as a problem caused by the racial other," for which the racial other must be punished.[8] Do the racial others—the people whose memories are targeted for eviction—blame themselves?

On March 23, 2010, from the ornate stage of the Max M. Fisher Center that was once (aptly enough) the site of the Paradise Theatre, Mayor Dave Bing gave a State of the City address in which he told his listeners that the "truth is most of the manufacturing jobs . . . are never coming back" and that Detroit needed to use its "140 square miles more productively." This speech that promised a new green future (financially, environmentally) for Detroit, reported by national news media, was important: it set the stage for the Detroit Works Project—the citywide planning process organized by a public-private partnership—which Bing would announce later in 2010. Bing had completed the term of Mayor Kwame Kilpatrick, who had resigned amid corruption charges. In November 2009, Bing was elected to a full term. Journalists contrasted him favorably with Kilpatrick, whom they described as a con man, and Coleman Young, whom they said had been racially divisive. In his State of the City, Bing stressed the need for austerity, blaming the city's challenges on a "culture of corruption" in city government and the inflexibility of a municipal union. No blame was cast on business and financial interests. This selective recall made the state of the city unintelligible: in 2005, at a black tuxedo event in New York, Mayor Kilpatrick had received a trophy from a bond market trade publication for borrowing $1.4 billion in a high risk deal that used derivative "swaps" to restructure pension fund debt.[9] This bad deal—more than Kilpatrick's much publicized sex and bribery scandals—pushed Detroit, which had been suffering for decades from the flight of capital, to the brink of bankruptcy when the global financial crisis of 2008 hit—a crisis set in motion by finance capital's capture of the state. Bing, a former basketball star of the Detroit Pistons, owned Bing Steel, a supplier to the auto industry. Like many affluent African Americans, he had fled Detroit, buying a suburban home. Yet he had kept his business in the city, and he had returned to live in the city before his run for mayor. The hushed, bespectacled demeanor of this man in his sixties was that of a church usher, belying his aggressive Horatio Alger life story: raised in an impoverished neighborhood of Washington, DC, the son of a bricklayer and a maid, he had overcome his early disadvantages—including a childhood accident that damaged his eyesight—reportedly making himself into a millionaire.[10] Bing, a Democrat, used his mild manner and business achievements to forge networks across race and party. In 1984—the same year that Mayor Coleman Young had accused President Ronald Reagan of neglecting cities and creating a "permanent underclass"—Reagan had honored Bing as the National Minority Small Businessman of the Year at the White House. Being liked by white Republicans might seem unnecessary in a black urban regime, but Detroit officials sought external aid to resolve the city's fiscal crisis. Equally important, Detroit's growth elites strived to overcome the city's bad reputation. In a 2006 Gallup poll that asked Americans to rate sixteen of the largest US cities in terms of their safety to live in or visit, Detroit was ranked least "safe."[11] The media reinforced these fears: journalists focused on Detroit's crime, corruption, and ruins, while comedians made Detroit the punch line for their jokes. Fear of Detroit hardened into contempt. Boosters hoped that the dignified, nonthreatening Bing would help to reduce fear of Detroit and to restore respect for the city.

Later in this section, I analyze Bing's State of the City address, comparing it to the inaugural address by the city's first black mayor, Coleman Young: a clear neoliberal shift is evident. But before we examine Bing's explanation of the crisis in Detroit—before we analyze how developers use green projects to silence talk of Monsters-on-the-Lodge—we must study the folk understandings of loss and ruin with which they contend. The Angel of History cannot stop progress from emptying streets of the people and shops of the old city, but the past lingers in old longings and fears. *Sankofa* (the return to the past)—represented by the Akan as a bird with its head turned backward—"flies again and again" against the winds of progress.[12] Urban projects rework the past that lies dormant in bodies and landscapes. Racial capitalism uses the past that it has crushed—a past older than Man—as mortar for eco-capitalist ventures. In doing so, it reawakens the pioneers pushing westward to drive out the savage. And again the resistance revives the warriors to fight for land and freedom.

Interior Architecture of Minoritized Space

THE BRAND OF a city or town emerges from its streetscape, its daily rounds, and its annual celebrations, which rely on investments by capital and the state. However, its *interior architecture*—which is more than its brand—can persist (at least for a while) even as investments or disinvestments transform its streetscape and calendar. By "interior architecture," I mean what people feel and dream about a city's streets. The basement of the interior architecture, a reassemblage of the past from multiple viewpoints, is like an Escher drawing: people on the same street at the same time do not always see and move through the same space.

Growth elites strive to dominate not only the physical design but also the interior architecture of a city. Political and economic elites have used public speeches, mass media, and think tanks to naturalize a memory of urban decline that blames big government, labor unions, and people of color for urban ruin to justify punishing the racialized and impoverished with austerity, surveillance, incarceration, and displacement.[1] The geographer Neil Smith describes this scapegoating as the ideology of the *revanchist city*—the vengeful city that the white middle and upper classes build as they return to the urban core:

> Revenge against minorities, the working class, women, environmental legislation, gays and lesbians, immigrants became the increasingly common denominator of public discourse. Attacks on affirmative action and immigration policy, street violence against gays and homeless people, feminist bashing and public campaigns against political correctness and multiculturalism were the most visible vehicles of this reaction. In short, the 1990s have witnessed the emergence of what we can think of as the *revanchist city*. . . . *Revanche* in French means revenge.[2]

Smith offers critical insights about the interplay between revanchism (vengeful policy making) and gentrification (class displacement), but he inadequately frames the racial struggle in US cities. His analysis focuses on capitalists returning to the devalued urban core to take advantage of a *rent gap* between actual land values and their potential value as existing structures on the land are rehabilitated and marketed to the affluent.[3] To trace how the return weds class dominance with white supremacy, we must place the black urban regime at the core of the analysis, and we must account for beneficent language and practices. The moralizing discourse of the return—echoing the paternalist discourse of the cotton plantation—does not simply speak of punishment; infantilizing black residents, it also speaks of care and guidance.

The return of middle- and upper-class whites to pockets of US central cities reverses the so-called Negro invasion of the mid-twentieth century.[4] The concept of *gentrification*—coined by Ruth Glass in 1964 to describe demographic shifts in London—is useful but not sufficient for framing this return. Gentrification, which refers to the class-based residential displacement that is happening in cities around the world, obscures the racial properties of the return in the United States. To be clear, I see no need for a new term to describe low-income groups (including the black urban poor) being driven out by rising rents as affluent newcomers (including black professionals) move in; *gentrification* adequately describes that process. Rather, I note that residential displacement is not the only effect of the return in the United States. People often use the term *gentrification* to signify all aspects of the return—it cannot meaningfully do so.

Most areas of Detroit—indeed, most neighborhoods in HBURs—are not gentrified (with the possible exception of heavily gentrified Washington, DC).[5] Gentrification is an important concern, but we also must analyze *minoritization*. The anthropologist Michel Laguerre describes "minoritized space" as a site that inscribes race and racial hierarchies—it does not necessarily involve a demographic shift.[6] He notes that the term "minority" has roots in the Justinian Code, which extended the status of *minor* (child)—a person unable to self-govern—to the enslaved. Laguerre relates this history to the evolution of the term "minority" in the United States, stating that the bodies and communities of racial others are represented as being on a lower stage of (intellectual, moral, economic) development and thus in need of governance and discipline by whites. Building on Laguerre's concept, I argue that white developers are not simply reinvesting in areas of HBURs with market potential; they strive to control citywide planning, using the gentrified greater downtown—the beachhead of the return—as the political, cultural, and economic hub of their operations. To be denied the right to decide the future of the place where one lives is to be kept in a state of infancy. White domination of city planning institutes a new white supremacist regime. The representations used by white elites—designed to change how city streets are experienced, imagined, and managed—legitimate this domination and its outcomes: uneven development and black political disempowerment. The gentrified enclave is window dressing; we must learn to see the range of places produced by the return. The return leads to the yuppie shop as well as the homeless tent. The return enriches areas with market potential as it furthers disinvestment in racially stigmatized neighborhoods.

In this book, my primary focus is minoritization (racial domination), not gentrification (a demographic shift). Yet gentrification is a useful concept to frame a critical part of the minoritization process at this historical moment. There is an interaction between the *minoritization* of black urban regimes and the *gentrification* of areas in central cities with market potential. As capital and the white middle class return to the core of central cities, minoritization decapitates the black urban regime and disciplines black residents for our supposed deficiencies in morals and intelligence. Thus, minoritized space imposes racial hierarchies as it bolsters a scheme for uneven development. The wedding of urban greening to fiscal austerity in HBURs is novel, but minoritization is not new. The "traditional black ghetto" of the mid-twentieth century struggled against minoritization, hemmed in by de facto segregation and devalued by redlining. The black urban regime was a response to this degradation, drawing strength from black voting power to improve the status of segments of the black middle and upper classes. Yet the regime struggled against minoritization as it was undermined by the rise of a racist neoliberal order. Minoritization is a fluid, always unfinished struggle among race-class fractions that erupts unstable degrees of domination across political, economic, and cultural domains, mediated by control of money, technology, and land. We should pay as much attention to the boardroom negotiations between white developers and old guard black elites as to the street conflicts between gentrifiers and low-income residents. The black middle and upper classes who led the black urban regime in the past are precariously positioned, at once privileged and minoritized. At times they side with white elites; at other times they battle them.

This contradictory position was evident before the return of the white middle class, as the black middle and upper classes suffered from, yet eventually participated in, the vengeful rhetoric and policy making of the federal and state government. The war on drugs exemplifies this process: whites and blacks use illegal drugs at similar rates, but blacks have higher drug arrest rates.[7] White racism drives but does not fully explain this outcome. James Forman Jr.—a law professor and former public defender—notes that, historically, black mayors, judges, and pastors in black cities such as Detroit have supported "tough on crime" policies that have led to the harsh policing of black neighborhoods and the mass incarceration of black youths.[8] A vicious cycle results: former inmates—finding it hard to get jobs because of the dual stigma of being black and a felon—often return to crime and then to prison. The cycle repeats. Compared to whites, African Americans are more likely to view social injustices as contributing to street crime, and African Americans are more likely to support government programs to address these problems. However, as the neoliberal order unfolded, it was easier to build coalitions at the federal and state levels for tough-on-crime policies than for social programs. So many African Americans—afraid of street crime, ashamed of black "thugs," and angry about the danger on their streets—accepted a focus on punishment. Forman traces this focus from the 1960s to the 1990s, as the black middle class reacted to drug epidemics (first heroin, then crack) and rising crime rates by calling for more policing and stiffer sentences. Forman notes the role of black media: in 1970, *Ebony* magazine ran a headline, "The Black Community Declares War on Dope." In 1973, the *Amsterdam News*—one of the oldest African American newspapers—editorialized that nonaddict drug pushers should get life sentences. Some black activists supported the conservative editorials of the black press, while others opposed what they saw as the parroting of white propaganda. In a 1970 letter from his prison cell, the black revolutionary George Jackson attacked "the little black tabloids" that, he said, "mimic the fascist press."[9] From the 1980s to the 1990s, the news media (including black media) stoked fear about "crack babies" and the rise of "super predators." As drug waves (alcohol, methamphetamine, opiates) hit white communities, there was no mass hysteria about the babies of white drug addicts growing up to be predators.

Fear of street crime has merged with nostalgia. In a 2002 nationwide poll, most respondents (73 percent) agreed that "Americans used to treat each other with more respect and courtesy in the past."[10] In a 2016 national survey, a majority of respondents (51 percent) report that the "American culture and way of life has changed for the worse since the 1950s."[11] A negative view is highest among white evangelicals (74 percent) and the white working class (65 percent). In contrast, 62 percent of African Americans in the survey report that American culture has changed for the better. One might ask why this percentage is not even higher, given the depth of racism in the 1950s. Perhaps many African Americans feel nostalgia too. Folk accounts of a biblical collapse in the moral order and the built-and-natural environment of central cities pervade urban ethnographies—I call this type of story the *narrative of the fall*. Sociologists Kasinitz and Hillyard describe white working class "old-timers" who blame African Americans and labor unions for the decline of their Brooklyn neighborhood.[12] Similarly, Timothy Gibson, analyzing the views of a group of white Philadelphians, notes that they blame African Americans for the decline of the moral order and the appearance of their community: "when neighborhoods turn minority, they, *they go down rapidly*."[13] This scapegoating is not confined to big cities: studying small southern towns, Arlie Hochschild notes that whites blame "the long parade of the underprivileged" for the problems in their communities and the nation.[14] And the story of a fall is not only told by the old: the political scientist Cathy Cohen—reporting the results of a nationally representative survey—states that 48 percent of white millennials "agree that discrimination against whites has become as big a problem as discrimination against blacks and other minorities."[15]

African Americans also tell moralizing accounts about decline. Elijah Anderson, studying an "Eastern City," notes that "old heads"—responsible black men past their young adult years—recall "better days when life was more orderly and civilized."[16] Mary Pattillo tells of "old timers" in Chicago who reminisce about the "high aesthetic standards" of the past: "It was gorgeous," a woman recalls the block that she played on as a child, "It didn't have no fences at all. And green grass."[17] Mitchell Duneier recounts the stories of black men in their fifties and above who "associate moral worth with the patterns of behavior . . . in the ghettos of their childhood."[18] Researchers often assume that these stories of decline—told by people old enough to recall the "golden age of capitalism"—mirror a real urban breakdown during the post-Fordist 1960s and 1970s, but that the claims in these stories about the *causes* of decline are products of neoliberal propaganda; instead of blaming neoliberal restructuring, people (including the victims of scapegoating) blame the racialized and impoverished. Addiction and crime are seen as the causes of industrial flight and crumbling infrastructure instead of their aftermath. Loïc Wacquant argues that this view has spread to some scholars who "skid from morality to moralism," subservient to propaganda that glorifies individual responsibility, discourages social movements, and abets the "ongoing construction of the neoliberal state."[19]

The life stories that I gathered from Detroiters are like the stories gathered by other ethnographers; however, I offer an alternative interpretation, and I have a different view of their political implications. If one wishes to find out whether disorder has increased, it is best not to rely on the reports of a single generation. It is common sense to interview the generation who lived through deindustrialization, but generations who did *and did not* go through this crisis may tell similar stories. As the anthropologist Clifford Geertz notes, social scientists often fail to analyze "how . . . elements of what we tamely call 'style' operate" in the stories that people tell about their lives.[20] As I listened to multiple generations, I found signs that their stories are neither fiction nor "fact" (if "fact" is defined as a reality that all see); they are collectively stylized accounts of shared experiences that affirm the past of the beloved community as an ideal. Neoliberal politicians did not invent these stories. These accounts, coming from the heart, are mined by the political right *and* the political left to build solidarity and advance their agendas. Bill Cosby's infamous "pound cake" speech at a NAACP awards ceremony exemplifies reactionary use of the Fall:

> Ladies and gentlemen, the lower economic and lower middle economic people are not holding their end in this deal. In the neighborhood that most of us grew up in, parenting is not going on. In the old days, you couldn't hooky school because every drawn shade was an eye. And before your mother got off the bus and to the house, she knew exactly where you had gone. . . . Looking at the incarcerated, these are not political criminals.

These are people going around stealing Coca Cola. People getting shot in the back of the head over a piece of pound cake! And then we all run out and are outraged. . . . 'The cops shouldn't have shot him.' What the hell was he doing with the pound cake in his hand?[21]

Across the political spectrum, one can find nostalgia for the black communities of Detroit's past. In a 2010 opinion piece for the black newspaper the *Michigan Chronicle*, Robert Young—a justice on the Michigan Supreme Court—stated that the black community in his Detroit childhood had higher moral standards:

I grew up in the 1950s being told that I had to work harder and be smarter to get ahead in our society. Getting an excellent education and doing well in school was, without doubt, my most important job as a child. In ways that now seem distant and quaint, in our community, children were expected to and did display respect for adults. Adults were expected to and did look out for children. . . . We need more . . . Black men . . . to stand up straight and stand clearly for something just and decent.[22]

Young, a judicial traditionalist, is on the political right. He considered running as a Republican for governor, and he was on Trump's list of potential Supreme Court justices. Radical activists in Detroit also invoke the past of the beloved community. Before his death in 2015, Ron Scott—a former Black Panther Party member in Detroit who spent his life fighting police brutality—advocated conflicts being resolved not by police but by traditional figures in the community:

From that tragedy [the police shooting of a young man who had gotten into an argument with his girlfriend] emerged a discussion within our organization on how to intervene in . . . neighborhood conflicts. . . . [T]here was an older woman who lived on the block who used to regularly calm Mr. Crawford down in these kinds of situations. This woman is iconic in our communities. She is known universally as "Big Momma." . . . We have to bring back the "Big Momma Factor" to the 'hood.[23]

The past can be made to serve the present—a political leader may stir crowds with an old battle cry. But nostalgia emerges from traces that are not fully under conscious control—longings, flashbacks, prejudices, phantom habits and tastes, love of a land and a people. The power of nostalgia—from the Greek nóstos ("return home") and álgos ("longing")—can get out of hand, driven not by what people see as real but what they sense as true about home. Growth elites strive to amplify elements of the narrative of the fall and suppress others, but racial solidarity and territorial stigma cannot be turned on and off like faucets. The tales of Monsters-on-the-Lodge that once served the suburban projects of white developers now harm their downtown investments. Ruins can be gussied up with trendy shops, the addict can be jailed, the poor can be evicted, but it is a hard thing to move ghosts.

Narrative of the Fall

IN THE 1950S—IN the days when Detroit's auto industry inspired factories in Europe and Asia—Hudson's, the tallest department store on earth, dominated the downtown skyline. Draped with an American flag that spanned seven stories and weighed a ton, Hudson's crammed within its twenty-five floors of brick wall (now only a memory) fur coats, diamond rings, pearl necklaces, birds and bird cages, a children's barber shop with a saddled menagerie for chairs (a hippo, a camel, a tiger, a moose), TV sets, ladies hats, maids' uniforms, golf clubs, bridal gowns, gas stoves, Oriental rugs, couches, beds, business suits, summer dresses, potted trees, house paint, artist supplies, frilly dolls, model trains, men's leather gloves, silk lingerie, Burgundy wine. As one listens to the men and women who fled Detroit, Hudson's reappears, in voluptuous decorum and polished excess:

> Hudson's at Christmas time was gorgeous. . . . It was a delight for every child just to look at the toy displays.—a white man

> There was gallantry . . . men opening doors for women, men taking off their hats. . . . Hudson's had great and very nicely appointed restaurants. . . . They had fabrics from all over the world. . . . It was all in order . . . the clerks could help you. They could lead you and show you things without you spending hours searching through racks.—a white woman

Fifty-one public elevators and forty-eight escalators transported Detroiters through a world of commodities made in the USA, manufactured from raw materials mined, harvested, and slaughtered everywhere on earth, a storehouse of everything needed to produce everyday life and to seduce desire for that life, with all of its costumes and its categories of work and pleasure and space and role. *Fordism*—the regime of mass production and consumption, secured by a government safety net, supported by US dominance of world trade—advanced the American empire. Named after Detroit's fabled industrialist (the shrewd automaker who instituted the assembly line and the

$5 per day wage—good pay in its time), Fordism had not simply girded the US economy in the Cold War, it had also sculpted the muscles and the dreams of workers. Promising freedom and prosperity if one kept in line and worked hard, Fordism and social welfare programs regulated the hierarchical relations between the US government and its citizens, between men and women, between whites and blacks, between western countries and the Third World, and between humans and nature. The laborers of Africa, Asia, and the Americas who harvested the cocoa, tea, and coffee served in Hudson's fine restaurants were told that if they followed the path laid out by Western advisors, they would eventually enjoy the free society and the high wages of westerners. This world, at once libertine and disciplined, seemed eternal, but it did not survive. During the years recalled as golden, the auto industry started to move to the suburbs for cheap land, low taxes, and a docile workforce. By the 1980s, Fordism had collapsed, as competitors in Asia beat US industries. As right-wing politicians used the crisis to justify dismantling the welfare state, income and wealth inequality increased. Forged in a compromise between capital and labor, Fordism had not brought freedom, yet it had fed dreams of mobility. As US factories closed, as Hudson's became rubble, uncertainty and anger grew among white workers. The past was not as great as they recalled: the dead from the Ford Hunger March open a window on a grim past. But the sense of loss that white workers report is true. Now that the Fordist city was gone, who could one be and become? Would America be great again?

Hudson's hold on family and community life endures in the annual Thanksgiving Parade. Begun in 1924 by Hudson's, the downtown parade evokes a time when merchants staged holiday spectacles to place their stores at the heart of city life. To do so, the merchants harnessed older spectacles—the ragamuffin parade, the medieval pageant wagon—that had roots in ancient harvest festivals. The parade continues with corporate and philanthropic support. Intriguing in its durability, this ritual unites city and suburb each fall in a selective reassembling of the past. The holiday—begun to commemorate a peaceful gathering of whites and Indians—does not speak to the indigenous past or present. The Thanksgiving Parade winds down Woodward Avenue without observance that it follows a trail built by the Anishinaabe.[1] At the 2010 parade, I noticed that white faces outnumbered black faces in the sea of people, shoulder to shoulder, lining the route. White marching bands joined black marching bands, who infused the martial beat with African American traditions of spinning cymbals, singing horns, syncopated drums, and elaborate steps. The parade preserved civility between city and suburb, yet the distraction of the bands, the floats, the clowns throwing beads, and finally Santa Claus also secured distance. There was something spectral about this jolly ritual through which one could see boarded stores and office buildings. The parade ended near the vanished Hudson's—reduced to a parking lot—where Santa once waved the crowd in to shop for gifts. Two black women tapped this unmet market, selling cupcakes to long lines across the street from the old Hudson site. An hour after the parade ended, the crowd disappeared, except for a few black street sweepers.

Many black Detroiters of a certain age remember Hudson's fondly, but they never had a secure position in the Fordist city and its dreamscape. Some black migrants got jobs that enabled comfortable lifestyles—they joined the labor aristocracy—but many were unable to do so. Racism forced them to take the

Thanksgiving Parade, Woodward Avenue, 2010.

most back-breaking, dirty, and stigmatizing jobs. A middle-aged black Detroiter told me that when his father blew his nose and coughed, his handkerchief was dark with the soot from his job that had buried in his chest. In the early twentieth century, black Detroiters could shop at Hudson's, but they could not work at its counters. Hudson's did not hire its first black sales clerks until the 1950s, amid pressure from civil rights groups.[2] Activist Sandra Hines recalled Hudson's:

> Best, biggest, more significant and magical store you could go to. But for black people you always had the history of the door man and the elevator woman. At one time nobody could be an elevator attendant unless they were white or a really light-skinned black person. . . . [Hudson's] wasn't for "us."[3]

A five-minute drive from the old Hudson site is the Max M. Fisher Music Center, once a legendary stop on the Chitlin Circuit—the Paradise Theatre. The Paradise was for "us"; it featured African American stars—Count Basie, Billie Holliday, Duke Ellington, Cab Calloway—whose gigs spanned the Regal in Chicago and the Apollo in Harlem. The black migrants who filled the Paradise—men in suits with handkerchiefs in their breast pockets, women in hats, gloves, and pearls—lived in Paradise Valley and Black Bottom. They had been lured from the South by tales of opportunity. Too often, housing in Black Bottom was rundown, yet former residents recall a rich street life, with black-owned stores, restaurants, clubs, barbershops, beauty salons, and doctor's offices. The Paradise closed in the 1950s as the big band jazz era ended. New music emerged—a choir in Black Bottom included the young Aretha Franklin, who would become the "Queen of Soul." But the street life of much of Paradise Valley and Black Bottom would soon be over; white mayors razed the streets to build freeways. White workers used the freeways to flee Detroit as the auto industry relocated to the suburbs. The loss of jobs, the loss of place, the persistent racism fueled the Molotov cocktails that exploded through store windows in 1967.

The narrative of the fall colors the disaster. I rewind in my head the story of the white suburbanite who told me about the Monsters-on-the-Lodge Freeway, past her terror of the city, back to when she recalled the things precious to her in Detroit—having the tea ready when her husband brought home

Chinese takeout as a special treat, taking her children to splash in the local pool, browsing for tiny treasures in the "knickknack store run by two little old ladies." That orderly world of quiet pleasures unraveled in the 1970s as the auto industry tanked. Someone robbed and murdered the two old women in the knickknack shop. Families split apart, neighbors became thieves, drug addiction exploded in her working-class neighborhood. She described thieves and addicts of all races, but she believed that black militancy—its attack on law and order—deepened the crisis. In her eyes, the beginning of the end was 1967 when the streets caught fire:

> All hell broke loose. . . . You could see the fear on everybody's faces. You pass people in a car and it was horrible. You wouldn't know if they were going to shoot and they felt the same way looking at us—it was mayhem.

The fires ended, but she eventually moved. Her dread of Detroit grew. The only solution that she could imagine was a steel-fisted police force. Yet her story veered back and forth from fear to empathy. She reflected, "I realized the black people were fighting for their rights and fighting for what they should have had and deserved." Her version of the narrative of the fall frames black militancy as a danger, but her story does not fit into an ideological box. Competing parties harness this mix of empathy and fear: the white swing voters in Michigan who cheered Obama's call for "Change" in 2008 applauded Trump's promise to "Make America Great Again" in 2016. White hate groups (which have a long history in Michigan) strive to channel the racial dread of individuals into organized rage. Political scientists report a sense of vulnerability among whites in the United States.[4] White anxiety is on an upswing, but it is not new. The Haitian revolution put terror in the hearts of slaveholders across the Americas in the eighteenth century, and Reconstruction brewed resentment among US southern whites in the nineteenth century. Racial capitalism is a menacing and menaced project—fear of the dark others recurs.

The narrative of the fall does not mirror a reality that everyone sees, but it is not pure fantasy; it stitches personal experience/dream/nightmare into a collective pattern. It weaves in stories about—but cannot be solely attributed to—the mid-twentieth-century flight of capital. Since the rise of the industrial city in Europe, successive generations have lamented the loss of a peaceful and beautiful place. Across generations, the arc of decline defies linear progression, forever beginning again in the telling, and thus it does not always correspond to historians' records. As I chatted with a twenty-one-year-old black Detroiter, he stated that when he was small, morals were stronger, neighbors kept an eye out for each other's kids. He said that, now, when he talks to "young people" (he volunteers at his old high school), he sees that things have changed. This twenty-one-year-old—born after Detroit's heyday—was telling me the narrative of the fall. Beyond Detroit, one can find cases in which young black interviewees in "revitalized" cities described witnessing a moral decline. For example, the archived interviews of Tomás Jiménez—a researcher who conducted a case study of interethnic relations in Silicon Valley—contains this account by a young black man between the ages of eighteen and twenty-four at the time of the interview:

> When I was living with my grandma you could go to them for anything. It was really just tight. They used to have block parties. We used to cut off the street and have block parties and everything. . . . Everybody got along on the block. . . . That's when everyone got along in (East Palo Alto) [*Interviewer: So what do you think changed?*] . . . Parenting has changed from me growing up till now. A lot of kids don't know what the word respect means. Because back then you learned respect, like you're not going to cuss, you're not going to say nothing foul or such in front of any elder. . . . Kids used to walk to school back in the day for a mile or two just to go to school. . . . And so it's not a lot of bonding. I know it's hard times but that's when you're supposed to gravitate to your loved ones.[5]

One might read this account as evidence of moral decline, but note the phrase "walk to school back in the day for a mile or two"—a catchphrase about the good old days that this young man echoed, which merged his childhood recollections with the mythic past. He described being a child in a more peaceful time—a time when everyone "got along"—even though homicide rates have declined sharply in East Palo Alto and throughout the United States since he was a child.[6]

The durability of the narrative of the fall is best seen when comparing the oral histories of black people who grew up in the same neighborhood before and after the decline of Detroit. Let's return to the other narrator at the

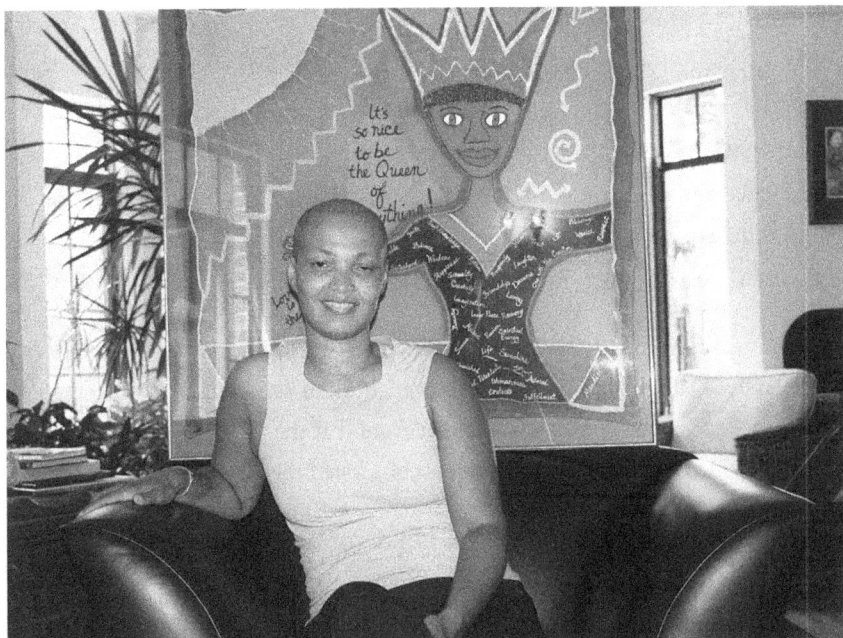

Cynthia Smith and her artwork, *The Queen of Everything*.

start of this section—the black woman in the palatial home. Cynthia Smith, an artist and small business owner, had risen in status, but she conveyed a different sense of her trajectory. In her home, one of her creations caught my eye—a picture of a crowned figure. The inscription read, "It's so nice to be the Queen of Everything!" On the queen's black robe (or in her interior/ soul) were affirmations, including the words "beauty," "respect," "cherished," and "One with the Creator." As we chatted, Smith bookended her memories, "That happened back in the days when I was a queen" in the Jeffries public housing project.

I interviewed Smith with the help of Cheryl Danley, a local scholar and food justice advocate. Like Smith, Danley is a black woman who was raised in the Detroit of the mid-twentieth century. Born in 1953, Smith spent her early years in a tenth-floor apartment at Jeffries. It opened the same year that she was born. Smith said that her parents and their friends at Jeffries were "upwardly mobile poor black people"—an appellation that described their tra- jectory yet rooted them in their origins. Over the years, her parents remained working class (her father's jobs included factory work and her mother was a store clerk), but their incomes rose. As their resources increased and Detroit declined, the family moved repeatedly. "My mother was always wanting to be in a better place." When Smith was small, there were still many jobs, but automakers had begun to automate processes and to leave the city. Young workers who lacked seniority were the most vulnerable to layoffs. Smith, reflecting on being a child during this period, recalled freedom, affirmation, and wonder as she interacted with the built-and-natural environment:

> I remember going to the store on my own for my mother when I was four years old, at an age that I would never think of sending my kids to the store. I remember playing in the playground at the projects . . . I used to walk to school. I liked to look at insects. I loved the butterflies.

As an adult, when Smith left home to do family chores, she was sealed in her car, often driving beyond Detroit to shop in the suburbs. As a child, she roamed the city:

> My mother and I would eat . . . and shop downtown. My mother liked to shop. . . . For special, special occasions, we would go to Hudson's. . . . Hudson's was the top of the line. That's where I got my first communion dress. . . . That would be part of the excursion, back in the days when I was the queen.

Hudson's appeared in her story as a royal "excursion" that she recalled with elegant yet sad phrasing. She mourned the loss not simply of Hudson's as a place to shop but also (and more importantly) as a space to feel special. Her school had nurtured her sense of specialness:

> Before I moved [from Jeffries], I was the queen of the universe. [laughs] The Catholic school that I went to near the projects was for me a really warm and wonderful and nurturing place. I felt like I was the smartest, the cutest, the most popular, the teacher's pet. It was a mostly black school.

When she was seven, her family moved to a white middle-income area in northwest Detroit that rapidly became majority black as whites fled. Her parents sent her to a majority white Catholic school in the nearby suburb of Ferndale:

Ferndale . . . back then . . . was blue-collar white folks. The children had never been exposed to black people. . . . They would say things like "God left you in the oven too long." I remember going to a [Girl Scouts] Brownie meeting, and they were singing "Eenie meenie miney moe, catch a nigger by the toe."

Smith's parents believed that she would receive a better education at the private school in the suburbs, so they told her to ignore racist remarks:

Their response was always, "Don't worry about that. Just tell them 'sticks and stones will break my bones but words will never hurt me.'" . . . Or my father, who was a little more on the aggressive side, would say, "Just haul off and hit them with your lunch box." [laughs, pauses] I wasn't that kind of girl, so none of those solutions worked for me. I internalized a lot of bad feelings about myself.

Smith said that her family today had many leisure "options" in the suburbs, yet she longed for the unboundedness that she had enjoyed in her black working-class community as a child: "It was a pretty carefree existence. In so many ways, we had a much better life because we had so much freedom."

Similarly, DeJuan Rice recalled his childhood at Jeffries fondly, although he had lived there two decades later, during the decline of Detroit. Rice was interviewed by Lionel Williams, a research assistant in his twenties who, like Rice, is an African American who grew up in Detroit. At the time that Rice was interviewed by my research assistant, he worked as a salesman. Born in 1971, Rice lived at Jeffries long after Cynthia Smith's family had fled for "a better place." In the 1970s, researchers documented the harsh environment for children in the housing projects of Detroit and other rust belt cities,[7] but Rice spoke warmly of his childhood: "My earliest memories are of hanging around . . . inside the projects. . . . I guess we were poor, but we really didn't notice it. We were just kids having fun." Rice's mother worked as a store cashier—the same occupation that Cynthia Smith's mother had. Unlike Smith's father, Rice's father was unemployed. As Detroit deindustrialized, "there was a dramatic fall in the employment of black men."[8] Before moving when he was thirteen, Rice, his mother, his grandmother, and his mother's brother and sister shared an apartment at Jeffries. In a 2001 *Detroit News* article, an eighty-one-year-old former resident of Jeffries recalled its history across the decades of Cynthia Smith and DeJuan Rice's childhoods.[9] The elderly man stated that Jeffries was beautiful when it opened in 1953, but the buildings began to fall into disrepair and the projects became more violent in the 1960s. Families who could afford to live elsewhere moved out. By the early 1980s, when Rice was in his preteens, Jeffries had become infamous for Young Boys Incorporated—a violent heroin-selling gang. However, Rice talked positively about being a child there: "It was, uh, it wasn't a bad area back then. . . . We would just do the same thing normal kids do. Play basketball a lot. . . . Things were a little bad. . . . You would hear stuff going on around the neighborhood, but you really wouldn't see that much." He detailed the fun that he and his friends had, hanging out at recreation centers where they "play[ed] pool, ping pong . . . basketball . . . you could win trophies and stuff." He also described caring adults, including the staff at a recreation center that gave him and his friends free meals.

There are hints in Rice's narrative that adults saw more neighborhood problems than he did. Rice said that his mother sent him to a distant public elementary school on the west side of Detroit because "she didn't want me to go to school in the neighborhood." Similar to Cynthia Smith's mother, DeJuan Rice's mother seemed to have wanted a "better place" for her child, but his mother could not afford the steps taken by Smith's mother—moving to a middle-income area, sending her child to private schools. However, he reported few problems in his childhood; perhaps if he had lived in Jeffries during his teen years, his story would have been different. He said that, since high school, he has seen the cost of living climb ("You spend three dollars now for a loaf of bread"), the streets become cold and dangerous, and young people become less serious about their education. Rice thought that a change in the student mix at his old high school had caused problems:

> Now I think more kids are going [to school] for a fashion show than anything else. Back then, it was a lot more poor black people going to the school. I have a nephew who's going there now, and he says that there are a lot of doctors' and lawyers' kids.

Far from lamenting a lack of black middle-class role models—which would be in line with neoliberal propaganda—Rice charged that their *increased numbers* at his old high school had contributed to consumerism and less focus on education. How could Rice—who was born after Jeffries descended into violent drug dealing—recall a lost moral order? And why did Smith compare her old neighborhood favorably to her affluent enclave? Their moralizing narrative *affirms* low-income black communities, constructing a Moral We that embraces the past of these communities as an ideal.

Miguel Martinez (not his real name) fondly remembered the 1970s in southwest Detroit. Martinez was interviewed by Ileana Cortez, a research assistant in her twenties who, like Martinez, grew up in southwest Detroit. Cortez is Mexican American; Martinez is of Afro-Latinx descent, with roots in Central America. He stated that he was born in "the best year in the world, 1971" (the same year as Rice) and that "everything was A-Okay" when he was small. His parents were drug dealers, but they hid this fact from him when he was a small child. After his early childhood, his life had been hard, including a stint in prison. After prison, he got a job cutting grass for a landscaping company. Since the early twentieth century, southwest Detroit has been the home of working-class families and small business owners from Europe, Mexico, and the Middle East. The Latinx population is mostly Mexican yet includes people from Central America and the Caribbean. Other ethnic groups in southwest Detroit include the Anishinaabe; some of them came here during the relocation era from the 1950s to the 1970s, when the federal government's 1952 Voluntary Relocation Program (a misnomer) pushed indigenous peoples into the cities and pressured them to assimilate. The American Indian Health and Family Services (AIHFS) center here is a hub for service provision. Southwest Detroit has not had the same levels of white flight as most of Detroit, but there are many vacant buildings, including the Michigan Central Depot—once the largest rail station in the world—which has become an icon of Detroit's ruin. The angle at which the building is typically photographed obscures the vibrant communities nearby. Over the past twenty years, there has been new construction. The commercial rebound is touted in the press: "From its Mexican Town restaurant district to the new shops of the La Plaza Mercado retail development, southwest Detroit is doing something it hasn't done in years—grow and prosper."[10] Southwest Detroit borders the suburbs, and the Ambassador Bridge links it to Canada. Business and government leaders seek to draw tourists to

Mural by George Vargas in southwest Detroit, near the abandoned Michigan Central Train Station. The train station often appears in depictions of Detroit as a place of ruins, yet there are vibrant communities nearby.

Mexican shops, yet the migrants who make these shops possible are not always made to feel welcome. Elena Herrada, a scholar-activist who runs a workers' center here, charges that Mexican migrants are "victims of unscrupulous employers, predator businesses, slum landlords . . . and law enforcement," including US Immigration and Customs Enforcement (ICE).[11]

The economic revival of southwest Detroit had been celebrated by the news media, but Martinez cherished its past, telling Cortez:

> I just wish Detroit was like it was when we were younger. . . . More better leisure, everybody had a little more self-respect for each other and themselves. . . . Now it's like nobody gives a crap.

He recalled that, as a child, he enjoyed going to Mexican restaurants with his family and playing in his neighborhood:

> Just about every other night in the summertime we would play hide-and-seek, my whole block, 15 or 20 of us, would play two blocks of

hide-and-seek. Like that, late at night. . . . [During the daytime] we'd go to the Boys and Girls Club, have fun, go swimming . . . go to the parks . . . play baseball and football. . . . It's too many gangs [today]. . . . Back when I was a kid . . . it wasn't all, everybody trying to be rough and tough, like it is now. . . . You can't hardly go to any of these parks now without getting shot at or stared at or somebody come messing with you.

Beyond fights, he suggested increased competition over "who is wearing what" had turned schools into "fashion shows" (echoing Rice). He remembered problems in his neighborhood—for example, he recalled that a big discount store had dirty floors and smelly rotten meat—but he stated that there were also good corner stores. He fondly recalled one grocery store: "There were really good people, Arabic people there, they would help you out if you needed credit." After Martinez's early childhood, he saw and was drawn into ethnic conflicts. He described a conflict between Latinx and Arab Americans at his high school. "I hung out with some guys . . . all the Hispanics. We got into a big ol' fight with some Arabics." As his interview drew to a close, Martinez voiced regret that the Detroit of the early twentieth century no longer existed. He described the Detroit of the 1930s as being like the Detroit of his early childhood. Martinez said, "I heard stories and seen pictures of Clark Park [in Detroit] back in the '30s and '40s and it looked beautiful. I wish it was like that again . . . like when we were younger." Like the young man in the East Palo Alto study, Martinez collapsed the distance between the early twentieth century and the present, linking his childhood to the mythic past.

This past was affirmed by Robert Yost, a white former Detroiter in his early eighties who worked for thirty-eight years in the Assessor's Office for the City of Detroit. Faced with deteriorating streets and heavy workloads, he and his co-workers had health problems. He told me: "Out of the forty real estate appraisers . . . eleven of us had bypass surgery." His first home was in a flat connected to his family's grocery store. After the stock market crash in 1929, auto production fell dramatically. The historians Robert Zieger and Gilbert Gall write: "In Michigan, the Ford Motor Company laid off all but 37,000 of its 128,000 workers. . . . Homeless by the hundreds slept in a downtown park [in Detroit] each night, while some families burrowed in the ground, using branches to cover the openings in the holes they dug."[12] Yost's account of this period was focused on play: "[At the age of five I'd wander] from where we had the house on McClellan . . . to Kercheval and Indian Village. . . . They had vacant fields there. . . . We'd go over there and play and do things." As a child, he and his family, German Americans, lived on Detroit's east side. During the 1920s and the early 1930s, the Purple Gang, a white mob, was in his area. The Purple Gang was infamous for bootlegging, extortion, and the murder of rivals and informants. Homicide rates in Detroit would not again reach the high levels seen during the Purple Gang's reign until the 1960s, when homicide rates would match then surpass these levels.[13] Yost told me that he had felt "perfectly safe" because of the big, no-nonsense policemen on patrol. Yet he recollected violence:

> One night there was a woman [across the street] talking on the phone. A guy came down the alley, turned and said, "You talked," bang, bang, bang shot her and ran down the alley. . . . And then another time on a Saturday afternoon, a car pulled up in front of our store and parked. . . . Monday morning it was still there. My dad called the police. They opened the trunk, there was another woman's body. . . . That sort of thing went on right in a normal neighborhood . . . in terms of Prohibition with gangs. Detroit had . . . the Purple Gang. . . . Young hoodlums.

Yost said that the police suspected his family's sparsely stocked store was a front for a "blind pig"—an illegal liquor joint—so they raided it. He laughed at the idea, stating that the store had little more than canned goods and a soda fountain because their customers had little money. People often asked for credit. From the store's 7:30 a.m. opening until its 11:00 p.m. closing, the cash register receipts were often only two dollars, yet he recalled being "happy" in his neighborhood:

> Times were hard . . . but we never had a problem [with people stealing]. . . . In the summertime . . . people would sit on either side of the door going into the store and converse on a warm summer night. Husbands and wives and some children. I'd be out there a lot too with the neighborhood boys.

Like Yost, Gwen Scales—a jazz singer with a German mother and African American father—fondly remembered the grocery store of her childhood and the tight-knit community surrounding it in Detroit. She told me:

We shopped at a black-owned market named Lindy's. . . . Every Sunday I had to go to Lindy's and pick out the greens and Jiffy cornbread mix. . . . Black farmers would bring their produce in, so we would get fresh fruits and vegetables. . . . Mothers were out walking with babies in baby strollers, so you had eyes on the street. . . . I had mommies aunties uncles, not blood [fictive kin]. . . . I am a product of the village. . . . We're disconnected today.

Scales described a history that is often overlooked: practices of economic solidarity between black rural farms and black urban stores.[14] She missed the black shops that provided fresh produce and anchored community life. Echoing Cynthia Smith, Scales also missed the pleasure and freedom of hanging out in green spaces:

I remember walking to school, walking home. . . . We had these wonderful chestnut trees . . . and fruit trees. . . . cherry trees. . . . I remember the smell of the trees. . . . We were always outside . . . we didn't come in till it got dark.

Then she was bused to a white school. She said that white kids hurled insults and snowballs, packed with rocks, at her and her friends. As an adult, Gwen felt a sense of solidarity with black Detroiters:

My husband and I preach staying in the city. . . . When the city became predominately black, it was automatically broadcast that we were going to fail. So I think it is important, I tell people, as long as I have energy, I'm going to carry this torch. I live in Detroit, send my kids to school in Detroit, I spend my money in Detroit. I understand that if we're ever going to thrive that we have to put our money back into the communities in which we live. We can't just keep on taking our money out of the community.

Echoing Scales, Shane Bernardo—a Filipino man in his thirties who works on food justice and Asian American concerns in Detroit—told me about the grocery store of his youth that served as a community anchor:

My family used to have a grocery store on the westside of Detroit for thirteen years. It was great [working in the store]. I was able to meet people who shared common interests, who ate the same kinds of food that we ate . . . that we loved. It was great connecting with people that I probably would never have gotten to meet or get to know. It was through this sharing of food that we were able to share values and cultural ideas. We used to get people who drove long distances just to see us. A lot of the foods we ate—root vegetables, tropical fruits and vegetables—were also shared by other cultures.

Bernardo recalled the family grocery store as a bridge between ethnic groups.

The narrative of the fall mourns the loss of earthly and consumer paradises (mammoth Hudson's, the mom-and-pop store, farmers with fresh produce, chasing butterflies, inhaling the scent of fruit trees). These remembrances are selectively reassembled into moving images in place-marketing campaigns. In a Pure Michigan ad for tourists, white children chase butterflies in slow motion near a sparkling river. Rooted in longings for a beloved place, the narrative of the fall blurs class distinctions. In her study of white towns, Hochschild quotes a white interviewee who reminisced about his working-class childhood: "We didn't know we were poor"—a refrain that Hochschild says she "heard often among those . . . on the far right, speaking of their own or their parents' childhoods."[15] Recall that DeJuan Rice used almost identical words to describe his childhood in Detroit ("I guess we were poor, but we really didn't notice it. We were just kids having fun").

I do not know the percentage of people who tell their life stories in this way, and I am unsure why this narrative recurs. Perhaps the life course sets up successive generations within working-class neighborhoods for experiencing a fall, and a storytelling style for expressing this sense of things has developed in their communities. As one grows older, adults no longer treat one as innocent; parents cease to buffer harsh streets. The childhood place that adults remember may never have existed as a reality that their entire community saw. They recall a reality shaped by their position as children. The arc of decline differs: some of my interviewees said that the fall began in their teens; others described its start in their adulthood. The narrative of the fall is perhaps a sign that families and communities of all ethnicities do their best to show small children love and beauty, even in hard times—and that they often succeed. It is also perhaps a sign that the play world of children persists in its joys. Detroit's decline has harmed the life chances of children. Political propaganda may influence how that harm is understood, and marketing campaigns may manipulate nostalgia. But the sense of a fall may have less to do with hegemony than with the structuring of the life course—and its collective framing within storytelling traditions—in places of perennial devastation. Deindustrialization is not the first disaster that the racialized and impoverished have suffered. To cope with disaster, every generation strives to revive the Moral We. In versions of the narrative, racial and class divides are evident. Note Rice's criticism of the black middle class and Smith's avoidance of the devastated working-class area. The desire of affluent African Americans to escape scenes of devastation, and the resentment of the black working class, may one day end their solidarity. But for now, the shared memory and reality of (symbolic, economic, physical) violence by white racists, combined with a love for African American placemaking, fosters some cohesion. Vaster assemblages are possible: the beloved communities of the past include people (Miguel Martinez, Gwen Scales, Shane Bernardo) with bonds that span nations and races.

There are parallels between the Moral We in the narrative of the fall (for example, Rice's criticism of growing materialism) and the Moral We in classic texts of the civil rights, black power, and anticolonial movements. Consider the moral decline that Martin Luther King describes in his essay "The World House":

> One of the great problems of mankind is that we suffer from a poverty of the spirit which stands in glaring contrast to our scientific and technological abundance. The richer we have become materially, the poorer we have become morally and spiritually. Every man lives in two realms, the internal and the external. The internal is that realm of spiritual ends expressed in art, literature, morals and religion. The external is that complex of devices, techniques, mechanisms and instrumentalities by means of which we live. Our problem today is that we have allowed the internal to become lost in the external.[16]

The justice-speak of King does not articulate a strategy to gain power: "we" have all sinned and must be redeemed. A young Nikki Giovanni, in conversation with James Baldwin in 1971, criticizes older generations of African Americans (including King and Baldwin) for valuing moral principles over power:

> For me the question has always been power. And for you all the question has been morals. I never wanted to be the most moral person in the world. . . . I mean I would sell my soul [*cold smile then stone-faced*]. . . . "What does it profit a man to gain the world and lose his own soul?" The world. That's the profit. . . . Y'all can have Jesus. Give me the world.[17]

Later in the conversation, Baldwin tells her:

> Baby, what we did with Jesus was not supposed to happen at all. We took that cat over and made him ours. . . . [White people] don't deal with God. God for them seems to be some sort of metaphor for purity and for safety.

Baldwin suggests that the black Moral We converts the religious gospel of white slaveholders to the mission of black liberation.

The black power and anticolonial discourses embraced by Giovanni's generation criticize the religious past ("*Y'all can have Jesus*"), and they reject the moral project of humanism; they regard appeals to conscience as useless. Yet they too enshrine a Moral We. Black revolutionaries frame the fall as a plunge from human potential, charging that rule by (European) Man has harmed the earth. This damage must be undone—if necessary, violently—for a future Moral We to emerge. Frantz Fanon articulates this critique in *The Wretched of the Earth*:

> Leave this Europe where they are never done talking of Man, yet murder men everywhere they find them, at the corner of every one of their own streets, in all the corners of the globe. For centuries they have stifled almost the whole of humanity. . . . Look at them today swaying between atomic and spiritual disintegration. . . . For Europe, for ourselves, and for humanity, comrades, we must turn over a new leaf, we must work out new concepts, and try to set afoot a new man.[18]

Social movements transform personal memories into a condemnation of world-historical injustices and a call for collective salvation. The degree to which the Moral We empowers low-income African Americans remains an open question.

The One

THE NARRATIVE OF the fall is not the only story that one hears on the street. One afternoon I sat reading by the Detroit River. White joggers and bicyclists passed by. On the next bench, two black men—one in his forties, the other maybe in his sixties—talked, swore, and laughed about their drug rehab. The older man kept saying "I've got to go take care of some business," but the younger guy told him to "c'mon, man, sit and talk." The older man begged change from a passerby and hurried off. The younger man got up and stared at the river. He was short and wiry; a black doo-rag fit tightly on his head and hung over his neck. The river tour boat passed, its passengers smiling and pointing. The man muttered: "Look at the whale," then turned and saw me looking.

What you reading? He folded his arms.

This book about Harlem and Chicago, I said.[1]

What's it about?

It's about how there's all these fancy stores and rich people moving in, but poor people aren't getting much from it.

He smiled, relaxing his shoulders. Sitting next to me, he said that his name was Michael. Nearby was the Gateway to Freedom—the sculpture of black people fleeing slavery. One of the statues pointed across the river toward Canada. The Caesars Windsor casino towered there now. Michael said that he wondered where all that casino money went. He told me that times were hard, and he wished he could open a place to help people. I asked him what kind of place. He did not answer. He said that he'd "gotten into bad things" and "been in a dark place."

He leaped from topic to topic—his daughter, politics, the economy, God. The running theme was trust: Who could believe in him? Whom could he believe? His answer to both questions seemed to be no one. He said that scientists claimed that there were millions of stars, and he asked if I believed them. Squinting at the wall of blue sky, I said that I did, and I asked what he believed.

He said that, years ago, he had worked in an auto plant, and he had learned that all the world was in a battle to be "The One"—the one that survived. The world appeared many things—stars, rivers, animals, trees—but only The One was real. An hour or so passed as he detailed his sense of things; reality shifted as I glimpsed the world that he saw. I told him that he should write a book. He beamed. . . . A sanitation worker lifted something from the bench where Michael and his friend had been sitting. Michael glanced at him, hesitated, then told him, You can just leave it, brother, it's mine. The sanitation worker nodded and moved on. Michael stared at the cargo ships. Finally, he said that he wondered what the men on the ships were doing. Said he looked at the statue pointing to Canada and felt like it was telling him that he should have a purpose, but what was his purpose? He stood and paced with a sour smile. Uneasy, I made an excuse and left.

Many Detroiters struggle with low wages, but most Detroiters do not live as close to the edge as Michael. A common defense against caricatures of Detroit (the Monsters-on-the-Lodge) is to stress that even most low-income Detroiters are not like Michael and his friend. The lurid stories that I read about the city obscure the people whom I see every day: Detroit is the mother who waits in the early morning on a dark corner with broken streetlights for an unreliable bus to her job; Detroit is the youth who juggles school and a job so that he can help his mother pay the bills; Detroit is the elder with a bullhorn who organizes for safe streets and good schools. Respect is due these everyday heroes, yet Michael is Detroit too. Rather than turning from him to "focus on positive people" (*Zong* ship logic), we need to see all. The supposed monsters alert us to perils that we do not see. As I reflect on Michael murmuring about a whale, then The One, *leviathan* comes to mind—both the Leviathan of the philosopher Hobbes and the sea monster of ancient myths. Embodying all, Leviathan is said to enable security and industry. Devouring all, The One churns a fierce industry that destroys security—its order is chaos. Leviathan is said to get its authority from the governed. The One commands from within, a form of possession. The One is not the self of warring ideals that Du Bois saw in the souls of black folk, and it is not the self at war with itself that Foucault viewed as disciplining the bodies of factory workers. The battle in Michael—which he saw in us all—consumes selves. Unlike the devil (*El Tío*) with whom Bolivian miners bargain for their lives in the dangerous tunnels where they must work, The One has no use for the other.[2] Similar to the philosopher Calvin Warren's articulation of "black being," Michael negated the politics of hope and its faith in black progress.[3] Michael was one with the black masses who had given up on voting, but his ontological terror was not *black* nihilism: The One finds no profit in the Negro Question. The political theorist Mbembé argues that contemporary power produces a fictionalized enemy to justify reducing populations to the living dead.[4] How do those erased by The One name their peril? Big Mama Thornton felt the threat, but her blues were a release. The ghost of Nikki Giovanni's unsmiling smile (*I would sell my soul . . .*) was on Michael's lips, but he did not find a soul to sell. George Jackson—the Soledad Brother who was labeled a "thief, burglar, gambler, hobo, drug addict"—would have understood Michael.[5] Writing from his prison cell as a soldier in the black power movement that rose from the streets and behind prison walls in the 1960s, Jackson stated: "trust is a difficult thing to build between men brought up under Anglo-American or Western cultures." But Jackson had faith in revolutionary solidarity: "My faith in life holds still to the principle that we men of color will soon make a harmonious world out of this chaotic travesty of fact." Michael had no such inspiration. As he was made to disappear into the blackness of the Monsters-on-the-Lodge—and then into the brilliance of the new downtown—he convicted himself and us. Beyond The One, there is no reality, no purpose. Its duplicity is doomsday. It extinguishes stars.

Michael's poetic naming of The One brings to mind the stories that Zora Neale Hurston collected from and told about black workers in the South:

> These poets of the swinging blade! . . . muscled like gods . . . Black men laughing and singing. They go down in the phosphate mines and bring up the wet dust of the bones of pre-historic monsters, to make rich land in far places, so that people can eat. . . . Some old-time sea monster caught in the shallows in that morning when God said, "Let's make some more dry land. Stay there, great Leviathan! Stay there as a memory and a monument to Time."[6]

Hurston puts me in mind of warm nights long ago in Los Angeles, the Temptations harmonizing on the record player and out the door left open for a breeze

(*I've got sunshine on a cloudy day . . .*). A three-year-old, I would peek from my room as my father and his friends roared with laughter and stomped their heavy work boots on the floor. Sometimes I'd slip in and steal a saltine or bit of cheese from their cold cuts platter, darting my hand between cans of beer and ashtrays with bitter-smelling stubs. I wasn't supposed to be there, listening to grown folks' conversations past my bedtime, but I hid and heard about Down Home (the pine woods of East Texas that my father and his friends had loved but fled) and the downtown jobs where they lifted and scrubbed and made and fixed. In contrast, Michael's account is postindustrial. His story cannot be reduced to a political critique of the neoliberal order or racism—he speaks of a danger in the constitution of reality—but a jobless streetscape is the backdrop for his story. Michael's despair, driven by the threat of disposal, differs from the sense of loss in the narrative of the fall. The fall recalls the Moral We. It is not the case that moral narratives discourage political action; they are the mortar that holds movements together. Beliefs about the fall can be used to rally the faithful. It is disbelief that there ever was (or ever could be) mutual support that hinders political mobilization. In Michael's eyes, the problem is not that the Moral We values moral principles over political power: the Moral We is a deception.

State of the City

AS MAYOR DAVE Bing moved to the microphone for his State of the City speech at the place that was once The Paradise, he needed to get the Moral We on his side. He had won office with promises of revival, yet his vague words to reporters in the weeks before his speech about the need to decide which neighborhoods were viable had stirred fear among Detroiters who recalled being driven from Black Bottom. Many families were struggling. The Great Recession had driven the city's official jobless rate to 25 percent, comparable to the US jobless rate in the Great Depression. City officials estimated that the real unemployment rate was closer to 50 percent, including part-time workers who sought full-time jobs and discouraged job seekers who had left the labor pool.[1] Thousands struggled to pay their mortgages or rents and their utility bills. Bing's own company had suffered a drop in sales. Bing saw the crisis in his company and his city through the same business lens. In interviews with reporters, Bing had underscored the need for rightsizing:

> You can't support every neighborhood. You can't support every community across this city. Those communities that are stable, we can't allow them to go down the tubes. That's not a good business decision from my vantage point.[2]

In the 1990s, Marie Farrell-Donaldson, the city ombudsman, had proposed removing residents from high vacancy areas, cutting off their services, and letting "mothballed" areas return to nature. The city council had rejected this proposal.[3] The revival of this idea stirred fear and anger. Hours before Bing's State of the City, municipal union members and a housing advocacy group began a protest outside the hall. The Pan-African Newswire—an alternative media site run by Abayomi Azikiwe, a Marxist organizer—had posted an online call for demonstrators:

> 45% unemployed in the City of Detroit—Families losing their lives due to DTE [electric and gas utilities] shutoffs—Our neighborhoods destroyed by foreclosures and evictions—Detroit schools continuing to fail—City

services diminished due to lay-offs. . . . Instead of hare-brained schemes to "downsize the City" and lay-offs and privatization at behest of the banks, it's time for the Mayor to stand up for the workers and poor who have been devastated by the economic depression. . . . [T]he Mayor must demand that the Governor apply to President Obama for money to bail out Detroit, the hardest-hit city in the country. We need funds to pay for jobs for youth to rebuild the houses that have been stripped and destroyed, and money to stop the destruction of public education and services in our city.[4]

Protestors charged that Bing's proposals were just the latest in a long line of planning schemes that had displaced low-income people. The bulldozing of Paradise Valley and Black Bottom had been followed by the demolition of Poletown, a mixed ethnic working-class neighborhood, for a new GM plant in the 1980s. Protestors reframed the problem of "abandoned" houses as a problem of people being forced out of their homes during repeated waves of financial turmoil. During the Great Depression, Detroit's mayor, Frank Murphy, had faced vast city debt, high unemployment, and homes threatened with foreclosure. Protestors noted that Murphy's response had been to battle the banks and to defend workers, and they demanded that Bing do the same. When Murphy's welfare program was attacked as "extravagant" during a downtown lunch for industrial and financial leaders, Murphy had reportedly exploded: "How dare you spend more money for each luncheon in this room than I need to feed a hungry child for a week! . . . The cold fact of the matter is that I'm saving the city of Detroit for you people."[5] Murphy ran the city at a time when labor power was building nationwide and businessmen feared revolution, thus they accepted reforms.

That time had passed. In his State of the City speech, Bing strived to gain the trust of Detroiters without alienating business interests. His State of the City won praise on the political right, including from a conservative pundit at *City Journal*.[6] By 2012, his language would turn combative as Governor Snyder proposed a bailout plan that transferred the power of the mayor and the city council to a state-mandated financial board, but there was no hint of conflict in the 2010 address. After welcoming the audience, Bing addressed the representation of Detroit as a dying city. His speech—delivered in his quiet, careful tone—could be condensed into bullet points, but that would hide the work of metaphor and allusion. There is a kind of poetry in Bing's words. Let's read the lines:

(1) There are those who believe the final chapter of our story has been written.

(2) They believe our city cannot come back.

(3) And the reality is if we allow ourselves to be defined by the crisis we inherited, Detroit's story will never change.

(4) This administration inherited a city near bankrupt financially, ethically, and operationally.

(5) A $325 million deficit and the threat of payless paydays by October of last year; unemployment approaching 30 percent and 50,000 homeowners facing foreclosure; a culture of corruption in city government and a mentality that we should continue doing things the same way simply because that's the way we've always done it.

(6) We could have listened to those who said our city was a lost cause.

(7) We could have allowed the statistics and stream of negative media coverage convince us that things would never get better.

(8) We could have continued politics as usual and promised change but continued down the same path that got us here.

(9) But we decided that the old way of doing things was no longer good enough.

(10) And in my ten months as your Mayor, I see a city whose collective ideas, spirit, and action are coming together as they never have before to turn the page and begin a new chapter.

(11) We began with a mandate to restore trust in our city and city government with a tough new ethics policy that shows no tolerance for corruption, conflict of interest, or abuse of your trust or your tax dollars.

(12) We've set a new tone of cooperation, transparency and accountability in City Hall, working with City Council, reaching out to regional leaders and our friends in Lansing and Washington to find solutions that work for Detroit.

The fused metaphor of storytelling/accounting frames the speech; to tell the story of the city is to give an account of its finances. Bing began by conceding that some people believed that the "final chapter has been written" and Detroit "cannot come back" (sentences 1–2). The term "final chapter" drew the value of his speech into question—if Detroit was finished, what was the use of more words? He distanced himself from this judgment (it is "they" who believed such things), but he continued the funereal tone by stating that there was little for his administration to "inherit" from the "near bankrupt" past (sentence 4). The suggestion that black officials had bankrupted the city resembled the narrative of the fall told by many white suburbanites. Bing's maneuvering was complex; he condemned and deployed negative representations of the city. In sentence 7, he blasted the "statistics and stream of negative media coverage" about the city, yet he had just used these representations himself (sentences 4 and 5). What, then, was the difference between his words and the words that "they" say? Their narrative suggested that Detroit was a "lost cause" (sentence 6). Bing suggested that the "reality" of the story could be changed if "we" redefined ourselves (sentence 3), rejected the "old way of doing things" (sentence 9), and united to "begin a new chapter" (sentence 10). Bing's "we/they" construction was not used to oppose outside interests. "We" referred to the Bing administration and to Detroiters, while remaining open to "friends" who might help rebuild the city. Bing expressed gratitude that "local, regional and state leaders are . . . working with us. . . . The philanthropic community is getting behind us. . . . And in Washington, we have the support of President Obama who I visited last week." Ethics, trust, and cooperation are referred to in almost a quarter of the 145 lines of Bing's speech.

The emphasis on changing the city's image and efficacy at the beginning of the speech (sentences 11 and 12) continued throughout the address. In lines 24 to 29, he repeated a phrase that foreshadowed the name of the Detroit Works Project, which would include austerity proposals to "make Detroit a city that works."

> (24) That's why tonight I believe we must come together with one voice and one vision to make Detroit a city that works.
> (25) A city that works for job seekers and small businesspeople struggling to survive in a tough economy.
> (26) A city that works for seniors living in fear of petty criminals and scam artists.

(27) A city that works for young people and prepares them to build a career and a good life.

(28) A city that works for neighborhoods, businesses, and churches.

(29) A city that works for all Detroiters.

(30) Together we can reinvent Detroit, bringing new jobs and investment, cleaning up our streets and getting tough on crime, finding solutions to improve education and schools and once again restoring trust and pride in our city.

The Great Recession was not mentioned until line 62, when it was made to rhyme with / structurally align with *concessions*:

(62) We have been hit hardest by what some are calling the "Great Recession."

(63) But the economic crisis in Detroit didn't happen overnight.

(64) It's been building for years and by now it should be clear to everyone that we simply can't afford to continue down this road.

(65) All across the state, unions in the private and public sector are recognizing that times have changed and [are] making tough but necessary concessions.

He made no other direct mention of the Great Recession. Lines 62 to 65 resemble line 5, in which economic hardship ("unemployment approaching 30 percent and 50,000 homeowners facing foreclosure") was paired with mention of local misdeeds ("a culture of corruption in city government and a mentality that we should continue doing things the same way."). Bing did not state that city government caused the Great Recession, yet no agents other than city government and "we" (Detroiters?) are identified in line 5, which consists of sentence fragments. It is a curious way of speaking (or not speaking) about the economy. Who/what (*subject*) did what (*predicate*) to cause the unemployment and foreclosures? Arguing that drastic measures are needed to achieve fiscal solvency, Bing chides a city union for resisting pay and benefit cuts:

(66) Unfortunately, one union continues to fight, delay, and undermine our efforts to move Detroit forward.

(67) Their refusal to recognize the fiscal realities we face costs the city half a million dollars every month; that's half a million of your tax dollars and half a million less for your city services.

Graphic 2. Comparison of 50 top words in speeches of Dave Bing (top) & Coleman Young (bottom). [The size of words indicate frequency]

(68) Now is the time to end the gamesmanship and begin the real discussion about the future of our city.

(69) We have lacked a true vision and viable plan in Detroit for decades.

At this pivotal moment in the speech, Bing—hitching the "final chapter" of the city to the Horatio Alger story and the narrative of the fall—suggested that a revival of the spirit of the old city (at once entrepreneurial and virtuous) would make Detroit great again:

(76) Now is the time for Detroit to *recapture the spirit of ingenuity and creativity that made our city great.*

(77) Detroit was once a world leader in innovation, a place where *entrepreneurs like Henry Ford and Berry Gordy* built thriving industries from the ground up, *where small businessmen in the auto supply industry like* me could grow from four employees to more than 500, and a place where local businesses thrived because we supported each other.

(78) I believe we can be that kind of city once again.

. . .

(81) For too long, *employers have had to deal with red tape, poor customer service, and a pay-to-play culture* that undermined our ability to attract new jobs and investment (*emphasis mine*).

In lines 76 to 81, Bing suggested that the spirit of the old city—embodied in its icons, Ford and Gordy (a symbolic union of the white and black entrepreneurial past)—could revive Detroit, making it a great city again where the Moral We support one another. Yet virtue was not the strong suit of the old city. Detroit has a long history of corruption, across good and bad economic times, involving Democrats and Republicans, blacks and whites. These cases include under-the-table payoffs to city officials in the late nineteenth century, the involvement of Mayor Richard Reading and the police department in graft during the 1930s, the conviction of members of the Wayne County Board of Auditors for accepting bribes in the 1940s, and the incarceration of former mayor and later city councilman Louis Miriani, "when he couldn't explain how he made nearly a quarter of a million dollars on a reported salary of only $25,000" in the 1960s.[7] Mayor Reading's venality harmed Detroit, but he did not cause the Great Depression. The same could be said for Mayor Kilpatrick and the Great Recession. Kilpatrick was but one of many players in the global financial crisis. The glittering skylines of New York and Chicago hide similar sordid histories, yet their positions in the global economic order set them on different trajectories than Detroit. To give a full accounting of the perils that Detroiters face, one must discuss the global order and US politics.

For decades, shifts in the global order and US politics have pressured black mayors to meet the demands of business and financial interests. Coleman Young and his successors pursued what they saw as pragmatic politics. Mayors Bing and Young are often framed as opposites, but there are similarities in how they downplayed class conflict. Framing themselves on the side of a Moral We that transcended race and class, both men sought to integrate Detroit into the regional and national economy. In 1974, Coleman Young began his first inaugural address by stressing mutual interests among blacks and whites, Detroiters and suburbanites, while demanding social equity:

(1) The first problem that we must face as citizens of this great city, the first fact that we must look squarely in the eye, is that this city has too long been polarized.

(2) We can no longer afford the luxury of hatred and racial division.

(3) What is good for the black people of this city is good for the white people of this city.

(4) What is good for the rich people in this city is good for the poor people in this city.

(5) What is good for those who live in the suburbs is good for those of us who live in the central city.

(6) It is clear that we have a commonality of interests.

So who was the "other" that must be fought? Young carried out the ritual of outrage against lawbreakers, framing himself on the side of the Moral We. Young is often misquoted as ordering whites to "hit Eight Mile Road" and leave Detroit. He actually ordered criminals to leave:

(18) I issue open warnings now to all dope pushers, to all rip-off artists, to all muggers.

(19) It's time to leave Detroit.

(20) Hit Eight Mile Road.

(21) And I don't give a damn if they're black or white, if they wear Super-
fly suits or blue uniforms with silver badges.

(22) Hit the road.

These lines reflected the move by Young and other black leaders toward "tough
on crime" policies. At a prayer breakfast before Young's speech, a prominent
African American judge had called on him to fight crime: "the drug pusher . . .
must be exposed and brought to the bar of justice."[8] Yet there are differences
in the speeches of Bing and Young. Young addressed street crime *and* police
corruption, and the most frequent words in Young's inaugural speech resembled the name of his plan to use federal development funds to revitalize the
city: "Moving Detroit Forward." In his speech, Young spoke about using federal and state funds to help move the city forward from racism and poverty,
and he expressed faith in the promise of the Fordist city: he celebrated Henry
Ford II's plans for building the Renaissance Center. In contrast, Bing did not
directly refer to race and poverty during his State of the City; both Young and
Bing delivered moralizing speeches, but (diverging from Young) Bing avoided
justice-speak. Facing backlashes against affirmative action and social welfare
programs, black mayors increasingly advance colorblind proposals and self-
help projects that do not rely on government. Bing did not break completely
with the Fordist past; indeed, he boasted in his speech about convincing GM
to house more of its employees at the Renaissance Center. However, black
mayors no longer see the Fordist city as viable—Bing suggested that Detroit's
days as a manufacturing powerhouse were over. The new vision was green
(financially, environmentally). Bing emphasized balancing the books, and he
identified service jobs and green industries as emergent opportunities. This
was, he said, an opportune moment to clear "blight" and then remake Detroit
into a "city with vibrant neighborhoods . . . thriving small businesses, better
mass transit, and community parks and green space."

In the State of the City, Bing mentioned urban greening as a means of dealing with blight and as part of his overall strategy to create jobs, fix the city's
business climate, and align the local workforce with business trends. However,
he did not emphasize environmental concerns. Faced with union protests outside the hall, his focus was on jobs. He elaborated on green redevelopment

in other forums. Urban greening was a colorblind proposal that many people considered good (morally, aesthetically, financially). After Bing's speech, I attended a Detroit Works meeting at which a Detroit city planner stated: "Certainly we want a sustainable community in the city of Detroit. . . . I think everybody brings different perspectives and thoughts to the table about how we get there, but I don't think we'll find lots of people who will disagree about wanting more green space."

Bing's interest in urban greening aligned with national policy making. Barack Obama had become the first black president a year earlier. In the early years of his administration, Obama emphasized the green economy, arguing that green initiatives can safeguard the public welfare and serve as engines for growth. Obama announced a "green jobs" adviser—the black activist Van Jones—and the freshly created White House Office of Urban Affairs listed "energy-efficient and environmentally sensitive development" as a goal. To coordinate green development, the secretaries for the Department of Housing and Urban Development (HUD), the Department of Transportation (DOT), and the Environmental Protection Agency (EPA) formed an interagency Partnership for Sustainable Communities. The American Recovery and Reinvestment Act (ARRA) of 2009 included funds for green projects, and the Department of Energy (DOE) offered loans and grants for alternative energy research and development. This green thrust should not be exaggerated; federal legislation to avert climate change got stalled in Congress. And Obama withdrew his support for Van Jones after conservatives accused him of being too radical. Nevertheless, in 2010, the green city was a popular goal. Between 2011 and 2016, the Obama administration entered into a federal-local partnership with Detroit that included support for green initiatives.[9]

Bing's interest in greening also reflected local realities: pockets of Detroit were being remade by green activism, entrepreneurialism, and philanthropy. Community gardens in Detroit, supported by private philanthropy, can be traced at least as far back as the Great Panic of 1893 when Mayor Hazen Pingree developed a "potato patch plan" to enable jobless Detroiters to cultivate food in vacant lots. The city government had little money to implement the plan, so Pingree encouraged churches to donate seeds and tools. During the Great Depression and World War II, public-private collaborations produced Relief

Gardens and Victory Gardens. In the 1970s, Mayor Coleman Young started the Farm-A-Lot program, offering permits to residents who wished to garden in vacant lots. Farm-A-Lot received seeds, tools, and technical assistance from Michigan Consolidated Gas Company, Ford Motor Company, and the 4-H Program (in collaboration with Michigan State University Extension–Wayne County). The difference between the potato patches of the nineteenth century and the gardens of the twenty-first century is the sense that urban greening should be a revitalization strategy, not an emergency subsistence measure. News of the greening of Detroit spread beyond the city as advocates publicized it via digital media. In place of photos of abandoned factories, images of vacant lots that had become spaces for community gardens, beekeeping, and recycled art appeared in e-zines and on YouTube. Instead of stigmatizing high poverty black areas as spaces of danger and ruin, talk of urban greening drew these areas and their residents (or at least select sites and individuals in them) into stories of personal and societal rejuvenation. Green activists and entrepreneurs cultivated a taste among college-educated, middle-class young people for "sustainable" practices, including eating locally grown organic food—a taste that the urban core could satisfy. Noting this potential for a lucrative rebranding of Detroit, even political rivals favored green initiatives.

In a radio interview in 2010, Bing stated that some of Detroit's empty lots could be converted into urban farms:

> We're blessed . . . with a massive amount of land that's being totally underutilized. . . . If we could start looking at more and more . . . community farmers growing their products in the city of Detroit, delivering them over to Eastern Market [an open air produce market near downtown], I think it's going to be an economic boon.[10]

Cultural workers nurtured the idea of a green future in pockets of the city long before Bing's election. A short drive from where Hudson's once stood, bordering the old Paradise Theatre, Cass Corridor (a.k.a. "the Corridor") offered a *narrative of redemption*—the crystallization of the communal past in a vision of bread and communion. This future-oriented narrative was connected to a long history of cultural work throughout the city, including D-Town Farm on the west side and the Boggs Center on the lower east side.

As downtown placemaking and Detroit Works unfolded, growth elites would try to revive the most charming ghosts of old Detroit (Hudson's Department Store, the mom-and-pop shop, lively streets with beautiful trees and gardens) while exorcising its demons (the Monsters-on-the-Lodge) from areas with market potential. To do so, they enlisted the storytelling power and placemaking of cultural workers in the Corridor and the black neighborhoods beyond greater downtown. These cultural workers often valued entrepreneurialism, yet some of them began to frame Detroit Works as an extension of the city's settler-colonial history. I turn to their narrative of redemption, while keeping in mind Michael's questioning of the Moral We.

III
Redemption

Downtown

"Bringing Hudson Back"

AT NIGHTFALL, ACROSS the street from the empty lot where Christmas displays once sparkled in the windows of Hudson's, the fire juggler tossed flames into snowflakes. Ice skaters started to spin round a brilliant plaza as black and white women with red lipstick smiles and Santa caps—too young to recall the flames of 1967—began to carol in front of a pop-up shop that appeared in an abandoned store. Nightly spectacles build up to Wonderfest—a new festival with food vendors and street performers that began after the 2011 Thanksgiving Parade. A year earlier, the crowd had fled when the parade ended. Wonderfest enticed suburbanites and Detroiters to linger together on the street and munch roasted chestnuts and kettle corn and fat sausages and drink German beer and take a picture with Santa and (last but not least) buy Christmas gifts. These remnants of harvest rituals have origins in a time when vast forests walled human settlements. But the commodification of seasons masks human dependence on natural cycles. The holly everywhere no longer invokes the magic of holly trees, but it still has power. In 2011, as families in winter coats passed the restored Kern clock at Woodward and Gratiot (a relic from Detroit's heyday), time restarted; the shopping season and ancient seasonal rites had been set once again in sync. A Wonderfest spokesperson stated: "Everyone around here remembers going to Hudson's downtown during this time of year and it being so beautifully decorated and really enjoying that. That's what we're working towards, bringing that back to the city."[1]

The following summer, Downtown Detroit Days, inspired by a sales event of the same name that Hudson's once held, was revived at the Hudson site: the red, white, and blue tent stalls of the outdoor market were set up where Hudson had towered with its seven-story American flag. A sky blue sign with bold white letters ("THEY'RE HERE!") announced the return. If you stared into the sky blue of the sign, you saw an optical illusion: a headless woman (only

Comparison of Hudson's lot in 2012 and 2018. In 2012, a sign ("They're Here!")—across the street from the lot—announces the revival of Downtown Detroit Days, a shopping event from the 1950s. Merchant tents are set up on the lot. The sign has a ghostly image of a 1950s woman's legs and shopping bag (barely visible) in the background. It also has a shuttle schedule from the suburbs, and it states that artists will entertain. In 2018, a sign announces a mixed use tower to be built on the Hudson site.

pale legs, a skirt, a shopping bag, and high-heeled shoes from a bygone era), rendered in the gray monochrome of black-and-white TV, appeared to walk again on the sidewalk. The sign listed the schedule of a shuttle to and from the suburbs. Nearby, a band played Motown oldies while a juggler in a top hat entertained kids. Hudson's is gone, yet it remains a magnet for commerce. When I visited Detroit in 2018, the old Hudson site was surrounded by a wooden fence, above which waved the US flag (bringing to mind the flag that draped Hudson's). A sign on the site announced a new building, planned to be the tallest in Michigan, that would have retail and residential space.

In a talk at New York's High Line, the directors of riverfront and park conservancies in Detroit's greater downtown touted their revitalization of public space. Modeled on conservancies in global cities that use lures such as the High Line, public-private partnerships in Detroit and other US cities in fiscal crisis have adopted *placemaking*—a strategy for increasing commerce and rents through vibrant streetscapes. Ford Motor Company led an effort in the 1970s to build the Renaissance Center on the riverfront. An office, retail, and hotel complex, the Renaissance Center was intended to be an economic catalyst, but it sucked pedestrians from the streets. Unlike the *architecture of fear*—the fortified office towers that secure suburbanites from the real and imagined dangers of urban streets—placemaking revives street life. As business and real-estate interests reconnect central cities to regional and global markets, they spotlight public space to make it appear a welcoming place for white gentrifiers that also benefits black residents. Suburbanites fight regional planning and revenue sharing, but they are drawn to the nostalgia of seasonal rituals in greater downtown, to its multicultural entertainment, and to its sports, arts, medical, and higher education institutions. Business and real-estate interests strategize ways of using these assets to turn tourists and commuters into shoppers and residents. In particular, they strive to draw young artists, professionals, and entrepreneurs. A young white waitress with ambitions to become a full-time writer (she writes part-time for an e-zine) told me that she moved here from the suburbs: "You hear so much about Detroit coming back, it's exciting. I want to be part of that." In 2009, a *Detroit News* opinion article coauthored by Brad Garmon, a director at the Michigan Environmental Council, and Gil White, past president of the Michigan Association of Realtors, called for private-public partnerships to support placemaking:

Michigan needs great, walkable, urban places if it is to mount a serious economic recovery. . . . In essence, the idea is this: If we build places where the best and brightest want to live, our economy will reap the benefits in job creation, skilled workers and entrepreneurial activity. If we fail to build them, those same folks will continue to go elsewhere. . . . The network of old wealth in the state has provided us with strong and engaged foundations, big pension funds and major institutions. These are the building blocks that can yield new private-public partnerships that provide access to the kinds of patient equity that build a higher quality urban environment.[2]

Downtown placemaking began by building on nostalgia for Detroit as a commercial paradise. The Detroit Shoppe, a new store that opened in the Kresge building, sold memories of the city's past—coffee table books about old Detroit next to treats such as Faygo soda pop (established in 1907) made in it. After the Detroit Shoppe helped to draw foot traffic back, it was replaced by a chain clothing store. In the early days of the revival, placemaking in the central business district capitalized on seasons, parks, and the river, but it did not try to seem eco-friendly—the bike share stations and the urban garden had not yet come. Over time, boosters enlivened their ornamental use of nature with marketable elements of the earth-conscious moral order in the artist enclaves near downtown and in the black neighborhoods beyond greater downtown. Experts advised developers that their college-educated target group valued the "culture of sustainability":

The talented are driven by . . . access to amenities, walkable healthy communities, recreational opportunities, availability of trails and bike paths, urban parks, [and] access to entertainment places. . . . [I]n the New Economy, economic development does not . . . come at the expense of depleted resources and social inequity, but is promoted by the culture of sustainability.[3]

When I visited the central business district in summer 2018, I stayed at a new hotel. Amid vintage photographs that showed the shops of old Detroit, the hotel sold new locally sourced goodies that it labeled as "gourmet." On the back of a potato chips package was a moral message:

Some of the potatoes for these chips were born on a vacant lot in Detroit's Hope District. They were nursed in our soup kitchen for the mentally and physically challenged. They are made by community activists in an effort to bring work, hope, and dignity to our vulnerable community. Some of the proceeds go to maintain the soup kitchen and to create other financially sustainable grassroots projects.[4]

The return may conjure to mind the white hooded redeemers of the old South—the racial nightmare beneath the surface of America. Indeed, some newcomers speak of Detroit in colonizing terms as a "wilderness." Yet it is the pleasure in goodness that sells (at least in the open) here. This goodness is more than a brand. The earthly paradise animates the market with a soul, drawing new residents and tourists past their fears of Detroit. But as the earth-conscious culture is made to revive the market, its nature changes. Like the chimerical colony of Libertatia, founded on the African island of Madagascar to unite and liberate pirates of all races—a seventeenth-century fiction that was an early expression of libertarian and anarchist ideals—Detroit's greater downtown has a buccaneer spirit.

The buccaneers include Schostak Brothers—a family-owned real-estate firm that pulled commerce from the central business district in the mid-twentieth century as it developed suburban shopping malls. In the early 2000s, as the market soured for suburban malls, Schostak Brothers converted abandoned department store buildings in Detroit into upscale lofts and contributed to street renovations. One brother, Bobby Schostak, was elected chair of the Michigan Republican Party in 2011. The most powerful downtown developer is Dan Gilbert, the billionaire founder of Quicken Loans, who moved his headquarters here in 2010. Quicken Loans is an internet-based mortgage lender. Gilbert describes his company as a "technology company that happens to do loans."[5] Born in Detroit during the 1960s, Gilbert grew up in Southfield, a nearby suburb. He worked at his parents' real estate firm then left to start his mortgage lending business. A short man with slicked-back hair, a five o'clock shadow, and a wary gaze, Gilbert began investing in real estate, in tech startups, and in sports and entertainment. He owns the Cleveland Cavaliers (he is perhaps best known nationally for his spats with LeBron James). His umbrella entity, Rock Ventures, oversees his mortgage business; his real-estate empire; his sports, entertainment, and tech enterprises; and his redesign of downtown Detroit. In 2014, Eric Larson, the former managing partner of Gilbert's Bedrock Real Estate, became CEO of the Downtown Detroit Partnership (DDP), which manages the Business Improvement District (BID)—a publicly authorized, privately administered entity that taxes downtown property owners for streetscape upkeep. With the blessings of city officials, Gilbert works with DDP not only to renovate downtown parks but also to develop an overall downtown plan:

> The process launched through a partnership of Rock Ventures, the Downtown Detroit Partnership (DDP) and the Detroit Economic Growth Corporation (DEGC). The team has engaged in a master planning process for the [central business district] . . . [hiring] four consulting firms that specialized in placemaking, retail strategy, and urban planning. The four firms were Shook Kelley from Charlotte, NC; TerreMark Partners from Atlanta, GA; Project for Public Spaces from New York, NY; and Gibbs Planning Group from Birmingham, MI.[6]

City government and the old manufacturing elite contribute to downtown placemaking, but Gilbert is the main driver. In the past, wealthy individuals such as billionaire "Matty" Moroun bought ruins in greater downtown and simply held on to them, waiting for property values to rise: Gilbert is different. When he came to town in 2010, his rapid purchases and renovations of downtown properties made him the largest and best-known private property owner in the central business district. Billionaire Mike Ilitch, founder of Little Caesars Pizza, also became prominent in Detroit redevelopment, until his death in 2017. Billionaire Roger Penske, chairman of the Penske Corporation (a transportation services company), continues to be a key player. Less visible, speculators in Asia, the Middle East, Europe, and the Americas pour millions of dollars into Detroit's downtown, driven by hopes of high rates of return.[7] Carlos Slim, the Mexican billionaire, bought the Marquette—a historic downtown building—in 2014. Black wealth is coming into the city too: Magic Johnson, the former basketball player, has made headlines for his plans to redevelop the city's former state fairgrounds. And there are the less publicized projects of black investors such as Michael V. Roberts, a Saint Louis businessman, who transformed a historic building on the downtown riverfront into the Roberts Riverwalk Hotel in 2010. Yet the most influential investment is being made by the white 1 percent. Over lunch, a black developer told me about a building that he wanted to buy, but he said that property costs in the central business district were becoming too high for him and other black developers whom he knew.

Nevertheless, old guard black elites have key roles in the redesign of greater downtown. Important figures include:

- Rainy Hamilton Jr. and Kent Anderson, cofounders of Hamilton Anderson, an architectural firm headquartered in downtown Detroit. Dan Gilbert has hired the firm to partner with SHoP, a New York–based firm, in the design of the showcase building planned for the Hudson's site. Hamilton Anderson was the lead day-to-day technical consultant for the Detroit Works Project, funded by the Kresge Foundation. In 2018, Hamilton Anderson is ranked #98 on *Black Enterprise* magazine's BE-100 list of the largest African American companies. Its 2017 staff are listed as seventy-three and its revenues as $14 million.[8]

- Faye Alexander Nelson served as CEO of the riverfront conservancy from 2003 to 2014. Her past projects include the development of greater downtown's research and technology park, Techtown. Nelson has been a vice president at DTE Energy and the president of DTE Energy Foundation, its philanthropic arm. She is a former board member of Compuware. In 2018, the Kellogg Foundation announced Nelson's appointment as the director of its Michigan operations.

- George Jackson (same name as the 1960s Soledad Brother but different politics) is the founder of Ventra Group LLC. His past positions including serving as the former head of the Detroit Economic Growth Corporation (DEGC) and as a director at DTE Energy. DEGC is a nonprofit that partners with the city to support development. Most of DEGC's budget comes from public funds, and it shares staff with the city government. In his role as head of DEGC, Jackson chaired Detroit Future City, the nonprofit implementing the citywide plan that emerged from the Detroit Works Project. Jackson resigned from his CEO position with DEGC in 2014 then founded Ventra. Ventra, a development and real estate advisory firm, has projects in greater downtown. Jackson sits on the DDP board.

Greater downtown also draws black elites from other cities. For example, David Tarver—a black engineer who left Bell Labs to cofound a tech company with two other black engineers in New Jersey that they later sold for $30 million— has advised young engineers in Techtown, and he has counseled Wayne State as the university expands its tech initiatives. Detroit has long had a black bourgeoisie. In the early twentieth century, these black leaders achieved a measure of success in their professions and businesses, had their own fraternal societies, and vacationed at the black resort town of Idlewild in northwestern Michigan, where they enjoyed horseback riding, fishing, swimming, and entertainment.[9] But racism limited their opportunities. None of them amassed the kind of wealth that would enable the Ford, Hudson, and Kresge families to create private foundations that would have an enduring influence on cities in and beyond Michigan. Black entrepreneurs and professionals had few opportunities in the central business district. Howard Sims, a black architect, reflects on those days in Detroit:

> Certainly it's true that at one time, black architects had only one major client: churches . . . and maybe funeral homes. . . . It wasn't until the mid to late '60s that black people entered the decision-making process so far as what might be built, and where, and how it should look.[10]

In the 1950s, Detroit activists pressured downtown department stores to hire African Americans as sales clerks. The legal and political protections these activists fought for—protections advanced by the black urban regime in the 1970s—enables some of today's black professionals and entrepreneurs to play roles in the redesign of downtown, benefiting from the return of capital. Rainy Hamilton, the black architect whose firm led day-to-day operations in Detroit Works and was later given a contract by Dan Gilbert to codesign the Hudson site, stated:

> If you think about a gentleman like Dan Gilbert, founder of Quicken Loans, I think we've all read about his investments. Mr. Gilbert owns over

65 buildings in downtown Detroit that he has put back on line and having them occupied by businesses, employees, and others, and basically is building an empire, and it's a wonderful thing.[11]

It is wonderful that black experts have opportunities to use their talents. After the Great Recession, the return of capital must appear miraculous. The problem is that, in the neoliberal order, it is hard to separate public and private interests as the 1 percent who are "building an empire" hire experts for quasi-public and private projects. It is not simply a question of individual integrity. Political scientist Lawrence Lessig notes, it is "perfectly conceivable . . . to imagine a corrupt institution filled with noncorrupt individuals."[12] It is problematic to have a city planning process that is led by private interests who can be rewarded by other private interests who have a financial interest in their decisions. This type of city planning should be avoided on ethical grounds, whether or not the decisions of specific individuals at a particular moment are swayed by promises of gain, and regardless of whether the process breaks the law.

One might counter that privatization is not the problem: city governments in the United States do not have a history of being responsive to their black and low-income residents. In the mid-twentieth century, Robert Moses—the "master builder" of New York who held unelected posts in government bureaucracies—imposed his vision of grand highways and bridges on the city, disregarding protests against his bulldozing of neighborhoods. During the same period, government-mandated urban renewal destroyed black neighborhoods in Detroit. And one might point to transformed streetscapes as proof that public-private partnerships are improving urban life in New York and in Detroit. Near the Hudson lot on Woodward Avenue, Campus Martius—a city-owned park that was once scorned as a deserted "pigeon plaza"—has been renovated through a public-private partnership into a popular lunch spot that anchors mixed-use development. The park won a 2010 award from the American Planning Association as one of the top ten great American public spaces. It also won an award from the Urban Land Institute, which stated, "What makes Campus Martius Park work so well is that . . . it's a place where people want to spend time. As a result, it's a magnet for investment. That's the definition of a successful urban open space."[13] Since Campus Martius's first renovations in 2004, there has been over $1 billion in investment nearby. This formula for turning space and time into money has been applied at the river. In 2003, the Kresge Foundation, General Motors, and the City of Detroit launched a riverfront conservancy, which added a walkway, a carousel, fountains, bike rentals, and a food court. A study commissioned in 2013 by the riverfront conservancy estimates that 90 percent of riverfront activity would not have taken place without the renovations, and that events there generate $16.7 million in annual spending.[14] During my years in Detroit (2010–13), the new ventures in and near Campus Martius and the riverfront seemed fragile. At certain hours there was a crowd, at other times golden oldies blared past unoccupied tables on empty sidewalks. Even when I visited in 2018, there was not enough foot traffic. But there is potential: the new ventures are in walking distance to major public and private employers and to entertainment such as Comerica Park baseball stadium and the Fox Theatre.

The statue of a woman warrior with a sword and shield faces out from Campus Martius. Unveiled in the nineteenth century as a monument to Michigan soldiers and sailors who fought in the Civil War, she has become the sentry of the new Detroit. A stone medallion in its walkway marks the "point of origin" from which Detroit's roads were laid out in the nineteenth century. Located on a median, the park is a hub of major streets, but its design—with a central fountain and a barricade of trees, water walls, and sculpture—draws the eye inward. It is its own world. There is a sense of privacy at each table; the roar of the fountain insulates conversations. Across a narrow street is Cadillac Square, a tiny park annexed to Campus Martius. A booth funded by Quicken Loans offers free game equipment. Depending on the time of day and week, you can see black men playing ping-pong or white men playing *pétanque*. A white couple held their wedding reception here, offering live jazz and free cupcakes for all as they declared their love for each other and the city of Detroit. On another day, the Salvation Army had an ice cream fund raiser. A flash mob with a French theme—*Diner en Blanc*—appeared one summer evening.[15] Modeled after a Paris event, diners of all races dressed in formal white attire and brought food and champagne.

In negotiations with the Dennis Archer administration, Compuware made Campus Martius's renovation a condition of its move in 2003 from the suburbs, desiring a "front yard" for its employees to enjoy.[16] It built its new headquarters across the street from the park. White Construction, a black-owned company, served as a construction manager. Compuware, the Ford Motor Company, and the City of Detroit funded the park's renovation. Schostak Brothers was part of the development team. The Detroit 300 Conservancy, a subsidiary of DDP, manages Campus Martius. Private space flows into public space: the fountain in the Compuware lobby and the fountain in the plaza were both created by WET Design, a water sculpture firm—founded by former Disney Imagineers—that also created showcase fountains for the Bellagio casino in Las Vegas.

This privatization of public space is taking place nationwide. By "public space," I mean a gathering place (a park or shop) that appears open to all, regardless of government or private ownership. "Privatized space" is a government-owned public space that is managed by business and real-estate interests. Privatization has generated a new *publicity regime* in Detroit and other HBURs. Scholars Staeheli and Mitchell define *publicity regime* as the property rights, social norms, and legitimation modes that form the public as physical space and social body.[17] Property rights produce public space and legal access to it. Social norms shape its design and use. Legitimation modes use stories to claim public space. Supporters and critics of the new publicity regime in Detroit emphasize market power. Yet cultural work also exerts force. Developers use cultural work to increase the appeal of public space and to justify its privatization.

A comparison of promotional films for downtown Detroit shows the shift in publicity regimes and their cultural messages. In the 1970s, a film by the Renaissance Center Partnership—led by Henry Ford II—touted Detroit's (hoped for) comeback. With the funk version of the classical European composition *Also Sprach Zarathustra* setting the tone, the camera flashes non sequiturs: Henry Ford II at a podium—Rodin's Thinker statue—the black mayor shaking hands with a white man in a suit—black and white blue-collar workers— downtown shoppers—a young white couple laughing—a model of men in suits inside the soon-to-be-completed Renaissance Center.[18] The narrator's smooth baritone reassures that the Renaissance Center will revive the city and "enrich our vision of society and ourselves." Contrast this film with Dan Gilbert's

Opportunity Detroit ad during the 2012 World Series, which breaks with the Fordist past.[19] Gone are the blue-collar workers; the handshake between government and business is nowhere in sight. As images flash of people (black and white artists, entrepreneurs, and professionals) and places (Campus Martius, an urban garden, street art, creative work spaces) in the new economy, white rapper Kid Rock narrates:

> Opportunity. It doesn't stare you in the face. It's not going to yell at you to come 'n get it. It doesn't knock. . . . You see, opportunity is not a right. It's definitely not equal. . . . It's molded. It's built. It's created. . . . An explosive high-tech corridor located at the intersection of muscle and brains? You bet. . . . What does opportunity look like? It looks like Detroit.

The ad conveys a neoliberal message: individuals with "muscle and brains" in the postracial, post-civil-rights landscape do not need government—they create their own opportunities ("opportunity is not a right. It's definitely not equal"). This vision of self-reliance, showcasing green projects, has appeal.

Privatized space has increased downtown investments that include the black middle and upper classes, and it has expanded local green amenities. However, the campaign to portray the new Detroit as solely the product of individual enterprise sidesteps reality: downtown developers, including Dan Gilbert, have lobbied for and gotten government grants, loans, and tax incentives.[20] And it obscures how real-estate speculation interacts with the history of job and housing discrimination to shape wealth disparities. This history tends to give white elites a privileged position to control development. The publicity regime has a *medieval logic*.[21] Seeking protection from the insecurities and violence of the world (dis)order, people submit to the (mostly white) wealthy and powerful oligarchy who hold fiefdoms—their private guards, their charity, and their patronage secure life and livelihoods. This domination brews resentment; some Detroiters refer to downtown as "Gilbertville." And it does not end insecurity; the beneficiaries of Gilbert's investments fear that if he were to leave, his streetscape might vanish.

The renovation of public space in downtown Detroit draws ideas from global capital, most notably from New York, where planners design lively, fun public spaces that encourage well-heeled foot traffic. Larson (the former

Gilbert executive who is the CEO of DDP) credits New York's Bryant Park Corporation (BPC) with inspiring DDP placemaking.[22] Billing itself as "the largest effort in the nation to apply private management backed by private funding to a public park," BPC drew gentrifiers to Bryant Park after New York's fiscal crisis in the 1970s, with help from the New York–based Project for Public Spaces (PPS), which has been hired to advise on Detroit placemaking.[23] Green nonprofits also help. In 2011, the CEO of Compuware started Lafayette Greens on a vacant lot. In 2014, Compuware donated the garden to Greening of Detroit, a nonprofit that supports urban gardens and forestry. Elizabeth Gordon Sachs founded Greening of Detroit in 1989, the nonprofit becoming a major resource for black urban farmers beyond downtown who used gardens for community affirmation and subsistence. The great-grandfather of Sachs's husband co-founded Goldman Sachs, the Manhattan investment bank. Rock Ventures is on the nonprofit's board, and the JPMorgan Chase Foundation, the philanthropic arm of the global financial services firm based in New York, is a sponsor. In 2015, JPMorgan Chase donated a closed bank building to Greening of Detroit to use as its headquarters, and a group of Chase employees served as volunteers to help Greening of Detroit develop a business plan for a project. New York did not invent BIDs and green placemaking. BIDs in Toronto and New Orleans preceded those in New York, and community gardens have myriad roots, including in black nationalist projects. New York's prestige, expertise, and money enable its mobile actors to play roles in a global network that shapes urban form. These actors do not have identical aims and politics. The diverse interests and institutions (commerce, finance, philanthropy, art) in the network generate tensions, but the privileged backgrounds of the actors and their need for collaboration make market solutions seem common sense.

This network invests in the gentrifiers who are coming into downtown Detroit. DDP projects have included D:Hive, a welcome center on Woodward. During my time in Detroit, D:Hive was a "one-stop shop" that offered Detroit tours, rental ads, job information, and networking opportunities. I attended D:Hive events that asked gentrifiers about the types of amenities that they desired, and it encouraged them to change the streetscape themselves by offering entrepreneur workshops and providing space for pop-up shops to jumpstart their enterprises—affirmative action for (mostly white) middle-class young people. A three-year project that ran from 2012 to 2015, D:Hive was supported by the Hudson-Webber Foundation (begun by the heirs to the Hudson's Department Store fortune) and Rock Ventures, which sought to increase "new, young, talented" people downtown.[24] In 2015, D:Hive split into new groups that focused on specific services for young newcomers. Hudson-Webber is part of a coalition of foundations whose goal is to "restore southeast Michigan to a position of leadership in the new global economy."[25] Some young, college-educated African Americans take advantage of the opportunities here: two black women completed the D:Hive entrepreneur workshop, started a successful catering business, and eventually opened a popular vegan restaurant. However, for impoverished young black Detroiters in the central business district who have not been to college, there is nothing comparable to D:Hive that boosts their self-esteem, provides them with resources, and engages them in the redesign of the streetscape.

One day in a downtown store, a muscular black man in his fifties, wearing a cap and work boots, asked me if I had seen the young man begging for change outside. I told him I had. The man in his fifties sucked his teeth and said that he had worked hard all his life, and it hurt him to his heart and made him angry to see a brotha so young out there begging—the young man needed to get a job, there were plenty of jobs. I was doubtful. The man in his fifties mentioned a job program beyond greater downtown. I suggested that he tell the young man about the program, but the man in his fifties said that young men today have hard heads, a lot of them are on drugs. He said that perhaps the young man outside would listen to me, because I am a woman. I didn't feel like getting into a debate about women's work, so I said nothing. As I left the store, I saw the skinny youth leaning on a trashcan. I asked him if he was hungry. He straightened up and said, Yes ma'am. I gave him a sandwich, chit-chatted, then I told him about the job program. His eyes brightened as he leaned forward, rapidly firing questions about the program and directions to it. I told him, but back in my loft, when I looked up the job program on the web, I saw that it had funding cuts. Perhaps I gave false hope. And he could have other problems that need to be dealt with first. Addiction is but one of the many problems that could put a youth on the street; he could have been dealing with domestic violence or mental health issues or a hard transition from foster care to adult life. Or he could have been one of the "throwaways" living on the street, tossed out of his home because of his sexual orientation. He needs to know how much we need him, and he needs to be invested in not just because it's "nice." There is work to be done that only his mind and heart can do. Maybe he could figure out a way to sell produce that the elders can afford or he could make the streets safe without all these guards and cameras. Or he could do or say who-knows-what unexpected and amazing and necessary to help change the structures in which we live.

Privatized space has increased downtown investments that include the black middle and upper classes, and it has expanded local amenities. However, it has also raised concerns about free speech and assembly in *traditional public forums*—government-owned sites that have long been gathering places. The US government does not have the right to ban or require prior notification for lawful activities in these spaces.[26] In 2013 and 2014, the security guards of Campus Martius and the riverfront prevented marches by an antiwar group and the gathering of petition signatures by an antiforeclosure group. In January 2015, the ACLU (American Civil Liberties Union of Michigan) filed a federal lawsuit against the Campus Martius conservancy and its security force, charging that they had violated free speech and assembly rights. In April 2015, the City of Detroit and the ACLU reached an agreement: the City would protect these rights but may apply "time, place, and manner" restrictions that fit Campus Martius's "unique" status.[27] The rules require noninterference with business operations and scheduled activities. Gilbert's plan for private management of downtown parks is tied to his plan for new retail. This monopolization of public space limits the ability of the public to choose when and how they appear downtown. Intensive security extends beyond the parks. During my years in Detroit's central business district, whenever I stepped outside my building, I saw either police in their cars or private guards on foot and bicycle patrols. A network of surveillance cameras monitors activity, including in the park.[28] The hope is that well-heeled visitors will feel comfortable and safe shopping downtown. Rock Ventures monitors the cameras from The Qube, in concert with police and other companies. Activists allege that the surveillance center monitors their social media to control downtown protests.

PPS—the New York–based nonprofit that Gilbert hired to advise placemaking—is inspired by sociologist William Whyte, who advanced the social psychological study of public space through the use of cameras to quantify and analyze the use of public space by different types of people. PPS extends his work by helping planners to enhance *place capital*, which it defines as the "shared wealth (built and natural) of the public realm" that can be combined with "cultural and social capital" to generate wealth in cities.[29] PPS promotes its merger of markets and hangouts as a nonbureaucratic, ecologically friendly response to interurban competition that boosts social integration and local economies. PPS asserts that placemaking increases racial co-presence in public space. Did it do so in downtown Detroit? I did not find any historical information that would enable me to compare racial contact before and after placemaking, so I compared public spaces that had and had not (yet) been privatized. Specifically, I compared racial head counts in two municipal parks (Capitol and Grand Circus) with two privatized spaces (Campus Martius and the RiverWalk). These spaces are within a ten-minute walk of each other. At the time of my head counts, the municipal parks had new benches and plants, but they did not yet have food vendors and music concerts. I did a count at each park on a typical workday in summer 2012 between 12:30 p.m. and 1:30 p.m. I did the RiverWalk tally between 11:30 a.m. and 12:30 p.m. on a Sunday. For all head counts, the weather was pleasant, and I selected times favorable to the claims of placemaking advocates. From casual observations while living downtown, I knew that, on a typical day, Campus Martius got most of its visitors on weekdays at lunchtime and that the riverfront drew weekend tourists. My counts support the argument that market-driven placemaking fosters racial co-presence (at least initially). Even when smaller in size (Campus Martius versus Grand Circus), privatized space drew more people, including more whites. Campus Martius was across from Compuware, which helped it to draw a crowd, but office workers probably would not have used it if it were still badly maintained. Many black retirees lived downtown. I saw black retirees at both Campus Martius and Capitol. During my years downtown, regardless of the time of day, I usually saw few whites at Capitol and Grand Circus. The ability of low-income black residents to use well-funded public space improved (for a time), and nearby venues became racially mixed. A black-owned café with soul food, hard liquor, and live music that had once floundered became a crowded retro nightspot.

TABLE 3. Head counts at privately and publicly managed spaces, by race

	Total acres*	Management	Black	White	Other	Total
Campus Martius**	2.5	Private	41	50	3	94
Riverfront***	--	Private	15	21	6	42
Capitol Park	.44	Municipal	10	1	0	11
Grand Circus Park	4.60	Municipal	12	1	0	13

* Data on park acreage are from the city of Detroit 2006 Detroit Recreation Department Strategic Master Plan, Cluster 4 Condition and Capacity Reports.

** Campus Martius tally includes Cadillac Square, an annexed strip of green space.

*** The Riverfront tally is restricted to the roughly one-quarter-mile portion of the RiverWalk that runs across the southern border of tract 5172, from Hart Plaza to the GM building.

Placemaking increased race-class co-presence but not necessarily social interaction or equity. During my years in Detroit (from 2010 to 2013), older black women and men in worn clothing typically sat on the periphery of Campus Martius, outnumbered by young people of all races in office attire at its center and in its bistro. Low-income residents had low priority in the planning of amenities; they could listen to music at Campus Martius, but they could not afford its bistro. On my visit to the bistro in 2012, I saw waiters (mostly white) in black aprons serving mostly white patrons who sat at tables with cloth napkins and wine glasses. The menu listed American and French dishes (Dijon saffron moules, filet au poivre . . .), and it boasted fresh local produce. In 2012, the Campus Martius website boasted that the plaza's "French tables and chairs . . . [offer] Detroiters a uniquely *European-feeling* outdoor space" (*emphasis mine*). Perhaps the European feel in the plaza and bistro—the "French flair" that conjured the soldier-trader Cadillac—made the space comfortable for middle-class and upper-class whites. In 2018, I noticed the bistro had new management and cuisine, but the menu had similar prices: $20 to $30 for lunch and much higher for dinners (oysters on the half shell, beef tartare . . .). Cheaper options appeared: food trucks began to stop near the plaza in January 2013 as part of a vending program by Rock Ventures, offering 50 percent discounts to downtown employees. Without the discount, a meal with soda was roughly $10. Social media advertised the deal. The patrons were office workers of all races. One afternoon, I watched as a black man—perhaps in his sixties, wearing worn clothing and pushing a bicycle with a sack tied to the handlebars—asked the office workers how much they had paid for their food, and then he got in line. The food truck owner asked the man if he worked downtown and told him the nondiscounted price. The man seemed embarrassed; he walked away with his bicycle without buying anything.

As placemaking increased gentrifiers, rising rents made it hard for the low-income black elders who were once the majority here to stay near renovated public spaces. Changes near Capitol Park exemplified this process. In 2012, a few blocks from Campus Martius, around the corner from the new shops on Woodward Avenue, past the stench of an alley where homeless men hid behind trash bins, Capitol Park sat on a median shadowed by vacant buildings and the Griswold, which provided Section 8 senior housing. On a typical day, most visitors were black, yet there also were hard, sunburned white faces, different from the white faces at Campus Martius. A few homeless men sat alone. Elders chatted on a bench. Their neighbors went by—a black woman with her grandchild, a black woman pushing an oxygen tank who stopped to gasp, a white woman with a walker, a black man in a wheelchair. The elders greeted them, asking about their day and health. One afternoon, I saw young, bare-chested white men hanging out a window, observing the park. Artists lived in the rundown building. The occupants were mostly white yet included black, Latino, and Asian artists. Another afternoon, I saw black men playing chess in the park while a radio played Motown oldies and youths—one black, one white—rode skateboards. Across the street, men hung out near a store that sold chips and soda behind bulletproof glass. This social world was near its end. In Dan Gilbert's placemaking plan, under the heading "Issues," Capitol Park's low-income users signify vacancy: "The park feels lonely. . . . Benches, chairs and tables are used primarily by the homeless with an occasional senior from the senior residence across the street. . . . Very little happens in the park except skateboarding."[30] To make the park (but not its users) less "lonely," the plan was to gentrify the area. In 2013, the Griswold elders got eviction notices so that their building could be renovated for market-rate units. The framing of "loneliness" as a problem of the park, not people, elides the risks that displacement from familiar ties and services poses to elders and the homeless. A sixty-one-year-old woman who had lived in the Griswold died less than a year after she was forced to move. She had expressed sorrow: "We don't like that we have to leave one another and make new friendships. We're like a family here."[31] A former resident attributed the woman's death to a loss of the social support that had helped her to manage her diabetes. Whether or not that was the case, it is problematic that Gilbert's downtown plan does not address the risks of displacement. The sixty-one-year-old appears to have been one of the signers of an open letter on Facebook to Detroit from the tenants:

> We . . . call on workers, retirees, young people, and the unemployed to support our fight against eviction. This fight is part of a broader opposition to the "restructuring" of Detroit in the interests of the rich. . . . What is happening to us is happening in different forms to every section of workers, seniors and youth throughout the city.

Like Detroiters battling evictions elsewhere, the tenants stressed their lives of hard work, their sense of community, and their social contributions. In August 2018, when I made a trip to downtown Detroit, I saw that the Capitol Park area had been transformed; trendy new shops had opened on the ground floor of the building where the elders had lived. In the park, black and white vendors hawked fresh produce and sweet potato and bean pies at tables. Tiny clear-walled pop-up shops sold books and clothes. A black musician played old soul songs with an electric violin. Young people of diverse races (white, black, Asian) moved through the park, chatting, buying food, browsing shops, listening to music. Sitting in the park at lunchtime on a week day, I counted roughly fifty people. The park had become a lively, diverse space with healthy food options. But the low-income elders who would have enjoyed the fresh produce and the pies and the soul music were gone, and the park was heavily surveilled: I saw three black guards on patrol.

The top-down urban renewal projects of the mid-twentieth century harmed black communities, but privatization is not the cure. Buses rumble through downtown Detroit, carrying working-class people from their neighborhoods to their jobs. Unlike public transit in New York, which has a diverse ridership, Detroit's unreliable bus system tends to be avoided by professionals. Workers voice concerns about late buses, job insecurity, school closures, violent crime, unsatisfactory policing, and dangerous vacant houses. They have little to do

New tables and benches at Capitol Park. In the background, the building that was once Section 8 housing for elders has become an upscale apartment complex, with new shops that appeal to gentrifiers on the ground floor (a Thai restaurant, a pizzeria and bar, a shop that offers Botox, chemical peels, and fat reduction procedures).

with the new downtown—the upscale lofts with valet parking, the euro-style coffee shops. Downtown placemaking is said to spur economic growth citywide, but high-poverty neighborhoods have spread across the United States, including within HBURs that revitalized public spaces in and near their central business districts. One might argue that we need to wait to see the full impact of downtown placemaking: sites such as Cleveland's Public Square and Detroit's Campus Martius are too newly renovated to generate citywide benefits. However, Baltimore's Inner Harbor and New Orleans' French Quarter have been in renovation for decades, while public infrastructure in low-income areas of Baltimore and New Orleans have crumbled.

Placemaking strives to distract gentrifiers from misery. To do so, it does not simply redesign streets—placemaking guides eyes and feet. In 2010, before most of the new shops opened, my first view of downtown placemaking was inside my building. When I moved into my loft, I saw graffiti on a vacant building from my window, but I got a mental picture of residing in a lively, affluent area from posters about Campus Martius, bars, restaurants, and a farmers market, which staff had placed in the elevator near the floor buttons—little commercials as I went up and down. After I brought up the last of my suitcases, I opened a folder that management had left on the kitchen counter. The folder contained local promotions, including ads for natural food shops in nearby Cass Corridor, an artist enclave. The Corridor's shops, connected to the urban agriculture movement and to regional farms, embedded daily life in relations with self, the other, and nature: a Moral We. This Moral We, rooted in the local, branched out to transnational networks of organizers who envisioned a global future that was not dominated by international corporations.

Developers have rebranded Cass Corridor and its surrounding neighborhoods as "Midtown," which they map as part of "greater downtown"—a 7.2 square mile area of reinvestment in and near the central business district. Downtown Detroit Partnership (DDP) and Midtown Detroit Inc. (MDI) take on quasi-government functions, hiring street cleaning and security services and coordinating redevelopment. Their boards overlap: a representative of DDP sits on MDI's board, and DDP includes a few MDI members. The DDP board has mostly FIRE (finance, insurance, real estate) industries and professional services. The MDI board has mostly ICE (intellectual, cultural, educational) industries and health/human services organizations. These differences initially shaped distinctive approaches to nature, which have become less apparent over time. On its website in 2012, DDP described parks and the riverfront as offering "beauty" and "entertainment." Similar to DDP, MDI associated green spaces with beauty and entertainment, yet it framed nature as more than ornamental. On its website in 2012, it described "reintroduc[ing] native vegetation" and teaching people about nature—goals consistent with the aims of MDI's service institutions. Listing spaces that promoted health, MDI stated that "Midtown boasts . . . an organic bakery, fresh markets . . . [and] walkable greenways."[32] The design of green venues has been less centralized in Midtown than in downtown.

Artists, shop owners, and nonprofits do placemaking in Midtown, with support from foundations, universities, and corporations. Unlike DDP, MDI had a "Who We Serve" statement on its website in 2012 that mentioned both "middle-income . . . and . . . low-income residents." In bohemian Midtown, "green" was a "visionary" space that met a "triple bottom-line" (earth, economy, community). Greater downtown also includes gentrifying areas such as Corktown—historically, a working-class neighborhood of Irish immigrants in southwest Detroit that became increasingly Latino and African American. As young white professionals and entrepreneurs began to move into Corktown, some of them framed "green" neither as ornamental nor moral but rather as part of Detroit's gritty authenticity. A young developer in Corktown stated: "It's real, it's honest. You can spend the day at an urban farm, and then head off to a Tigers game or the opera, just like the locals do."[33] Yet Detroit can get too "real." This developer led a Corktown group of white newcomers that dubbed themselves the "Conquistadors" in meeting minutes leaked to the press.[34] On an online board, a poster wryly commented: "At least they're honest." The minutes, outlining the group's efforts to stop a church from giving free food that drew the homeless, led to charges that they sought to "recolonize" the area. The group said that they used the name in jest and that they had simply wanted to reduce crime and nuisances. They said that they had helped to fund charities, preserve historic buildings, and develop green spaces. DDP and MDI have better public relations, yet their activities also have led to concerns about gentrification.

Like other newcomers, I knew little about DDP and MDI when I arrived in 2010. I found a CVS drugstore that sold (limited) groceries a block away. It was a rare point of intersection for gentrifiers and longtime residents—everyone needed laundry detergent and toilet paper. The customers on a typical afternoon: A young white man in a suit trying to decide which juice to pull from the cooler . . . a heavy, middle aged white woman in a faded flowered dress, sitting in a wheelchair, buying cigarettes . . . a fiftyish black man in work boots who asked the cashier for a lotto ticket . . . an old black woman who picked up her prescription and bought canned food that she rolled in a small shopping cart back to her apartment. I liked the friendly black store clerks, but I wanted fresh food. From reading the ads on my kitchen counter, the healthiest options seemed to be in the Corridor, so I went there.

The Corridor

"Being Open"

IF YOU WERE to drive to Cass Corridor at lunchtime as white faces increased on its streets and the Detroit Works Project began, you would have to battle for parking at Goodwells, a black-owned natural foods shop. Goodwells is gone now, but before Whole Foods opened a few blocks away, it brought together gentrifiers and longtime residents who like organic and Afrocentric markets. The space was small but airy. The storefront windows, open to a tide of light, let you feel the time of day. A black man with a neatly clipped moustache and a white apron took your order at the hot food counter. The black woman who spooned your steamed vegetables and brown rice was in African garb; a scarf bound her locs. A short, serious black youth in a cap and a lanky young white man with an easy grin helped to serve customers. The menu had daily specials—today greens, black-eyed peas, and cornbread, tomorrow vegetarian chili—and regular items such as the popular Pocket Pita Sandwich with fresh sprouts, crisp veggies, avocado, a soy patty, Havarti cheese, and special sauce. Beyond the hot food counter, a cashier rang up groceries amid racks of cereals, canned goods, medicinal herbs, and Detroit-grown produce. You could pull Nikki's Ginger Tea from the cooler or a Sweet Potato Sensations pie from the deli case. Both were made by black vendors in Detroit. If you had roots in the black South, the greens and cornbread seemed (almost) Down Home. Yet the customers were multiracial. Perhaps they longed for the store in their old neighborhoods or the neighborhoods recalled by their grandparents. Goodwells brought to mind the mom-and-pop store run by Robert Yost's parents, the place where neighbors sat outside talking on warm summer nights . . . and the shop of the kind Arab family who let Miguel Martinez's family buy food on credit . . . and the grocery store with tropical fruits, run by Shane Bernardo's family, that bridged cultures . . . and the black-owned store with fresh produce—grown by black farmers—that drew mothers pushing baby strollers in Gwen Scales's childhood. Longtime residents who shopped at Goodwells described the store as tied to the Corridor's past: the store was new (opening in 2006), but its owners had been part of the Cass Corridor Food Co-op—its motto "Food for people not for profit"—that operated for thirty years before closing in the early 2000s. Goodwells served more than food; it was an opening to the heart of Detroit, its interior architecture. Flyers in the shop announced political and cultural events in the Corridor and in the black neighborhoods beyond it. Goodwells' own flyer showed silhouettes of a Moral We—without obvious race or gender—sharing a well beneath tag lines "Eat Well and Live

Goodwells

N A T U R A L ✦ F O O D ✦ M A R K E T

Naturally Good to Go Menu

The Famous Pocket Sandwich! $4.25

Tasty vegetarian soy patty topped with baby spinach leaves, crisp romaine lettuce, fresh-sliced tomatoes and cucumbers with energy packed alfalfa sprouts, topped with Goodwells House sauce inside in a whole wheat pita pocket. w/cheese or avocado $4.50 w/cheese & avocado $4.95

Vegan Pocket Sandwich $4.25

All vegan version
Sauce on the side $.35
Extra sauce $.65

Raw Pocket Sandwich $4.25

All raw ingredients on sprouted multi-grain bread.
Extra sauce $.65

Falafel Supreme Sandwich $5.50

Baked falafel, tomatoes, cucumbers, onions, hummus, lettuce, pickled turnips with tahini sauce inside a whole wheat pita pocket.

Avocado Delight $5.50

Avocado slices and creamy havarti cheese are layered between tender baby spinach leaves, crisp romaine lettuce, fresh-sliced tomatoes, cucumbers and energy packed alfalfa sprouts, topped with Goodwells House sauce inside a whole wheat pita pocket.

Steamed Vegetables & Brown Rice $6.95

An organic medley of seasonal market-fresh vegetables from broccoli, carrots, cabbage and onions - steamed to perfection and served over nutritious and delicious aromatic organic brown rice.

Soups Soup of the day Cup $2.99 Bowl $3.75
Vegetarian Chili Cup $2.99 Bowl $3.75

Call ahead and place your order! 313-831-2130

Eat Well & Live Well with Goodwells

Fresh Organic Fruits & Vegetables
Groceries & Bulk Food Items
Dried Fruit, Nuts & Snacks
Soup, Salads Sandwiches & Specials
Vegan Baked Goods & Desserts
Fresh Juices, Natural Soda
and Bottled Waters

YOUR HEALTH IS YOUR WEALTH!

HOURS
Mon-Sat 8 AM - 7 PM
Sunday 10 AM - 5 PM

418 W. WILLIS ST.
WEST OF CASS – MIDTOWN DETROIT

WELCOME TO A MODERN DAY WELL – A GOOD WELL – IN THE CITY

Goodwells Flyer, circa 2010.

Well with Goodwells" and "Your Health Is Your Wealth." Under their feet, the tagline ("WELCOME TO A MODERN DAY WELL—A GOOD WELL—IN THE CITY") rooted them not in any particular ethnic history but rather in a future of shared well-being. The flyer brought to mind revolutionary posters that rallied people to realize human potential and liberate the earth. Yet the flyer did not articulate a political ideology.

For a different dessert, you could go next door. It was hard to find a seat at Avalon International Breads—a white-owned bakery with a gay flag out front and composting posters inside. From the 1970s to the mid-1990s, the

Peace pole outside Avalon Bakery, 2013.

space was the Willis Gallery, a hangout for (mostly white) artists and rebels to view each other's paintings and read poetry and play music and drink beer. Gilda Snowden, a black artist who ran the Willis from 1983 to 1984, stated: "There was this network that really was wonderful."[1] In 1997, two Jewish women from the suburbs remade the building into a bakery. The space still wove together artists and rebels across backgrounds and generations *(Gilda Snowden: "Every time I go into the Avalon Bakery I look on those walls and . . . I can remember where each one of my pieces was on those walls.")*.[2] Now it sold artisan breads and fair trade coffee. Nikki's Ginger Tea—the black-owned soft drink sold next door at Goodwells—was in the cooler here too. On Fat Tuesday there were pączkis. Sandwiches, salads, and quiches made with Detroit produce and with eggs, meat, and vegetables from nearby rural areas were on a menu that listed each item's supplier. Shelves displayed regional jams. The shop's name had roots in legends of a healing island paradise, while the bread—Paradise Valley Raisin Pecan, Poletown Rye, Corktown Cinnamon Raisin, Hastings Street Challah—recalled the old working-class neighborhoods of black migrants and white immigrants in Detroit. The white woman wearing glasses at the counter would slice your loaf of Motown Multigrain on request. If you looked behind the counter, between metal shelves of bread (an edible library), you would see black and white workers with sacks of flour on their shoulders and trays of dough in their hands. A rickety wooden bench—seesawing as customers sat and stood—lined the window in front of rickety tables. A narrow aisle separated customers from the counter, with wiggle room between tables. The closeness and the seesaw led to conversations among strangers, and regulars greeted each other by name. The white man with glasses sitting next to you asked what you thought. The older black gentleman wearing a gold embroidered African cap pressed a card in your hand; he taught about ancient Kemet. Talk of art, books, news, and daily life filled the air. A language other than English would drift in. If you sipped coffee here long enough, you would see artists, revolutionaries, mystics, and scholars from all over the world. A wooden pole outside Avalon proclaimed "peace" in four languages. In 2017, Avalon added a location in the central business district, but in 2010 the eccentric little shop was synonymous with the Corridor.

Shopping in the Corridor connected you to an imagined community that spanned nations. It also connected you to rural Michigan. While searching in a white, rural area for a room to rent near campus on the days that I taught in East Lansing (my Detroit loft was a snowy two hour drive from my classroom in winter), I met the woman who supplied the eggs that went into my breakfast sandwich in the Corridor. I recognized our link because the organic food shop named its suppliers on the menu. The woman gave me a tour of her farm. A farm activist, she mentioned individuals, nonprofits, and academic groups whom I knew from studying Detroit's urban agriculture. She said that she might attend a Detroit forum that would bring together some of these groups. The regional food market fostered overlapping networks, with the Corridor as an important hub. Similar to the Corridor, gentrification was a concern in rural areas of the region. Urban sprawl—driven in part by rural gentrifiers—had reduced farmland and harmed the ecosystem.[3] As the value of the land increased and the profitability of small-scale agriculture declined, some farmers had sold their property to developers. Other farmers saw a future in organic farming for local "natural food" markets—a strategy that fed urban gentrifiers. The gentrification concerns of longtime urban and rural residents overlapped, but their interests did not always coincide.

The Corridor—reviving the memory not only of its own history but also of other places threatened with erasure—was a crossroads for people and information. It was not quite downtown or the neighborhoods; historically, it had been a portal for flows in and beyond Detroit. The area was named after Lewis Cass—a territorial governor, slave owner, and advocate of Indian removal—who farmed here. A woman told me that she shortened "Cass Corridor" to "the Corridor" to avoid honoring this racist. I do not know when or why most people began shortening the name. In the early twentieth century, the area was an upper-class enclave with Victorian homes, where prim ladies played croquet on their lawns and families in elegant attire attended stately churches. Some residents called their enclave "Piety Hill."[4] Fortune shifts. By the mid-twentieth century, Piety Hill had become a working-class area and then a "red light" district with bars, addicts, sex workers, drag queens, single-occupancy room hotels, pawn shops, and homeless shelters. After Detroit's old skid row was demolished to expand the Lodge Freeway, the city council decided to corral vice from other parts of the city into Piety Hill:

> "The businessmen [e.g., bar owners] who operated along Michigan Avenue and the men who lived there are going to turn up somewhere," Ravitz [a city councilman] told the *Detroit News* in November 1962. "Why can't we control and designate a specific area for them, before we find the effects of a new Skid Row appearing throughout the city?"[5]

The area that was once Piety Hill became Jumbo Road for a while and then was widely referred to as Cass Corridor. For decades, the Corridor has had diverse residents—whites, blacks, Chinese, Native Americans, LGBT—whose hangouts come and go as their percentages shift. During my years in Detroit, North Cass had a heavy concentration of students. South Cass had older, low-income residents. Wayne State University is on the northern border of the Corridor. The neighborhoods surrounding the Corridor have a concentration of arts, educational, and medical facilities. The Detroit Medical Center—the largest health-care provider in southeast Michigan—and the Henry Ford Hospital are east and north of the Corridor, respectively. Nearby cultural venues include the Charles H. Wright Museum of African American History, the College for Creative Studies, the Museum of Contemporary Art Detroit, and the N'Namdi Center for Contemporary Art. The University of Michigan and Michigan State University have outreach facilities bordering the Corridor, and the Ecumenical Theological Seminary offers a program for "spiritual nurture and social justice." Techtown, located northwest of the Corridor, was cofounded in 2000 by Wayne State, Henry Ford Health System, and General Motors; it serves as an incubator for tech start-ups. The most prominent cultural venue near the Corridor is the Detroit Institute of Arts, whose collections include *Detroit Industry*, the famous mural by Diego Rivera, painted during the Great Depression.

As capital fled Detroit in the mid-twentieth century, the Corridor became known as a place of crime, drugs, and prostitution—one of the most feared and maligned areas of the city. Yet it also was known for its avant-garde art; its painters and sculptors used drills and saws to create industrial abstractions with found objects and faux antiquing. A British artist drawn to Detroit recalled hearing about the Corridor while studying in the United Kingdom:

"Two of my instructors at Hull College of Art knew of it, telling me that 'there's stuff going on there. . . .'"[6] Beyond the visual arts, the Corridor has been an incubator for music and the alternative press. In 1969, CREEM—a rock magazine—began publication in the Corridor. Over its run, it would showcase a wide array of Detroit music. One collective that appeared in its pages—the Detroit-based Parliament-Funkadelic—would serve as an inspiration for Afro-futurism: a vision of black cultures generating technologically advanced uto-pias. The Corridor also has been known for its radical politics. In 1965, Viola Liuzzo, a member of the First Unitarian Universalist Church in the Corridor, was murdered by the Ku Klux Klan in Alabama after she went on the Selma to Montgomery march. Also in 1965, seventeen-year-old Harvey Ovshinsky founded the *Fifth Estate* newspaper in the Corridor, which would become a clarion for green anarchism nationwide. Its writers included John Sinclair, the manager of rock band MC5 and a cofounder of the White Panther Party. In the late 1960s, John Watson, a member of the League of Revolutionary Black Workers (LRBW), headed the Wayne State student newspaper. LRBW culti-vated transnational links. In 1968, Watson spoke at an anti-imperialism con-ference in Italy. Radicals in the "motor cities" of Detroit and Turin shared ideas about fighting for worker autonomy from corporate power and bureaucratic unions. In the 2000s, as capital returned to Detroit's central business district, the counterculture art and politics of the Corridor mingled with calls from its rehab programs, its sidewalk evangelists, and its meditation circles (shades of Piety Hill) to heal the self, the community, and the earth.

On sunny days, the lunch crowd from Avalon and Goodwells spilled out on sidewalk tables. The customers gulping icebox-cold Nikki's Ginger Tea here beneath umbrellas might appear as the same as yuppies in Chicago or New York sipping iced lattes at Starbucks, indifferent to the bulldozers scooping the rubble of public housing or the police stopping and frisking black youths. One must look closer: there are a mix of subcultures in Detroit, with distinct terri-tories (as there are in Chicago and New York). More than the central business district, the Corridor drew newcomers who wanted to transform themselves and the world. Two or three street people, asking for change, leaned against the brick wall; lunch crowd regulars greeted the sidewalk regulars by name and chatted with them. Bohemian shops nestled nearby—a black-owned bookstore with titles on vegan cooking, Malcolm X, and women's spirituality . . . a tiny clothing store that featured local designers . . . a natural hair care shop owned by a dreadlocked former model who used the aromatic herbs from her garden in hair potions . . . an art gallery. A few blocks away, Green Garage had converted an alley into a green pathway for pedestrians and bicyclists, using native plants and reclaimed bricks. Green Garage held start-up workshops for "triple-bottom-line businesses" that aimed to be "good for the environment, economics, and the community." A farmers market was held at Wayne State University. The growers included Detroiters and regional farmers. Newcomers, drawn to the Corridor for a meal or a shirt or a book, went on to learn in its spaces about the politics, history, and culture of Detroit, and they were urged to be creative, start their own ventures, and transform the world. To do so, they were told they must heal and share their true selves. Some newcomers felt drawn to this world that was aggressively open to difference/making a difference.

The Spiral Collective, which occupied the building that was once the Cass Corridor Food Co-op, exemplified this aggressive openness. As you wandered into the Spiral Collective, the Source bookstore owner, Janet Jones—a small brown-skinned woman past middle age, with a direct gaze, round glasses, a flowing scarf, and a curly white mane—greeted you:

> Welcome! You've been here before, haven't you? Well, welcome. Welcome, welcome, welcome. They're three businesses that share this space. I'm the bookseller. Then there's the person who sells the body products. She might be in today, I'm not sure. Then there's the person who runs the art gallery. You're welcome to walk around and enjoy

The Spiral Collective had book readings, art exhibits, exercise classes, and Tai Chi and Qi Gong workshops. The bookshelves reflected the eclectic interests of Jones: titles on the history and culture of black Detroit . . . women's studies . . . health and well-being . . . world spirituality and metaphysics. If you chatted with Jones, she might tell you about the Detroit Housewives League in the 1930s—a forerunner of black food security groups. Or she might slide into a discussion of Buddhist thought or Stephanie Rose Bird's writings on African American spirituality or Pierre Teilhard de Chardin's religious philosophy. After a few visits, I asked Jones if I could interview her. She agreed. It was a quiet morning. I stopped the tape a few times as she answered the phone or greeted customers with her "welcome, welcome, welcome." A middle-aged black author came in with copies of his book about the history of a Detroit neighborhood. They chatted a bit. Then a white youth in a hoody from Ann Arbor, perhaps in his late teens, asked her advice: should he stay in Detroit or go on a study abroad? She told him to go, see the world, expand his mind, and then come back to Detroit. As I turned on the tape again, she told me that she rejected narrow definitions of community. She said that her space was open to everybody:

> I often say this is a community bookstore, because it is open to the community. Anybody who comes in or approaches this place, I accept, because I'm sitting inside a community and not a multilevel corporate operation. . . . We want to make money, but that is not the key goal. Our key goal is Read. Inspire. Live.

I asked her to define community. She said,

> I feel that community is anybody you touch and anybody who touches you. The science fiction writer Octavia Butler says "All that you touch, touches you." That's true. You can live in isolation, but you become more and more dehumanized by being in isolation. Those innate qualities of love, companionship, hope, dreams, become skewed and reduced.

In the Corridor, I often heard mention of Octavia Butler—the African American novelist who speculated about the nature and future of the human. Like Butler, Jones did not define community in racial terms, and she did not speak of membership in community as an abstract "right":

> I think "right" is an overused word. You are a member of the community because you simply are—you were born into this society and shaped within its culture. . . . Every human being shares in and is shaped by this earth. Because I'm here, you're here. Certainly when you're in an urban setting—and more and more people around the world are moving to large urban areas for multiple reasons—it changes the tribal-ethnic dynamic.

Jones said that sometimes people use the term "community" to exclude others; she considered her bookstore a space for the "public." I asked her who was the "public":

The public is just the people, that's what it means. For example, the people that come through this door. . . . There's this one guy, he's a handsome dude, a good looking fellow, probably in his forties, but when he talks, you can see he's really in another kind of space. He has this homeless look about him. But he's part of the public. Sometimes he's kempt, sometimes he's not kempt. He's in and out of shelters. But he loves buying books. I let him buy them some times. Other times I tell him, "You have enough books now, you can't buy anymore. Right now, you're not caring for yourself, so you've got to use your money for that." I jump into his business a little bit [*gives a little laugh*]. I accept him, but I don't accept his behavior. If he's been drinking, I tell him, "You have to leave. You can't be in here with alcohol on your breath. And you can't smoke in here. You can do it outside. But not here." So far people haven't gotten back at me for telling them what to do. I rely on my oldness and my white hair [*giggles*]. So maybe they just shrug and say, "Yeh, that old lady's tripping."

For Jones, public space was not simply a *place that was open for all*—it was a space in which *people were open to others*. Being open was not simply tolerating the other. One recognized, shared with, and respected the other, and one expected recognition, sharing, and respect in return. This mutual recognition emerged neither from a Hegelian battle between "master and slave" nor a claim about "the right to the city" (as articulated by Henri Lefebvre and David Harvey) but rather from a cultural / spiritual / earth-based interdependence that made one "jump into the business" of others and allowed others to jump into one's own business. Traditions such as respect for elders regulated public space but did not bound who belonged. I asked Jones if she thought that the homeless man felt part of the community.

Well, he's not rejected for one thing. I have a friend who works in one of the libraries, and he says, "Yeh, we know him." People like him need a place to sit down and just be for a minute. Some places are more welcoming than others. . . . That's why I get a little nervous about an overuse of the term community. When people say they're going to have a rally for the community, I think, "Who are you talking about?" We all have those same needs. . . . Everybody, everything has to have access. . . . Everything according to physicists is energy and information. And we are that too—we are energy and information. So when you look at me or I look at you . . . we can draw . . . a conclusion . . . or we can remain open.

Being open does not end in a conclusion; mutual recognition does not fix identities; exchanges and transformations go on and on. Jones framed these interactions in the cold language of physics ("energy and information") and in warm, intimate terms ("touching" and "being touched"). Jones suggested that government was needed to help maintain this virtuous spiral. She wanted to see more businesses in Detroit, but she worried that privatized spaces—especially public spaces privatized by corporations—could become spaces of indoctrination and control. In her eyes, freedom did not equal the absence of government. She said that funding cuts for schools, libraries, and the mental health care that would help the homeless man who visited her shop had harmed the public and public space.

In those days, it was typical for people in the Corridor to speak about sharing resources and preserving the commons, but not everyone here agreed with Jones about the need for government. The politics of the Corridor were diverse. It drew anarchists seeking an autonomous zone, so-called primitivists desiring a return to nature, Marxists fighting for revolution, black nationalists calling for collective self-determination, feminists and queer activists transgressing gender roles, and religious groups striving for the good community. Some came to live here, others to study or work, still others just to sit in its cafés. The unifying force was more sensual/spiritual/communal than ideological: a Moral We enjoying each other. Adrienne Maree Brown, an environmental justice activist drawn from the Bay Area to Detroit, writes about seducing people to revolt—making revolution so pleasurable, so appealing to the senses, the mind, and the heart, that people long to take part.[7] Scholar Benjamin Shepard tells about generations of artists and activists—the situationists in France during the 1950s, the community gardeners in New York during the 1970s— who used *play* (street theater, BBQs, games, music) to reclaim streets, build solidarity, revive their spirits, and experiment with ways of seeing and being in the world.[8] Long before the situationists in France or the pleasure activists in the Corridor, Congo Square in New Orleans served as a gathering place for enslaved Africans, who were allowed to use it on Sundays for drumming, dancing, and socializing and for selling deliciously tempting goods such as pralines. Their seductive rhythms drew whites (no doubt tapping their feet) until terror of Congo Square being used by the Africans to organize a rebellion caused slave owners to end the gatherings.[9]

Midtown's arts, educational, medical, and tech facilities were prized by planners and developers as engines for revitalization. Between 2000 and 2009, a public-private alliance reportedly poured $1.8 billion in investments into the rebranded Midtown.[10] Data Driven Detroit states that, between 2000 and 2009, small business growth in North Cass was 80 percent and job growth for all businesses was 15.7 percent.[11] Perhaps dataset errors inflate the figures, but it is notable that economic growth occurred here even during the global economic crisis. Observers beyond Detroit have asked its entrepreneurs to tell the secret of their success. Avalon bakery has been profiled by radical blogs as well as by *Business Week* and *Forbes*. Shops in the Corridor have created jobs, enriched street life, increased tax revenues, and contributed to local charities. Some entrepreneurs and their patrons claim that these environmentally and socially conscious ventures are a way of transforming society from market-oriented to people-oriented. These shops offer more than goods, but do they lessen the power of the market?

Radical placemaking is always in danger of being crushed or subverted. Over the centuries, capitalism has survived crises by adopting a new moral code—a new "spirit of capitalism"—that enables its revival and legitimation.[12] By assimilating the ideas of its critics, capitalism disarms them. The market (re)appears as progress. Midtown's best known artwork—Diego Rivera's *Detroit Industry*—is an homage to and a critique of progress—the work of a Marxist, paid for by a capitalist. Henry Ford's son, Edsel, commissioned it. The mural depicts a landscape of time: a human fetus in a womb of plants . . . the races of the world as red, yellow, white, and black mountains holding elements for industry in their rock-fists: iron ore, sand, limestone, coal, diamonds . . . a multiracial workforce in synchronized production at Ford's River Rouge auto plant . . . a doctor and nurse vaccinating a haloed baby . . . insect-like chemical weapons workers in gas masks. The panorama depicts progress as a constant reassemblage of nature, myth, and technology, at once awesome and monstrous, constructive and destructive.

In the 2000s, progress came (again) to the Corridor. MDI sought to break with the area's infamous past while preserving marketable aspects of its history and culture. To do so, MDI restored historic buildings, developed new properties, promoted cultural venues, led crime reduction campaigns, and engaged in beautification projects—historic style street lights, new sidewalks, flowering trees. Its activities were funded by member dues and by public-private partnerships. Brownfield and historic preservation tax credits helped to finance its projects. Some cultural workers voiced concern that redevelopment would evict the memory of the Corridor's past and displace longtime residents and shops. As public housing on the edges of Midtown was cleared for mixed-income development, the demographics of local tracts changed. Between 2000 and 2010, in North Cass, the population shrank from 2,211 to 2,038. Blacks dropped from 59.6 percent to 42.4 percent, while whites and Asians increased (from 25.5 percent to 36.1 percent and from 10 percent to 16.7 percent, respectively).[13] This demographic shift has stirred fears about the second wave of gentrification. The first wave brought the bohemian shops of North Cass. These shops invoke the working-class past and include working-class patrons (men in hard hats can be seen in the food shops). Yet these shops may appear more inclusive than they are. The Corridor has high poverty rates, especially among older people in South Cass. What percentage of the patrons of North Cass shops were below the poverty line? I do not know. It seems likely—based on the prices ($3 cinnamon rolls, $4 coffee) in some shops—that their regular patrons, including the scholars in glasses and the men in hard hats, were middle income and above. Some newcomers to the Corridor praised their bohemian hangouts as resources for poor and rich. They said that they saw people of all races in the shops. This bridging was valuable, but racial mix should not be conflated with income mix. A low-income black resident of the Corridor told me that the price and taste of food were better at McDonald's than at the natural food shops and that he did not feel comfortable inside them. He fondly recalled a "bacon-and-eggs place" with down-to-earth folks and cheap coffee Down Home. Similarly, a retired auto worker from another part of town did not patronize the bohemian shops. He preferred the stale donuts of a coffee shop bordering the Corridor—a place that drew working-class black people like himself. I watched the gravelly voiced waitress call him by name and laugh hard at his jokes as she poured his coffee. Amid conversations in the shop about everyday life, there was talk about labor concerns in Detroit and teacher strikes in Chicago. The Corridor would be a more life-sustaining and politically dynamic place if its shops included affordable, down-to-earth, bacon-and-eggs places that offered the fresh fruits and vegetables recalled from Down Home. A mix of places would make the street culture less dominated by bohemians and more pleasurable for all—not just the pleasure of personal consumption but also the pleasure of being in a place where everybody can exercise their placemaking power. But the market defines demand in dollars. Rising commercial rents make it hard to start and sustain affordable shops with healthy food and multicultural relevance. The second wave of gentrification in Midtown, bringing in young professionals and Whole Foods, threatens even some bohemian hangouts.

The lingo of downtown libertarians and Corridor anarchists overlapped. In both places, you heard people advocating creative communities that do not rely on government. One afternoon I walked past a restaurant in the central business district with a banner publicizing its Ron Paul event, and I heard people railing against big government. Days later, I listened to activists in the Corridor talking about collective self-determination that relied neither on government nor corporations. The language was similar across places, but their visions of public space and green placemaking differed (at least they did when I first arrived in Detroit). Downtown public spaces were less open and much more visibly policed. Every time I stepped outside my downtown apartment, I saw city police or private guards on patrol and security cameras everywhere. The Corridor also had security systems, but its most in-your-face regulation was its culture: people called each other out and "got into each other's business" and self-critiqued their actions as they gathered in public spaces.

As I walked to a block party in the Corridor sponsored by its shop owners on a clear blue June day in 2011, I saw a stage with a sound system and a white awning set up in the cordoned-off street. On stage, black children played violins. There were long lines at Avalon and Goodwells. Two black women who ran the clothing store had pushed their racks outside; customers swarmed around them. The beauticians from the shop around the corner had come to watch the festivities: they tossed their locs over their shoulders as they stood in a row with arms folded in flowing clothes. The crowd included blacks, whites, Asians, biracial people, a woman in a hijab, a videographer with earphones, a troupe of teenage drummers and dancers in yellow and red African-inspired attire, a man in a blue dashiki snapping photos, young people in shorts and t-shirts who might be Wayne State students, a couple of panhandlers, mothers hugging babies, some elders, lots of children, a few dogs.

I recognized local artists and activists, including Grace Lee Boggs—a Chinese American activist in her nineties who lived on the lower east side and was revered here. She was given a microphone. Boggs said a few words from her wheelchair and then went inside Jones's bookstore to sign copies of her new book, *The Next American Revolution*. In her book, she argued that the crisis in cities was not simply economic but also moral and ecological. She wrote about the ruined landscape of capitalism as an opportunity:

> When you look out and all you see is vacant lots, when all you see is devastation . . . do you look at it as a curse, or do you look at it as a possibility, as having potential? And we here in Detroit had to begin doing that for our own humanity.[14]

Boggs argued for a Gramscian *war of position*—a war of ideas.[15] The daughter of Chinese immigrants who owned restaurants in New York, Boggs earned a PhD in philosophy from Bryn Mawr. Her dissertation focused on the pragmatist philosopher George Herbert Mead, which contributed to her lifelong interest in how individual potential emerges in relation to community. Facing racism that limited her opportunities after graduation, she became involved with radical groups, eventually moving to Detroit. Her late husband James Boggs—a black migrant from Alabama who became a labor organizer in Detroit—advocated direct democracy and a localized economy as remedies to worker alienation. In the 1950s, the Boggses were part of the Johnson-Forest Tendency, a radical offshoot of the Workers Party that included C. L. R. James, the famous Trinidadian historian. Rejecting capitalism and Stalinism, the Boggses emphasized the potential of oppressed people for self-organization and creativity. In his 1963 book, *The American Revolution*, James Boggs said that US industrial workers were becoming obsolete because of new capitalist strategies and technologies, yet they did not create a new reality because of racial divisions and blocked imagination. In 1966, James and Grace Boggs co-wrote an essay, "The City Is the Black Man's Land," that provided an ideological foundation for the rise of black urban regimes.[16] In the essay, the Boggses stated that African Americans would soon be the majority in many large US cities and that "in accordance with the general philosophy of majority rule and the specific American tradition of ethnic groupings (Irish, Polish, Italian) migrating en masse to the big cities and then taking over the leadership of municipal government, black Americans are next in line." The Boggses argued that African Americans—the group most harmed in the United States by corporate strategies and technologies—would use their voting power to transform cities and society. However, the Boggses became disillusioned with Detroit's black urban regime. Before his death in 1993, James Boggs called for Detroiters to rebuild their city through enterprises such as greenhouses and bakeries that would establish local commerce in harmony with nature. As the twenty-first century brought fears of job loss from corporate use of artificial intelligence, new generations began to read the work of James and Grace Lee Boggs. Jackie Victor, co-owner of Avalon, told journalists and students that the inspiration for her store comes from the Boggses, combined with advice from a Zen priest:

> Jimmy used to say, you can't rely on the big boys to supply our needs. If we want to see this city become a different city, we have to start today. . . . I think there are a lot of visionary people, a lot of idealists [in Detroit]. The post-industrial carnage around us, what the car has done, what industry has done—we have an opportunity to make a difference. You almost have to ignore the mainstream, ignore City Hall, ignore the casinos, because they aren't going to do it. We have to do it.[17]

This statement exemplified the entrepreneurial discourse of the Corridor. Invoking Boggs and Buddhism, Victor blended the gospels of economic self-reliance, spiritual practice, and community solidarity—traditional American virtues restated with unconventional citations. In this discourse, the "big boys" (government and corporations) were critiqued in passing, but they were neither petitioned for help nor challenged for power. Indeed, "they" were almost ignored—"you"/"we" (the listener hailed as a member of the collective) was entreated to supply "our" needs. Victor's philosophy overlapped with the ideas of the bookseller Janet Jones, but Jones underscored the need for government-funded public institutions. Noting that James Boggs urged Detroiters to "make our own bread," Victor advocated an "imagination economy" built by "entrepreneurs, farmers, grassroots leaders, architects, artists, visionaries and homesteaders" that furthered "sustainability, local economy, and community." She did not mention class interests. To some extent, her vision resembled the cultural nationalist strand of black political thought, yet in place of a focus on the black community, the entire city was framed as a collective. It was also reminiscent of the language of nineteenth-century utopian socialists and welfare capitalists. Generation after generation, this language has appeal: Empire cannot suppress its power. However, the ventures inspired by it tend to flop or assimilate because they must compete in the market, and they do not control the land, infrastructure, and investments that they need to thrive. As new generations articulate the Garden, they fail to learn from or even recall this past. I do not mean that today's visionaries are wrong when they articulate the unique promise of now. Empire's capture of the Garden is a constant refrain, but the verses—the historical moment and its risks and opportunities—change. The challenge is to make a difference in the new moment.

After Grace Boggs spoke, Ill—a young, Jewish, nongender-conforming rapper known as "Invincible," raised in Ann Arbor—took the microphone, adjusting a newsboy cap over their short hair. They wore a t-shirt with the words "Detroit Summer": the name of a youth leadership program that was cofounded in 1992 by Grace Boggs and other local activists. Ill introduced Wajeed—a young, bearded African American—who stood at a turntable. Wajeed announced a "special guest," saying: "Many of you know this gentleman." He told the audience to "make some noise" as he called a fiftyish black man with drumsticks and plastic buckets from the crowd. The street musician was known on the block for his sunny disposition. As the drummer went up, he raised his arms and waved at the cheering audience. After welcoming the drummer, Ill turned to the audience:

> This area is called the Cass what? [*Audience: "Corr-i-dor!"*] The Cass what? [*"Corr-i-dor!"*] It's not "Midtown," for all the developers who try to change the name and make it seem snazzy for all the rich people who want to push the poor people out.

Ill urged respect and support for the shops and for longtime residents:

> Okay, so we're going to respect the culture and history of this neighbor-
> hood, we're going to respect all the beautiful people who built this neigh-
> borhood, and this block is a big part of that. . . . It's beautiful to have so
> many community-owned businesses, so be sure to support them.

Ill did a rap about the area, including the destruction of public housing ("up
the street from where they knocked the Jeffries down") and its drug addicts
("You gotta ask where they live / Who they were before here / Hustling in
the aftermath of chemical warfare.") that included a "bucket solo" from the
drummer. As the drummer reached his crescendo, the white videographer
with earphones and the black man in the blue dashiki moved in with their
cameras. Next Ill did a song, "Apple Orchards," which warned of corporate
agriculture: "Have you seen the apple orchards / Where the trees are trapped
and tortured / But the captives all look gorgeous." Ill, in collaboration with
Wajeed and other artists, would go on to form Complex Movements—an arts
collective that blends high tech creations with social and environmental justice
concerns and cross-place organizing. The collective, inspired by the philosophy of emergence (derived from quantum physics), seeks to bring together
the local and translocal to solve problems and transform communities. The
collective is tied to a strand of cultural work in Detroit that critiques "corporate science"—technology that causes poverty and alienation—yet embraces
innovations (digital media, 3D printing, microgrids) that facilitate the localized production, translocal connections, ecological harmony, and direct democracy that the Boggses advocated.

After the trio performed, Joe Reilly—a guitarist of European and Native
American heritage—came on stage. He flapped his arms in a "turkey vulture
rap" ("Uh uh yeh I'm a turkey vulture dude . . . fly in a v-shape . . . make a turkey
vulture beat") as children dance and laugh. As he shifted to a slow song about
water, a mother danced with her baby in her arms. There was little greenery
on the block—the crowd was told to imagine and embody water, plants, and
animals as they danced and sang along to songs about the earth. The performers urged the crowd to think about the effects of their actions on their bodies,
each other, and the earth. In the central business district, nature tended to

be concretely framed (by renovated parks, the RiverWalk) not playfully embodied. The fish carousel on the RiverWalk was fanciful, but it left less to the imagination than becoming a turkey vulture in the Corridor. In the central business district, developers described nature as a resource that enterprising people harnessed for pleasure and profits. In the Corridor, artists talked about the pleasure and freedom that came from realizing the self as nature and a force of creation (profits mattered, but they were not emphasized).

In the central business district, I only saw one space that was as open as the Corridor: the defunct Canticle Café. Brother Al Mascia—a Franciscan friar—ran the café, serving free muffins and fair trade organic coffee in a space that had a piano, computers with internet access, and poetry slams. To help support the café, he sold bags of fair trade coffee to affluent patrons. The café was named after the Canticle of the Sun, a praise song for God and nature by Francis of Assisi. If we were to travel back in time to the medieval revival of cities in Europe as hubs for world trade (a moment with parallels to our time), we would see the rise of religious orders—Franciscans, Beguines—to serve the urban poor. Yet the Franciscans would go on to help invading armies destroy indigenous cultures in the Americas. Extending the service mission of these mendicants while breaking with their ethnocentrism, Brother Al spoke of making the café into a place where people from different backgrounds and religions could come together, enjoy the uniqueness of each other, and reconnect with what he described to me as the "temporal-and-spiritual"/"tangible-and-intangible"—for example, sharing a meal while being moved by a song. The café mostly served homeless, drug addicted, and mentally ill street people yet also welcomed the retirees and office workers housed downtown. As the central business district gentrified, the newcomers viewed Canticle with alarm. Struggling with financial challenges and hostility to its presence, the café closed in 2011. A café owner offered his kitchen for the friar to warm up food. Brother Al used a bicycle cart for deliveries. He said that he tried to create a moment of fun and respect; he did not want the people he served to feel that they were being doled scraps. As he parked his bicycle food cart—a bright yellow vehicle with "Canticle Café" in attractive letters—gentrifiers occasionally would mistake him for a street vendor and ask the price of his sandwiches and hot cocoa. He told me that he once got a $50 tip when he explained his "business." Brother Al cited Dorothy Day and Peter Maurin as influences on his work. Day was a New York bohemian; Maurin was a French immigrant from a peasant background. Together, they founded the Catholic Worker movement. Catholic Workers advocate the collective growing and sharing of food to put people in touch with each other and the land. Brother Al also cited the scholar Martin Buber as an influence. Buber posited that humans have two stances toward the world: "I-It" and "I-Thou." In the "I-It" relation, I see the Other (whether tree or sculpture or friend) as an object of my interest, my project, my desire. Thus, I see only a fragment of the Other, its function as a thing among other things that I experience, categorize, and put to my practical use. This way of seeing and being in the world fragments the "I." I become merely the set of my roles (worker, parent, shopper . . .) and the sum of my isolated uses of this, that, and the other thing. In the "I-Thou" relation, I open to a process in which my whole being—and the whole being of the Other—are in dialogue. By "dialogue," Buber meant a moment of boundless communion, whether with nature, another human, or "intelligible forms" (for example, art). In this embrace, I do not seek for our differences to disappear. Dialogue illuminates "I" and "Thou" as unique beings whose sharing begets possibilities. "I-It" is essential for survival; "I-Thou" opens the Self to take part in Creation.

Sociologist Elijah Anderson suggests that residential integration should not be used as the sole measure of racial contact; we also must consider "cosmopolitan canopies"—public spaces of people-watching and brief, friendly exchanges across race and class.[18] In downtown Detroit, many spaces—including Campus Martius and the bleachers of Comerica Park—are cosmopolitan canopies. Yet spaces of aggressive openness—the now defunct Canticle Café and the Corridor's bohemian shops and block parties—are rare. These spaces are *spiral collectives* (to use the name of Jones's shop to signify a type of public space)—points from which exchanges deepen and spread and go on and on. These sites push people to seek out and form enduring, transformative relations with the "other" even when they feel unsafe. Drawing on diverse traditions, these spaces strive for a new moral order. To do so, they struggle against global capital, which fragments people (through displacement and segregation) and discourages spatial re-visions (through top-down surveillance, regulation, and commodification).

The Corridor's Moral We has (or had) muscle. Before the affluent became commonplace on the Corridor's streets, back when gentrifiers wandered here from the central business district for quiche and coffee, the artists made it clear that if you wanted to hang out and fit in, you had to appear to care for the earth and seem open to difference. The Corridor was open, but it was not a place where anything goes. Newcomers were welcome, but they had to show respect. I heard newcomers nervously correct themselves ("Midtown—I-I-I m-mean the Corridor!"). One young newcomer told me that soon after she arrived in Detroit, friendly residents took her for a ride through the Corridor, showed her popular hangouts, and advised her not to call the area "Midtown." The Moral We of the Corridor shaped street interactions. Months after the block party, as the leaves turned color, I saw the drummer who had played at the block party. He stood outside the shops as usual, chatting with a young white guy about music—they laughed and shook hands. I never saw that kind of exchange in front of the upscale shops downtown, but it was common between street people and the café crowd here. Yet street regulars tended not to sit *inside* the Corridor shops—none of the eateries sought to be a Canticle Café. I didn't see the drummer again for weeks, and I wondered if he was okay. One evening as the shops closed, he resurfaced. He had crutches and seemed thinner, more frail, shivering alone as the temperature dropped near freezing. The Corridor was not as open and caring as it seemed at sunny block parties. Or rather, the Corridor lacked structures to bring into being the open and caring society that the Moral We (the heirs of Piety Hill) desired. The area had charities and casual sharing, but it lacked political and economic institutions that secured the well-being and the dignity of all residents on an everyday basis. Thus, it had not (yet) become the good community that it dreamed.

The Moral We of the Corridor did not agree about the path to the good community. Not all longtimers feared that the return of capital and the white middle class would harm the character of the Corridor; some shop owners called the neighborhood "Midtown" *and* "Cass Corridor," valuing the redevelopment projects of MDI. The residents who insisted on calling the area "Cass Corridor" or "The Corridor"—not "Midtown" or "greater downtown"—described themselves in a fight to claim home.

The Neighborhoods

"Putting the Neighbor Back in the 'Hood"

DETROIT NEIGHBORHOODS INCLUDE Mexican Americans, Native Americans, and Arab Americans in southwest Detroit; Hmong and Bangladeshi residents on the east side; white workers in UAW caps on the west side; and affluent whites in Indian Village on the lower east side. By and large, however, the neighborhoods beyond greater downtown are mostly African American. There is pain and danger and death here—streets on which tennis shoes dangle from power lines above stuffed animal shrines—but there is also life and love and fun. Children munching cotton candy and snow cones at street festivals, block parties with barbecue and laughing and dancing, families playing board games on porches, church ladies singing in the choir, bicyclists peddling on sunny afternoons, teens shooting hoops, chess groups competing, theater groups rehearsing, poets reciting, musicians playing to packed clubs. The neighborhoods preserve black history—a sign marks the homesite of Elijah McCoy, a black inventor born in the nineteenth century. And they celebrate new generations of innovators—people such as Ali Dirul, a young black engineer who built a solar power plant out of recycled materials for urban farmers.[1] Art projects are everywhere—from the whimsical street art of the Heidelberg Project near downtown to the gold "Mother Ship" of the North End (O.N.E.) Mile Project. Reinvestment has begun in areas of black Detroit that have market potential: scenic locations near the river, old commercial corridors. Activists remind newcomers that their neighborhoods are not a "wilderness" or "blank slate." In a hip-hop video by Chace "Mic Write" Morris, the camera pans Detroit from downtown to the neighborhoods. Mic Write scorns newcomers who have what he calls a "savior complex." He rejects their pity, performing an inventory of his origins that counts the entire city as a "stock" that is collective and embodied:

This our crib, This our rib,
Y'all can't take what I aint gone give[2]

Gentrification is not the only threat to home. In high poverty areas, street crime, bad infrastructure, and home foreclosures drive out-migration. Community organizers speak of "putting the neighbor back in the 'hood"—restoring mutual respect and support. To do so, some cultural workers organize gardens. Not all longtime residents like the urban farms; the sight and sound of crops and chickens remind them of the oppressive South that their parents and grandparents fled. Jesse Jackson, visiting Detroit in 2010, told the Detroit City Council that urban farming is "cute but foolish. . . . We need industrialization, not farming."[3] Some Detroiters agree with him. At a public hearing on land use, one woman asked:

> And I just want to know, when did an industrialized city become an agricultural city? We went backwards. How about this is the city of Detroit. I don't want to see corn growing all up and down the streets. I'm not used to that. I'm used to houses and buildings and apartments and people. I mean, if you want to grow farms, go back to Itta Bena, Mississippi. That's where that's done. This is a city. We need homes. We need people.[4]

Some residents are angry about nonprofits planting trees and crops on their streets—they feel that the nonprofits do not give longtime residents a say.[5] One

A bicyclist in a black middle-class neighborhood of Detroit.

day I saw an older woman, fist on hip, cross-examining a new farmer about where he was from and who was paying him. They both had black skin—black gentrifiers did not escape suspicion. Based on interviews and observations that they completed in Cleveland during July 2016, Joshua Akers and his colleagues argue that black residents get involved in gardening, tree planting, and neighborhood cleanups to improve their conditions, but the narrative of urban greening comes from white elites who promote green projects to further right-sizing.[6] If Cleveland is like Detroit, the truth is more complicated. Green nonprofits, headed in some cases by gentrifiers, sometimes overstate local support. But green projects and their promotion have myriad roots, including in black social movements. In Detroit, Gerald Hairston, a black Detroiter from the South, started a group called Gardening Angels in the 1980s, which planted gardens to beautify vacant lots, provide healthy food, teach children, and build community. During the same period, James Boggs framed local food production as part of a larger movement for direct democracy. From 1986 to 2014, the Catherine Ferguson Academy served pregnant teens and young mothers, with an urban farm on its grounds:

> A beautiful red barn built by the students flanks the academy's small farm, home to several goats, a huge sheep, rabbits, a pony, a beehive, two horses, ducks . . . a dozen hens and roosters . . . [and a] vegetable and flower garden (with one plot for each student). . . . [The farm teaches] teen moms and their young children about the cycle of life. . . . Down the hall, girls are getting ready for dance class while music plays; a goat stands outside the window looking in. . . . There's something very old-fashioned about the school . . . in a very poor area of Detroit. . . . several "grandmothers" . . . part-time workers . . . watch over . . . tiny people [students' babies].[7]

These school and neighborhood gardens build on the practice of black families from the South growing vegetable gardens in their yards. Black cultural workers (ministers, teachers, artists) help to shape the design and meanings of these gardens, and they publicize these projects in and beyond Detroit. The danger is that these projects, which sometimes get funding from growth elites, will be used to further neoliberal agendas and discarded the moment that they do not.

A corn field in a Detroit neighborhood (*top*). Goats at the Catherine Ferguson Academy (*bottom*).

Malik Yakini, an educator and musician who is the director of the Detroit Black Community Food Security Network (DBCFSN), describes hunger as a complex problem (physical, spiritual) that requires a mix of government and community programs to solve. Yakini is a nationally known advocate for food justice and sustainable food systems, and he has served on various boards, including the Michigan Food Policy Council and the Detroit Food Policy Council. He sees neighborhood gardens as a way to build community, further collective self-determination, and heal spiritually: "By putting your hands and feet in the soil, you begin to connect with that energy and it helps to ground you and helps you to kind of be more in tune with the flow of life."[8]

The dream of the Garden connects black urban and rural farmers. A black farm advocate in Detroit gave me a flyer about a Juneteenth celebration to be held by a black rural farmer in the region. The event's schedule included reading the Emancipation Proclamation at sunrise, a farm tour, forums about how to be "independent, self-reliant, and self-sufficient on the land," and sessions with "words of wisdom from the elders." Historically, the US farmer has been portrayed as white and male. Yet there is a long history of black and brown farm labor, and women of all races have done much of the community garden and food justice work in cities. There is an "interrelationship between city spatial structure, women's household work, and urban policy" that links constructions of gender and urban environments.[9] In the 1930s, the Housewives League of Detroit (HLD), a black women's organization, supported cooperative economics and food justice. Founded in 1930 by Fannie Peck, the HLD urged black housewives to use their buying power to fight for affordable, healthy food and to help black-owned businesses survive the Great Depression.[10] The HLD, headquartered in Detroit, spread nationwide.

As tourists and new residents come to Detroit, lured by narratives of redemption or ruin, gatekeepers try to control what they see and don't see. To do so, the gatekeepers use the *tour*, the *mission*, the *forum*, and the *march/parade*. The *tour* highlights ideals and spectacles; the *mission* recruits volunteers; the *forum* frames grievances and agendas; the *march/parade* reignites allegiances and displays power. The *tour*—the urban agriculture tour, the shopping tour, the cultural heritage tour, the tour of ruins—is used by business owners, activists, nonprofits, and profiteers of all races to rebrand areas, draw tourist dollars and new residents, and gain volunteers and donations. Whenever I read an article about Detroit by a journalist or scholar who has spent only a few days here, I suspect that the article is based on a tour—the people and places that they mention often correspond with various tours. One afternoon, I rode on a tour bus that had been organized by a nonprofit that showcased gardens. Most passengers were white suburbanites; I was one of a handful of black passengers. As the bus moved through black neighborhoods, I eavesdropped on white passengers pointing out places that their families fled. A middle-aged father told his son that the city should make it easy and cheap to take over vacant homes and shops. "You see that?" The father nodded at a boarded-up building. "In the old days, the family would live on the top floor and run the store below. Imagine what we could do with that place. It could be a good business." The tour directed longings for roots—the mom-and-pop store, the old neighborhood—to the Garden. At stop after stop, white passengers stepped out and chatted with black urban farmers about the need to restore relations among food and family and community and nature and spirit.

The *mission* does not always involve interaction between volunteers and residents. I attended a charity event on the west side that had recruited mostly white suburbanites to board up homes and clean debris in vacant lots. I noted the race of volunteers as everyone assembled in a gym and got a pep talk from Mayor Bing before being randomly split up into cleanup teams. On my team, I was the only black member. Media cameras followed us. Images of a mostly white crew helping a poor black neighborhood reached beyond the United States; a student of mine studying abroad emailed that he saw me and the rest of the cleanup crew on the news in France. As our team loaded debris on a truck, I saw a few black residents staring from their porches. I walked over. They wanted to know what was going on, and they told me that no one had told them about the cleanup. I learned about it from Google Alerts that I'd placed on the names of growth elites and their organizations. The event *was* publicized in advance, but perhaps the residents did not see the news or did not realize it would involve their block. I returned to my crew and overheard a white teen telling others on the team that a purple stain inside a vacant house looked like blood: "Someone was murdered here!" He whispered. Perhaps other teams worked with longtime residents; the lack of contact between my team and the residents of the area reinforced negative images of the black urban poor and the city.

The *forum* enables people of different backgrounds to share their stories. On a different hot Saturday afternoon, I drove out to D-Town Farm on the west side to attend a public discussion, "Undoing Racism in Detroit's Food System." Will Allen was scheduled to speak. Allen was a former basketball player who won a MacArthur "genius" grant after founding Growing Power, a Milwaukee-based urban farming project. D-Town Farm was run by DBCFSN, which negotiated with the City of Detroit to use land in Rouge Park. DBCFSN, founded in 2006, builds on traditions of food justice projects in Detroit. The weekend event included Allen's talk as well as workshops in hoop house construction and vericomposting. As I got out of my car and walked on the farm, vegetable rows stretched in front of me. I chatted with the black women at the sign-in table, whom I'd met at other events. To my left was a green tent with folding chairs inside. The back of the tent was open. It was shadowy inside—a relief from the scorching sun. About forty people, mostly women, sat on the folding chairs. Will Allen—a tall, muscular older man in a billed cap—stood in front talking with a microphone. The director of DBCFSN, Malik Yakini, sat nearby. I sat in back, near two black women and a white woman who ate from paper plates. As they lifted their forks to their mouths, they swatted mosquitoes away from one another. One of the black women hit a mosquito hard on the white woman's arm. The white woman gave out a cry. The three broke out in laughter. The mood was casual, a conversation between Allen and the audience. He said that when he hires someone, he doesn't consider the color of their skin, but whether they fit with the organization. He said that a lot of people were getting involved in the food movement now. An older white woman turned to me and said, "That's because of these economic hard times." I nodded. Allen said that it was hardest to get white men—especially older white men—involved because they feared "they're going to get roasted" because of their race and they felt uncomfortable in an environment in which "women are doing 80 percent of the work." A young white man who grew up in Detroit said that he didn't identify with the white newcomers and that he didn't feel comfortable in all-white environments. Complicated identities of race, class, gender, and place were discussed, and the ways in which identities combined to shape access not only to food but also to the publicity and money—investment capital, foundation grants—for food entrepreneurs and nonprofits. Nationwide, white men dominate management positions in green sectors, and people of color have limited access to green entrepreneurial opportunities and career ladders.[11] Monica White—a Wayne State professor—took the microphone. She talked about white people coming into Detroit to "save" black people. She said that the news rarely showed black people working to provide food for their communities. She said that newcomers must be educated about black Detroit and its history.

The gatekeeping of local organizations extends beyond their neighborhoods into greater downtown. I attended workshops that DBCFSN organized in greater downtown that socialized newcomers to propagate an antiracist critique of the food system. This narrative infiltrated the downtown discourse. I went on a tour sponsored by corporations in the central business district, led by a young white tour guide. Most participants were young white professionals. In between touting Campus Martius and showing the gentrifiers where to buy the best cheese, artisan bread, and organic vegetables, the tour guide mentioned and echoed DBCFSN about the history of racial inequities in the food system. She introduced the gentrifiers to black and Latino Detroiters who grew the organic vegetables, and she advised the gentrifiers to read Thomas Sugrue's *The Origins of the Urban Crisis*. Removed from a critique of the current order, the antiracist discourse loses some of its force, yet it still unsettles the meanings of race and place. During my time in the city, black tour groups (Black Scroll Network, Us Too Detroit) also cultivated an awareness of the history of black Detroit and promoted black-owned shops.

Neighborhood groups use parades and marches into the central business district to affirm solidarities and to show their strength. In 2013, I attended a commemoration of the fiftieth anniversary of Martin Luther King's march in Detroit. I saw mostly black marchers, along with whites, Arab Americans, and Latinx. Downtown gentrifiers watched from cafés and shops. The procession marched into downtown, moving down Woodward Avenue past Campus Martius to the river. Some people carried 1963 posters, while others held signs about current issues: signs that protested emergency management, called for fair wages, requested immigration reform, pled for safe staffing at hospitals, and demanded justice for Trayvon Martin. Many signs called for moral integrity and solidarity: "Thou Shalt Not Kill," "Let There Be Peace," "Marching for Justice," "We Are One." A black family carried a banner: "It Takes a Village Y'all!" A white man held a sign: "Women, Unions, The Poor, Anti-War Activists, LGBT Activists/Stand Together/Fight the Fight/It's One Issue: Human Rights." People marched with their labor unions, high schools, and religious and fraternal groups. African diasporic traditions sustain movements across generations by mobilizing networks across grassroots institutions and using music, storytelling, and chants to honor past sacrifices and reignite zeal. At the riverfront, there was a call-and-response, to an African drumbeat, that recalled radical groups such as the Dodge Revolutionary Union Movement (DRUM) in the 1960s. The names of "heroes and sheroes who were martyred during civil rights and human rights struggles" were called out. The invocation ended with a communal pledge, led by a woman in African garb: "We stretch our arm as a symbolic link that binds us together as one family. As I drink from the *kikombe cha umoja* [unity cup], I say what is good enough for me is good enough for the community." Unity has never been a reality in Africa and

Commemoration of the fiftieth anniversary of Dr. Martin Luther King Jr.'s 1963 "Great March" down Woodward Avenue in downtown Detroit, June 22, 2013.

its diaspora. Nevertheless, diasporic traditions sustain a thirst for unity that makes these traditions resilient at mass mobilizations.

Forums to shape how people view and engage with Detroit neighborhoods extend beyond Detroit and include social media. In September 2010, I attended the National-International Urban and Small Farm Conference at State Fair Park in Milwaukee—hosted by Will Allen's Growing Power—which drew hundreds of farmers and planners. DBCFSN gave a workshop at the event, and Grace Lee Boggs spoke to the crowd on a huge screen from her home in Detroit. Also in 2010, Compuware announced a plan to use some of its property to grow food for charities: this project became Lafayette Gardens. On his blog, Compuware's founder—Peter Karmanos—asked artists and gardeners to join his project. He described gardens as ways to "improve [the] appearance" of the city's vacant lots. He noted: "Others are talking about farms and gardens in the city. I hope Detroit will be inspired . . . to start planting." Who were the "Others"? His hyperlink to "Others" opened not on a story about black urban farmers (who had been talking about urban agriculture for years) but rather a news article about a wealthy white developer seeking to buy city-owned land on the lower east side for a farm—a controversial effort that some black urban farmers called a land grab. A reply to Karmanos's post called it "great news," comparing Karmanos to Will Allen. In a 2011 post, Karmanos wrote that Obama wanted to tax the wealthy to solve the debt crisis. Warning that taxes reduce philanthropy, Karmanos stated that it was "rich guys" such as John Rockefeller and Bill Gates who "endowed universities, battled diseases, and fed the hungry." Karmanos neglected to mention that before government support for public education and health—in the days when the urban masses depended on the charity of "rich guys"—they were even more badly educated, disease-ridden, and ill-fed than they are today.

Some food justice activists talked about the need to make the food movement less dependent on philanthropy. In 2011, Will Allen accepted a $1 million grant from the Walmart Foundation. Nevertheless, in 2017, Growing Power—faced with mounting debt—shut its doors.[12] Growing Power lacked the capacity for scaling up its operations, and it hurt its reputation by accepting the Walmart grant. Some activists charged that the grant helped Walmart to greenwash its exploitation of workers. When I attended meetings at nonprofits in Detroit, the host would often say, "Let's see who is in the room." People were asked to state their names, their organizations, and where they were from. It was a point of pride for people to say that they were born and raised in the city. To see who is in the room, it also might be useful to ask how people get paid and what they get paid to do. After meetings, I checked the funding sources of attendees. A few folks were what I call "old money"—they depended on the grass roots. For example, clergy who relied on church collection plates. Most folks—whether longtime or new residents—were "new money"—they relied on foundations and corporations. Grantees of the same three foundations that funded Detroit Works—Kresge, Ford, Kellogg—were almost always "in the room." For over a century, wealthy individuals have funded artists and charities in black communities. But the dependence on foundations and corporations is more recent, arising over the past few decades. Some "new money" groups have strong community ties, but many others lack the street knowledge and outreach of the old grassroots groups. Decades ago, Malcolm X and countless behind-the-scenes folks blossomed in redemptive, grassroots spaces.

I attended a forum on food and housing security held at a nonprofit that got corporate and foundation funding. The neighborhood was over 80 percent African American, yet half of the attendees were white. The forum talked about the poor but the event was geared for its middle-class attendees—professionals, entrepreneurs, graduate students—many of whom were new to Detroit and got corporate and/or foundation support. I did a shift at the sign-in table. A tall African American man in a rumpled black suit wandered into the building, with a leather-bound book under his arm. I greeted him and asked him if he wanted to sign in. He smiled nervously; his eyes were confused. He began pulling things from his pockets and placing them in front of me: a handkerchief, an empty medicine bottle. Finally, he pushed the leather-bound volume toward me: it was a law book. I told him that there was no charge and that he could keep his things. He pocketed his handkerchief and bottle. I handed him a pen. He signed his name then looked around, frightened. I asked him if he wanted to sit next to me. He sat down and asked in a whisper, what is happening here? I told him about the event, and I asked him about himself. He said that he lived up the street in the basement of a place where no one lived. It was cold there—no heat or lights. He mumbled; I could not understand everything he said. He once put doors on cars; he pantomimed the motion. I asked him if he used to be an auto worker. He nodded, but he said that he was really a music teacher. The confusion and fear left his eyes as he tapped a beat with a pen. I really looked at him now, the intensity in him. His long dark face and sculpted cheekbones reminded me of the musician in the old husband and wife duo of Ashford and Simpson. He handed me a pen and encouraged me to tap along. I studied his beat, shook my head, and said I couldn't. He opened the law book and wrote a music note on the last page and waved his hand for me to sing it. I told him that I could not read music or carry a tune, and that back in the days when I was in school, my music teacher had given up and told me to just mouth the words. He said, No—you should sing! Let the others work around you! I smiled; his students must have loved him. When my shift ended, I asked him if he wanted refreshments. He loaded his plate with fruit and pastries and got coffee. He seemed transfixed by a talk about the beauty and oneness of the earth. I left him and went to another workshop. I sat at a table with a grim black man and a grinning white man. The grinning white man said, isn't it wonderful how people from all backgrounds get to know each other here! The grim black man said, I don't see much diversity. The grinning white man said, look at us! The grim black man said, all of us are middle class and that there is going to be hell to pay when the neighborhood folks realize that the money pouring in isn't for them. I left. As I drove away, I saw the music teacher being held by his lapels and pushed backward, stumbling, down the stairs of the nonprofit by a black guard. Perhaps I could have helped the music teacher, but I hesitated then drove on.

The Transnational

"Another World Is Possible"

DURING THE SUMMER of 2010, the Allied Media Conference (AMC) and the United States Social Forum (USSF) were held in greater downtown. The AMC is an annual event that brings together artists, activists, and technologists from cities in and beyond the United States who use media in social justice organizing. The 2010 event, from June 17 to 20, included panels at Wayne State University and a bus tour of Detroit neighborhoods. On the bus, the conversations among the cultural workers were more intellectual than those I heard on the agricultural tour for suburbanites that I had attended earlier. Yet the passengers on both tours were captured by the Garden. A young man, looking out the bus window at vacant houses, said that Detroit should allow homesteading, and he recommended a book on the topic to other passengers. The tour included a stop at Manistique Garden, cofounded by Myrtle and Wayne Curtis. The visitors gathered around the couple in the garden, snapping photos and holding up digital recorders. Wayne Curtis—an artist who is a former member of the Black Panther Party—spoke about the garden's purpose:

> What we're trying to do is develop this culture, that will develop the norms, that start with little children, learning how to work together. Throughout history, it's been work that has sustained and developed societies and cultures, language, music, and this is all that we want to do.

Curtis invited the visitors to become part of the Garden:

> I hope that everyone brought their bags and everything so that we can all stay here and develop this land [*laughter from visitors, Wayne Curtis smiles*]. I'm serious. I remember when people from Zimbabwe, Nicaragua, would come here and say that they needed the resources, the human resources, the money, whatever, to come back to the land. Because of globalism, I'm asking you to come here and liberate this territory. We want to create a Peace Zone. What's a Peace Zone? All of the things that

I just mentioned that we can do with ourselves and between ourselves. Creativity and consistency is what this system stops. This is why things look the way that they do.

Curtis argued that the global market, investing and disinvesting around the world without regard for place, stopped the "creative" and "consistent" work of community building, thus communities fell into ruin. He suggested that the global order could be reshaped by solidarities that revalue the earth; development must be made to mean the cultivation of land and culture—a peaceful space of creative work that enabled the good life. These solidarities would not be isolationist; the transnational flow of labor, ideas, and resources into places that need them would "liberate territory" (freedom as mutuality). Detroit is often depicted as cut off from the world, but its activists move across cities, and they host activists from other places. Wayne and Myrtle Curtis are part of a centuries-old black radical tradition that spans countries, interacting with indigenous battles in the Americas against settler colonialism and class struggles in Europe over hereditary privilege and the market.

Soon after AMC ended, USSF began. From June 22 to 26, USSF drew thousands of activists to the Cobo Center in downtown Detroit, with actions that fanned out to the Corridor and to the neighborhoods. Attendees included youth, elders, indigenous peoples, immigrants, people of color, labor organizers, queer activists, deep ecology advocates, environmental justice activists, antiwar activists, and international allies. USSF was inspired by the World Social Forum, which first met in Porto Alegre, Brazil, in 2001 as an alternative to the World Economic Forum in Davos, Switzerland—the annual meeting of business, political, and academic elites to discuss ways of solving global problems. The World Social Forum and the USSF, arguing that the World Economic Forum serves international financial and business interests, offer "peoples' solutions" to global problems. The first USSF was held in Atlanta in 2007. Organizers stated that Detroit was chosen for USSF 2010 for two reasons: (1) the city shows the devastation caused by the global market, and (2) Detroit is a "movement city"—a critical hub in transnational activism.[1] USSF began with a downtown march to the Cobo Center for the opening ceremony, where there was indigenous and African drumming and dancing, under a banner:

Bus tour of Manistique Garden by artists and activists who attend the 2010 Allied Media Conference in Detroit. From left to right, the tour guides are Myrtle Curtis, Richard Feldman, and Wayne Curtis. The Curtises (husband and wife) cofounded the community garden. Feldman is a board member of the James and Grace Lee Boggs Center. The "D.C.O.H." on the t-shirt stands for "Detroit City of Hope," a grassroots campaign to reimagine the city.

"Another World Is Possible. Another U.S. Is Necessary. Another Detroit is Happening." Some attendees joined brigades on urban farm and mural projects, and they marched with local labor and religious leaders to the downtown Chase bank. The protest against Chase combined concerns about the bank's

US Social Forum, Cobo Center in downtown Detroit, June 2010.

home foreclosures in Detroit and its role as a lender to R. J. Reynolds, which was accused of abusing farmworkers in North Carolina.

Veterans of movements that shaped the twentieth century spoke at USSF. Some of these veterans died a few years after USSF ended: General Baker, a cofounder of the League of Revolutionary Black Workers (LRBW) and the Dodge Revolutionary Union Movement (DRUM); Grace Lee Boggs, a humanist philosopher and activist who wrote about social revolution, cultural evolution, and ecological liberation; Ron Scott, a former Black Panther who fought for peace on the streets and an end to police brutality; John Trudell, a poet and activist who had participated in the indigenous occupation of Alcatraz Island and then became chair of the American Indian Movement (AIM) in the 1970s. In their talks at USSF, these veterans urged youth to reimagine the world:

> Detroit was never one of the intellectual centers of the movement. Those intellectual centers of movement mainly came from the east coast and west coast. But here in Detroit, we can find our way to carry out this fight

in a practical manner, without a lot of talk and not a lot of press. We're not trying to make heroes out of people. We're trying to be victorious.

—General Baker, 1941–2014, USSF 2010

Detroit is a city of hope. Detroit is not just a city of poverty. It's not just a city of devastation. It's a city of hope because every time they do something to us, we find something else to do. And we stand above all of them, and they know it.

—Grace Lee Boggs, 1915–2015, USSF 2010

As my young brother and friend . . . Yusef Shakur said, "We're putting the neighbor back into the hood." We're rebuilding community where communities are being destroyed. We're challenging capitalism on its basic roots. . . . They said we were down and out. They said we were useless. And we're creating communities where there were none, creating values and relationships which were meant to be destroyed, and building a framework so that young black people, young people of color, and young people, in general, can retake neighborhoods and reshape them for the future, not only of Detroit, but the future of the world. This is not the world that Rick Wagoner [former CEO of General Motors] and that General Motors wants, but it's the world that we will see.

—Ron Scott, 1947–2015, USSF 2010

Technological civilization . . . suppress[es] and erase[s] the memory of the human being from us, and turns us into citizens, and turns us into race and culture and class . . . that they then make divisive. . . . All things of the earth have the same relation to sun sky universe. All things of the earth have being. Being is energy. . . . That industrial ruling class . . . mine the energy of the being through how they imprint the human to perceive reality, the same way that they mine oil. . . . Our intelligence is the fuel that runs this system. . . . This mining . . . leaves behind poisons and toxins . . . our fears and doubts and insecurities. . . . Once this sets in, we participate in this reality. . . . It is time for us to understand that we need to not cooperate. . . . This is about taking the power of our intelligence and using it clearly and coherently, rather than chaotically and distortedly. Because every time we do that, we're cooperating with them. No matter how good our intentions.

—John Trudell, 1946–2015, USSF 2010[2]

Baker emphasized practical action; Boggs affirmed Detroiters' ingenuity; Scott urged for this ingenuity to be focused on community building; and Trudell warned that global elites "mine" intelligence. The common thread was (mental | material) liberation. How was it to be realized? On the last day, some attendees joined locals to protest the municipal incinerator. Then people went home. There were toasts: people said the event expanded their minds and networks. And there was critique: many Detroiters did not know USSF was in town, and some attendees felt that more time should have been devoted to movement building. And there was creative sampling: Sacramento Knoxx, an Ojibwe/Chicano rapper based in southwest Detroit, wove Trudell's words at USSF into his music.[3]

That fall, a different kind of creative sampling emerged; a forum began in Detroit that had some of the redemptive, earth-conscious justice-speak of USSF—and like USSF, it drew people and ideas across cities—but growth elites organized it. This forum, which "mined the intelligence" (in Trudell's words) of cultural and technical workers, would last two years: the Detroit Works Project.

IV

The Forum

Detroit Works Begins

"Fear Factor"

IN SEPTEMBER 2010, the Detroit Works Project held five forums to kick off public outreach. For months, Mayor Bing had promoted rightsizing. Activists charged that he has been co-opted by "outsiders." Kresge, the main funder of Detroit Works, is based in Troy, a white suburb of Detroit. Bing said at his State of the City address that all Detroiters would have a "voice and role," but suspicions persisted that public outreach was just a show and that powerful elites already had a plan. Anxious residents packed the first meeting at Greater Grace Temple—a megachurch—to learn whether rightsizing meant that they would lose their homes. Startled to be put into brainstorming groups, they demanded to hear the mayor's plan. Bing said that he wanted to hear their ideas and that he had no plan (which stoked fears of the plan). After this chaotic forum, the meetings were given a town hall format: a speech from Bing followed by Q&A.

The last town hall, held at the Charles H. Wright Museum of African American History at 6:30 p.m. on Wednesday, September 22, 2010, framed the future of Detroit within the history of the diaspora. The museum, designed in the 1990s by the black-owned architectural firm of Sims-Varner & Associates, has a glass-domed entrance with columns that bear a rope motif (the nobility of Benin had a similar pattern on their residences).[1] Ninety-two flags, representing lands with people of African descent, circle the rotunda. A circle on the tiled floor—the terrazzo *Genealogy* by the artist Hubert Massey—sums up diasporic history as a (spiritual | material) quest from slavery and death toward knowledge and elevation:

> The central and largest figure represents the Supreme Being and the importance of spirituality in strengthening African Americans. To the right, an African woman kneels beside a body representing young slaves who died during the Middle Passage. An African American woman on the left embraces a body that symbolizes the loss of lives to violence in

the United States. . . . On the lower left and right are two figures. One clutches a book, symbolizing hunger for knowledge, and the other's arm is outstretched seeking upward mobility.[2]

This point of origin can be read as a cross-generational petition; the ancestral spirit with outstretched arm on the floor appeals across time to the diaspora to fulfill its elevation. The main exhibit, *And Still We Rise*, continues the theme. The tour begins with the start of human life in Africa. You move through the rise of African civilizations, see the horrors of the Middle Passage, travel the Underground Railroad. The century changes, and you glimpse the lives of black industrial workers and see the civil rights movement. The tour ends with the first black US president. Yet Obama's elevation did not liberate the diaspora. The tour can be seen as triumph. Yet its spiral also brings to mind the "boomerang" of history seen by Ellison's Invisible Man from his underground hiding place—the cynical double of the yearning figure on the terrazzo.

Detroiters filled the museum theater for the Detroit Works forum. The attendees included people in suits and people in jeans. When the theater reached capacity, the overflow was directed to other rooms in which the forum was simulcast. Black women had prominent roles: Toni Griffin, an architect and planner based on the East Coast who had been hired by Kresge to lead the Detroit Works Project, shared the stage with the mayor, along with Karla Henderson, the city's head planner. Griffin—a tall, forty-something woman with glasses—folded into a chair. Dressed in black, she leaned back solemnly, her arms crossed at the wrist over her lap, as she listened to Bing. Griffin, raised on the south side of Chicago, had made a name for herself in a field dominated by white men: only 2 percent of all architects are African American, and less than 1 percent are African American women. She got her bachelor's degree in architecture from the University of Notre Dame, and she was a Loeb Fellow at the Harvard Graduate School of Design. She had taught at Harvard and the City College of New York, and she maintained a private practice.

A school band performed, a bible verse was read, and Mayor Bing came to the podium. He began by reassuring the audience that their participation mattered and that he would tell the truth:

Detroit Works Project Town Hall held in the Charles H. Wright Museum of African American History on September 22, 2010. *Upper photo*: Mayor Bing is at the podium. Consultant Toni Griffin, DWP director, sits on the far left, in a row with city staff. A sign language interpreter stands in the foreground. *Lower photo*: Q&A session.

Let me thank all of you for coming, for listening, and hopefully for participating by giving us a lot of direction. . . . My integrity is very important
to me. I have not lied to anyone, and let me tell you something, I do not
intend to. . . . I . . . recognize that there is a fear factor because there are
a lot of unanswered questions . . . but the key is getting you involved in
this whole process.

Bing was conciliatory but vague; he alluded to but did not address the fears
that people had about rightsizing. He briefly mentioned that the plan would
help people in "desolate areas" obtain "better situations." Why had he changed
his language? In the past, Bing had told residents the plain truth: the plan was
to rightsize the city. Some Detroit Works staff told me later that Griffin and
others in the project were upset that Bing had talked about forced relocation to
reporters, and they made him change his words. I understand why they might
be upset about his talk of forced moves, but forced moves are not the only
way that rightsizing is done. Rightsizing means to align infrastructure investments with "needs." It is misleading to replace the term *rightsizing* (a process)
with the phrase *better situations* (an uncertain outcome). Growth elites talked
about the challenges of rightsizing in expert circles. Reducing investments in
high vacancy areas seems common sense—the equivalent of cutting off the
lights in a room when no one is in it. But water pipes and power lines are
interconnected—the breakdown of aging infrastructure in a high vacancy area
may impact other areas. The costs of decommissioning infrastructure are not
well known and may outweigh savings. And there are legal hurdles to reducing
services and getting people to move. Most seriously, there are ethical concerns:
some rightsizing strategies may deprive low-income people in high vacancy
areas of critical resources, and investments in areas with market potential may
deepen social inequities. Detroit Works planned to rightsize, but it was unsure
how (legally, practically) to do so and *what language* to use. Staff worried that
terms such as *rightsizing* "rub residents the wrong way."[3] They saw their challenge as engaging Detroiters without provoking fear and anger. In his speech
at Wright Museum, Bing urged residents to participate so that their children
could have better lives, he reassured them that the plan would focus on "people who are here" (translation: longtime residents, not gentrifiers), and he affirmed local know-how:

We are at a point . . . in this city's history, to make significant change, and we need to do it. We need to do it for our children, and we need to do it for our grandchildren. My focus is going to be on who is here today. We've got to take care of the people who are here. . . . Once we stabilize, we'll start looking at how do we grow. I don't think in my lifetime, for sure, we're going to get back to two million people. But we're still going to have 139 square miles and the city will be different. They're different industries that we can look at, there are a lot of things that I think we can do in the 21st century that we're not doing now, so, I need your intellect, I need your feedback, we've got a lot of smart people in our city. We don't have all of the answers in city government. Help us to help you.

At the close of his speech, he promised that—after the outreach, before the design was finalized—he would bring the plan back to the residents, which suggested that he and the residents would have decision-making power. I assumed that he was talking about a formal process of approving a city plan, but time proved me wrong. Bing did not actually say who would make decisions or where resources would come from to implement the plan. He expressed faith in the process and team:

And then we will put this plan together and bring it back to you and then we will finalize the plan and then we will execute the plan. So I am looking forward to it, it's a challenge, but it is a tremendous opportunity. So I'm going to thank the young ladies behind me because they have a yeoman's job and they have my respect, they have my support. We have a great team that I think we can put together, but we need you to stay engaged and help us put this plan together. Thank you so very much for coming out tonight. [Applause]

Q&A did not erupt in the angry chaos of the first forum. Most people stated their concerns and suggestions calmly. Detroiters asked questions of their mayor, unaware that he and they would have little control over the plan. The black urban regime was near its end.

After the town meeting at the Wright Museum, I observed two phases of Detroit Works outreach over two years. Across the phases, the city government was involved with Detroit Works, but private foundations funded it. Reports about the amount of grants differ. I use *Crain's Detroit Business* and the

Philanthropy News Digest as sources. Reportedly, Kresge—the major funder—gave $3.9 million to the project and pledged $150 million to implement it; the Ford Foundation awarded $1.5 million to University of Detroit–Mercy to design civic engagement for the project; the Kellogg Foundation gave a $400,000 planning grant.[4] During the first phase, city planners led outreach. The use of clickers to control crowds incited anger. In the second phase, private consultants took the lead. Using cultural workers to build bridges, Detroit Works expanded its outreach with innovative exercises and technologies. Everyone was invited to be at the table for discussion and to have "boots on the ground" for implementation. However, decisions about the long-term future of the city were made by elites.

Since the outcry against the top-down urban renewal ("Negro Removal") projects of the mid-twentieth century, democratic deliberation has been championed, drawing inspiration from the deliberative councils of small towns. The contention is that voting merely aggregates individual interests, while democratic deliberation produces mutual understandings that guide and legitimate government action. However, critics charge that public engagement is a ploy to make elite decisions appear as though they came from the grass roots. Around the world, some grassroots groups have stopped dealing with city planners, viewing them as complicit with global capital and racism. Abahlali baseMjondolo—a shack dwellers movement in Durban, South Africa—has developed its own projects while boycotting elections. S'bu Zikode, a leader of Abahlali, states that "those in power are blind to our suffering. This is because they have not seen what we see, they have not felt what we are feeling every second, every day."[5] Elites "ventriloquize" public discourse, undermining the potential of democracy to bring about change:

> Much of what passes for contemporary democratic life around the world
> has not been able to insist on or create what Baldwin . . . called in *The
> Fire Next Time* a "consciousness of others," such that the institutional
> trappings of democratic governance necessarily mean the end of white
> supremacy.[6]

At a planning meeting for Detroit Works, Heaster Wheeler, head of the local NAACP, argued that Detroit Works should reassure Detroiters that it would protect their interests: "We can't negotiate away our commitment to poor people, our commitment to city residents, our commitment to self-determination." In response, Marja Winters, a city planner, stated that Detroiters must be willing to engage in "conversations that traditionally have been uncomfortable to have" about the future of the city. Who would Detroit Works discomfort and comfort?

Phase One

"Democracy Is Noisy"

AFTER THE TOWN hall forums, the Mayor's Advisory Task Force (MATF) for Detroit Works met with project staff (city planners, private consultants) to discuss next steps. MATF consisted of business, church, and nonprofit leaders, including DBCFSN (the collective of black urban farmers and environmental justice activists). Not all of the MATF meetings were open to the public. I attended open MATF meetings on two different days in northwest Detroit. At each meeting, I sat with roughly thirty observers; MATF sat at a distance, facing project staff. MATF and project staff discussed the chaotic first forum. The project staff proposed that, in future outreach, the audience should be made to use clickers to answer multiple-choice items. (A few observers gasped.) This change was framed as a crowd control measure and a way to collect needed data. Charity Hicks, a member of MATF, warned her colleagues on the task force:

> Let people have democracy. Let people have their voice. Otherwise, it's going to blow up when it hits the streets. When we open up forums and engage, know that it's going to be noisy. If we're not prepared to deal with democracy, then this is all for nothing. You will get pushback, but what's wrong with that? We should ask people: "What would you like to see?"

Detroit Works did not address her concerns. The *Detroit News* reported that Detroit Works' private funding let it bypass Michigan's Open Meetings Act and Freedom of Information Act:

> City officials wouldn't publicly release contracts of companies paid to assist with the effort . . . the effort is funded by the private Kresge Foundation and advised by a task force of volunteers [MATF]. That's allowed the process to bypass laws requiring meetings and contracts be public. Meeting minutes of the 55-member advisory task force [MATF] aren't posted publicly. Its last session, on Jan. 6, was private. Kresge's

$1.5 million donation to the project was funneled to the Detroit Economic Growth Association, a nonprofit that told *The Detroit News* this month that it doesn't have to release records because it's not a public body.[1]

When I asked a Detroit Works outreach person whether MATF meeting minutes would be made available, she told me that they would be posted soon on their website. However, the minutes did not appear. The discussions covered important topics—for example, Detroit Works consultants told MATF about the health risks of brownfield sites: "We began to look at some statistics that clearly demonstrated that city residents have higher exposure to very serious diseases such as heart disease, cancer, or diabetes that have not just social and economic factors but also have really strong environmental links." The consultants did not ignore community problems, but they were unwilling or unable to address the power relations (including within Detroit Works) that hindered residents from learning about their risks and fighting for their lives. Mark Purcell, a political scientist, describes the suppression of local democracy as part of neoliberalization:

> Democracy is . . . squeezed into irrelevance by the competitive discipline of neoliberalization. . . . Truly democratic decision-making tends to involve political wrangling and vigorous debate; it values transparent disclosure and openness to considering new options. It takes time. It is therefore seen as slow, messy, inefficient, and not likely to produce the kind of bold entrepreneurial decisions that attract and keep capital. . . . [P]ublic-private partnerships, appointed councils, and quasi-public agencies are increasingly making decisions that were formerly made by [elected] officials.[2]

Worries about privatization could be heard even within MATF:

> When you bring up issues like water and sewerage, we want to see as much emphasis placed on . . . that Detroit owns it. We don't want to talk about privatization [*clapping in the audience*]. . . . If you bring up DTE [utilities] . . . we also want to talk about affordability.

Another MATF member expressed concern about equity:

> Is there an office or a person who is giving some thought to how the folks work into this and what is the probability that we will have people falling

through the net and that sort of thing? And I'm concerned about, uh, poor folks, real poor folks, and folks who don't have nothing.

A woman in the audience murmured "Amen!" A planner reassured the MATF member:

I would certainly say that it is our responsibility to see, to make sure that . . . it's not a plan that benefits some at the expense of others. . . . So far as an individual office, that has yet to be determined, but I think there's a mixture of structures in place within the City to make sure that that . . . is vetted.

Detroit Works staff soothed concerns with reassurances that no final decisions have been made:

We want to give you the opportunity to react to things. These are ideas that are not final. . . . I appreciate your comments.

Weeks later, the neighborhood cluster meetings began (eleven in total). The number of attendees is unclear. After the meetings concluded, Detroit Works reported 1,630 respondents to its "cluster-based" survey.[3] Asked whether they "had an opportunity to share their opinion," most respondents agreed.[4] Whites and senior citizens were overrepresented. African Americans were 83 percent of the city's population, but only 42 percent of respondents were African American. Perhaps poverty lessened attendance by African Americans. Public transit was bad in Detroit, and many low-income residents lacked cars.

I observed cluster meetings in three areas of the city: a high-income, majority black area in northwest Detroit, a low-income, majority black area on the lower east side, and a low-income, majority Latinx area in southwest Detroit. The first cluster meeting was on Thursday evening, January 27, 2011, at the University of Detroit–Mercy (UDM), a Catholic institution in northwest Detroit. Most whites fled the area after the 1960s; UDM and its mostly white student body remained. In 2010, the estimated median family income in the tract north of the campus was $94,107, compared to $34,741 for the tract to its south. Only 2 percent of families were below the poverty level in the north, compared to 19 percent of families in the south. In the affluent northern tract, 88 percent of residents were non-Hispanic blacks and 8 percent were

TABLE 4. Comparison of city demographics and cluster attendees*

	Detroit	Detroit Works Project Cluster Meetings (11 total)
Total Population	*713,777*	*1,630*
Female	52.7%	56%
55 years old and over	23%	41%
Race/Ethnicity		
African American	82.7%	42%
White	7.8%	42%
Asian	1.1%	--
American Indian	0.4%	--
Hispanic/Latino (of any race)	6.8%	5%
Other	--	8%

* US Census Bureau. Profile of general population and housing characteristics: 2010. Retrieved from http://factfinder2.census.gov; Detroit Works Project. Close-Ended Feedback Summary: Cluster-Based Meetings January 2011–March 2011. Detroit, MI: Author.

non-Hispanic whites. In the less affluent southern tract, 80 percent of residents were non-Hispanic blacks and 12 percent were non-Hispanic whites. On the night of the Detroit Works meeting at UDM, I waited in a line with other drivers for the guard to wave us in. My car radio droned about a snowstorm hitting the East Coast that shut down JFK International Airport and left thousands stranded. The Blizzard of 2011 hadn't hit Detroit yet, but the wind was blistering cold. I crunched in my winter boots through the parking lot with other attendees. By the time I entered the bright Student Center Ballroom, it was past the scheduled starting time, but the meeting had not begun. Reporters and cameramen roamed the floor. A projection screen displayed the Detroit Works logo on the blue-curtained stage next to the podium. I chose an aisle seat near the front. Each blue plastic chair had five items:

- a black electronic clicker remote control (the size of a key chain)
- a registration and comments form
- a green question form for the Q&A session
- a blue service request form (to report neighborhood problems)
- a pen

Despite the weather, the room was packed—roughly 250 people. A white woman who introduced herself as a teacher passed out flyers, asking us to go to an "important union meeting" to "talk about real change in the city." The flyer had the seal of Local 207 of the American Federation of State, County, and Municipal Employees (AFSCME). It announced a church rally to resist rightsizing, service cuts, and attacks on labor contracts. Local 207 represented public utility workers.

The cluster meeting began with remarks from the black president of the Sherwood Forest Neighborhood Association. Sherwood Forest is an affluent enclave near the university. The president proudly described new stores, art galleries, and infrastructure in the area. Next, Heidi Alcock, a white Detroit Works consultant, explained clicker use. Finally, Karla Henderson—the head city planner—talked for half an hour. She did not detail a plan. Rather, she made the case that increased density would benefit residents: for example, by lowering their property taxes. She used the clickers to get feedback. The audience was silent, except for murmurs ("oh!," "wow!") in response to slides. Most people seemed receptive. However, in the Q&A that follows, the anger of some attendees became clear. Detroit Works staff collected the question cards and selected some for Henderson to address. She read a question about "ticketing" people for peeling paint. A white woman stood and said that it was her card. She stated that she wanted to know whether the city's blight reduction campaign was meant to penalize her neighbors for living in homes that they could not afford to repair. She went on to criticize the clickers: "The process of pushing these buttons is kind of crazy and, you know, creates the illusion that we're participating. I think it's ridiculous." Some in the audience murmured agreement. Others frowned, perhaps disapproving of her words. The woman told people to attend the rally listed on the flyers. (I could not see her clearly, so I do not know if she was the same woman who passed out the flyers.) An elderly black man stood. He agreed with the woman about the clickers, and he protested the process by which Detroit Works screened and read comment cards. Rather than submitting questions, he wanted to hear and respond directly to Detroit Works and his neighbors. He said: "A dialogue is where you say something, then I say something, and we exchange ideas."

The southwest meeting was on Saturday morning, January 29, in Odd Fellows Hall. In 2010, the median family income in the tract was $27,309; 36 percent of families were below the poverty level. A hundred years earlier,

Mexicans began coming to southwest Detroit in large numbers, recruited for factory work. During the Great Depression, the US immigration bureau deported thousands of them. Labor demand during World War II pulled Mexicans back. The Detroit Works meeting in southwest Detroit was the most raucous of the three that I attended. The tract was 72 percent Latinx, but most attendees were non-Hispanic whites and blacks. A Mexican American activist told me that Detroit Works had done a poor job notifying residents. Some black and Latinx attendees loudly protested the clicker questions. When asked, "which . . . is most critical to your quality of life . . . education . . . health care . . . grocery stores . . ." people called out: "We need them all!" "I want schools *and* food!" They muttered that other questions had obvious answers ("How important is it for Detroiters to have access to jobs in Detroit?"). One person called out that whoever thought of the clickers should be fired.

The lower east side cluster meeting was held on Monday night, February 28, at Gleaners Food Bank. Gleaners distributes food donations in southeastern Michigan. Its tract is mostly African American (89 percent). In 2010, the median family income was $28,964, and the percentage of families below the poverty level was 20 percent. Similar to much of the lower east side, the tract has suffered from flights of people and capital. One can see boarded-up homes and businesses on the lower east side, and there is much poverty, yet there are also blocks with the well-maintained homes of working-class, middle-class, and upper-middle-class families. The lower east side has grassroots institutions that are known among activists outside Detroit, including Peace Zones for Life and the Boggs Center. During the Detroit Works meeting here, there were no outbursts during Q&A. A question card asked whether Detroit Works knew about the Lower Eastside Action Plan (LEAP), suggesting that Detroit Works should talk with LEAP. Funded by the Erb Foundation, the Community Foundation for Southeast Michigan, and the Local Initiatives Support Corporation, LEAP brings together local groups to develop uses for vacant land.

The use of clickers by Detroit Works got bad press, but they could have been used to enhance discussion. The clickers collected useful demographic data: it is important to document who is present. However, many clicker questions were obvious or leading—for example, one question asked: "What is the most important benefit of creating light rail in Detroit?" The meetings were not structured to help residents calculate impacts and to air opposing views. The outrage at the clickers was not just about technology; people wanted full disclosure of project intentions, and they wanted their concerns to matter. Two types of attendees attacked Detroit Works:

- People who wished to have a dialogue with Detroit Works but felt frustrated by its procedures. They did not view the local black and white elites who shared the microphone with Detroit Works staff as representing their communities.
- People who did not seek dialogue with Detroit Works because they believed that it was set up to serve corporate interests. Tied in some cases to labor activism, the people in this group came to Detroit Works meetings to rally opposition.

As attendance by the latter group declined, the forums became less explosive. After the cluster meetings, Detroit Works held summits that focused on entrepreneurs, artists, youth, environmentalists, immigrants, seniors, and faith-based representatives. Labor did not get a summit.

> Mr. Mulholland of AFSCME Local 207 . . . calls the Detroit Works Project proposals "nonsensical" and "racist" because he says the majority of people who would be invited to move [during rightsizing] are black. "The problem is [city leaders do not] fear us anymore and they can do anything they want," he says.[5]

The neoliberal order suppresses labor unions (who demand bread) but relies on artists' collectives (who transform bread into communion). It is hard to separate these groups and their messages in Detroit. In spring 2011, the Detroit People's Movement Assembly (PMA)—a coalition of labor activists and cultural workers who had helped to organize USSF 2010—called for "disinvestment from Detroit Works." In a PMA video, Will Copeland—a hip-hop artist who works on environmental justice projects—stated: "The mayor thought it would be a pushover . . . he would bring in some experts and the experts would make some pronouncements and then everyone would be okay with that. It wasn't a pushover. . . . We're going to see what the next phase is."[6]

Phase Two

"This Is a Conversation?"

KRESGE BECAME DISSATISFIED with the progress of Detroit Works, and city officials began to bristle under Kresge control.[1] In summer 2011, Detroit Works was split into a (1) "short-term" team, led by city officials, to deal with current problems and conduct demonstration projects, and (2) a "long-term" team, led by private consultants, to devise a fifty-year plan. In other words, city officials no longer served even as figureheads in planning the city's future. Toni Griffin, based on the East Coast, headed the long-term team, but I never saw her again at any of the public meetings that I attended. The public face of Detroit Works became white and male: Dan Kinkead, a local architect, became the lead planner responsible for day-to-day operations, and Dan Pitera, another local architect, became spokesperson for civic engagement.

Pitera, a professor at the UDM School of Architecture, co-led long-term outreach with Heidi Alcock (the consultant who had assisted with cluster meetings). Describing himself as "an activist masquerading as an architect," Pitera directs the Detroit Collaborative Design Center (DCDC) at UDM, which works on projects for nonprofits. According to DCDC's 2013 program report, Detroit Works grants have helped the center to overcome its budget problems:

> The Design Center landed the biggest grant in their history from the Ford Foundation.
>
> $1,500,000 was provided to support the Design Center's role in the innovative "Detroit Works Project" to develop new land use and economic development strategies for the city. This enabled us to hire many new contract staff members for the development of this project and to open a satellite location downtown. An additional $300,000 was provided by the Kellogg Foundation, to provide gap financing for a limited period of time for the Detroit Works Project. . . . [T]he Kresge Foundation has funded the Detroit Collaborative Design Center for 3 years at $125,000 per year.

This has helped eliminate a budget short fall and puts the Center on more stable footing.[2]

Detroit Works financially benefited DCDC, yet it posed public relations risks. Pitera had a good reputation among activists. In 2010, he collaborated with Young Nation in southwest Detroit on an outdoor art space. In 2001, he advised Adamah, a UDM-led plan for an agricultural community on the lower east side. Adamah was never built, but it excited cultural workers. Grace Boggs spoke favorably of it:

> The Adamah vision . . . includes community gardens, greenhouses, grazing land . . . a tree farm, lumber mill, and windmills . . . and living and work spaces in the former Packard auto plant. . . . Community residents draw from Adamah ideas. . . . Out-of-towners start wondering how they can spend time in Detroit to help build the movement.[3]

The Boggs Center has shared the Adamah video with visitors.[4] During the second phase of Detroit Works, Pitera and his outreach team talked about strategies that sounded like Adamah, so some cultural workers credit Pitera with getting Detroit Works to adopt a green vision. This is not true: talk of urban greening is common in planning, and it is intrinsic to smart decline, an approach for coping with depopulation. Before Bing's State of the City speech and before Detroit Works began, Rip Rapson—the head of Kresge—talked about the need to rightsize and green Detroit.[5] In 2009, Dan Kinkead—the architect at Hamilton Anderson who would later become the day-to-day lead for Detroit Works—blogged that Detroit should "develop woodland areas" and "transform the community garden into a true city-wide asset."[6] During phase one of Detroit Works, Karla Henderson, head city planner, spoke of devising an urban agriculture policy. Detroit Works included Stoss Landscape Urbanism, which describes its work as bringing cities and ecologies into relation. The approaches of these key players to greening were in line with smart decline, which frames vacancy "as an opportunity for creating a new kind of place" with a sense of community, innovative enterprises, efficient infrastructure, and small ecological footprints.[7] John Gallagher, a journalist for the *Detroit Free Press*, exemplifies advocates of smart decline. In *Reimagining Detroit*, Gallagher argues that cities do not have to be big, industrial powerhouses to be good places to live—small can be beautiful if shrinking cities turn their vacant land into sustainable spaces.[8] Planners increasingly embrace smart decline, which combines greening with rightsizing. Smart decline has been described as a paradigm shift in urban planning, but it has antecedents. Decades earlier, Roger Starr, the chief housing administrator in New York City, stirred charges of racism when he proposed "planned shrinkage"—the relocation of residents and the reduction of city services (fire protection, police patrols, garbage collection)—in the heavily black and Latino neighborhoods of Harlem, the South Bronx, and the Lower East Side.[9] In these areas, population loss had resulted in vacant buildings. Starr argued that the city's budget crisis necessitated consolidating residents into a more compact space to lower costs. Opposing Starr's relocation plan, Herman Badillo, a South Bronx politician, stated that if there were not enough funds to rebuild depopulated areas, empty buildings should be demolished and money given to community members for planting "crops and flowers" to make the land attractive and thus halt flight.[10] Badillo (a fiery Democrat who later switched to the Republican Party) became an early driver of federal support for urban agriculture.[11] Similar to early efforts at planned shrinkage, smart decline is driven by fiscal concerns. However, smart decline sweetens rightsizing with an appealing "crops and flowers" proposal— originally, the Garden was an opposing argument. Smart decline (also called "smart shrinkage") may appear to be Adamah—the opposite of the growth machine—but smart decline advocates resemble growth coalitions in areas of Detroit with market potential.

Pitera's unique contribution to Detroit Works was to bridge technical and cultural work. Perhaps the funders wanted to leverage the goodwill that he enjoyed. Pitera had ties to the artists, clergy, and intellectuals with a green vision who were hostile to Detroit Works. Similar to them, he spoke of stories and landscapes as fused—narratives inspire people to reimagine and rebuild places. The story into which he drew cultural workers was the redemptive narrative of the Garden. Pitera opened the Detroit Works "Homebase"—with its warm, welcoming name—in an easy-to-find site next to Eastern Market, a large farmers market near downtown. Rural and urban farmers sell produce here. This siting placed Detroit Works at an important location of green projects. Pitera and his team worked in a plain space without partitions, perhaps to convey transparency and egalitarianism. The public was invited to view exhibits by local photographers and to see diagrams of the future city on the walls. Pitera began a series of "community conversations," at which he said that Detroit Works had learned from its past mistakes. In phase one, residents of southwest Detroit and the lower east side had asked for better outreach. Pitera addressed these concerns. I saw Mexican Americans from southwest Detroit arrive to speak with Pitera. Another day, I saw Pitera meeting with LEAP from the lower east side. During phase one, some activists had complained that Detroit Works staff had disrespected residents by describing them as illiterate and irrational. In phase two, Detroit Works produced *iDetroit*, a three-minute video that it placed online.[12] The video begins with waving US flags at the GM building then pans to scenes of Detroit architecture, artists, and entrepreneurs, while the voiceover states descriptions of the city that begin with "I": "I am industry. . . . I am intelligent. . . . I am imaginative. . . . I am Detroit." Some residents who had voiced anger about Detroit Works during phase one spoke favorably of Pitera's outreach. Others remained hostile to Detroit Works and suspicious of Pitera. He softened but did not end opposition.

Pitera was "new money" (funded by foundations), but his style resembled "old money" (grassroots groups that relied on community contributions). Detroit Works began to use a "roaming table" to reach out to people on the street. Pitera told a reporter, "The intention is to get out and interrupt people's flow . . . [for example, at] the transit center. . . . We're not sitting inside in the warm. We're out there in the cold."[13] A member of Pitera's team added, "We won't be standing in front of a room with a clicker and a microphone." The table reached Detroiters without cars who found it hard to come to meetings. Pitera recruited diverse residents to help with outreach. These helpers included cultural workers and nonprofit heads. For example, he got advice from cultural workers who blended art, activism, and digital media to help develop an online planning game called "Detroit 24/7." The game increased youth participation. Toni Griffin acknowledged that help from people with grassroots ties had made a difference: "A lot of times, it's all about the technical team coming in and doing this thoughtful work and presenting it to the community: 'This is what I think you should do.' One of the big lessons that we learned in Detroit is that there's something called community expertise."[14] In phase one, the technical team had been met with what Griffin describes as "the equivalent of tomatoes being thrown at us." After locals became the face of Detroit Works, it got easier to build relations. I spoke with a few cultural workers who did outreach. They said that the history of urban renewal made them cautious, but Detroit Works had money to redesign Detroit, so they had decided to work with Detroit Works to make a difference. I also interviewed Pitera. He voiced pragmatism about urban projects, saying that what is possible to build differs from what is ideal: "Capitalism is built on inequality. I don't know if we can ever have justice, but we can further justice."

Pitera and his team made outreach more inclusive and creative, and they used respectful language. However, growth elites had the same power. Residents could make suggestions but not decisions. Detroit Works embraced LEAP and other green projects, drawing ideas from existing neighborhood plans. However, Detroit Works did not facilitate democratic deliberation. It framed engagement as an opportunity for residents to creatively implement top-down decisions. Inside the Homebase, the recommendations wall framed feedback as support: "How can you make the framework a reality? Share your thoughts." Detroit Works showed promotional slides and videos with stirring music and images. At a Detroit Works meeting in northwest Detroit, Lila Cabbil—a PMA activist who had been a friend of Rosa Parks and the program director of the Parks Institute—muttered, "*This* is a conversation?" An upbeat staffer—perhaps not hearing the sarcasm—told Cabbil that she was in the right place and handed her materials for a planning exercise. The exercise included questions as superficial as the clicker questions. I asked Pitera why Likert scales were placed under vague statements such as "We must be strategic and coordinated in our use of land." He said that engineers who lacked skills in questionnaire design added the items. But the problem was not that the items were clumsy; the problem was that they did not seem driven by a desire to get input that could inform design. The items appeared to serve didactic or "rubber stamp" functions. Most seriously, Detroit Works refused to admit rightsizing and its risks to residents. At professional meetings around the country, Detroit Works consultants used the term *rightsizing* to describe their vision for Detroit.[15] However, the outreach staff preferred to use less politically charged terms such as *repurposing* when they spoke with residents.[16]

Their representations of "repurposing" were always sunny. In conversations that I observed with a community group that asked Detroit Works staff about whether they planned to do rightsizing, the Detroit Works staff responded that rightsizing was a "rumor" and a "misunderstanding," changing the subject to their ecological and economic strategies. In the final meetings, attendees were put in groups, given short drafts of the plan to read, and asked for comments. A few attendees said that the proposals sounded like rightsizing. Detroit Works staff repeated their denial ("rightsizing is only a rumor"), and they insisted that their aim was to expand "options" about where people could live. These reassurances calmed some people. In phase one—alarmed by Bing's words—attendees had expressed fear that relocations might destabilize receiving neighborhoods, given the history of residential flight when demographics changed. They also had voiced concerns that service cuts in high vacancy areas might harm residents. These were reasonable concerns. Whether service cuts occur through policy or "benign" neglect—whether moves are forced by mandate or worsening conditions—rightsizing has risks. Perhaps good intentions motivated some Detroit Works consultants to be silent about the risks; they may have wished to avoid alarming residents because it might lead to fights that would impede necessary action. However, the assumption that planners know best reduces residents to the status of children. When residents are not told potential costs and benefits, they cannot make informed decisions about their future. After a Detroit Works meeting, I shared beers with UAW organizers—a black man and a white woman. The white labor organizer told me that the experts should tell Detroiters and suburbanites about the monetary and environmental costs of the decades of sprawl. She said that white suburbanites might "shut down" if charged with racism, but she thought that they would be open to a conversation about the costs of existing policies for everyone. That would be a good place to begin—it is a richer, more respectful conversation than Detroit Works attempted—it would provide a foundation for all adults in the region to reason together. However, some costs are particular to black Detroiters because of the history and persistence of racism, and that needs to be said too.

Detroit Works released *Detroit Future City: Detroit Strategic Framework Plan* at a press conference with Mayor Bing in January 2013. The plan provides a fifty-year agenda for Detroit, detailing goals for the next five years, years five to ten, years ten to twenty, and years twenty to fifty for five planning elements: economic growth, land use, city systems, neighborhoods, and land and building assets. Justice-speak combines with Moral We language to frame the plan. DFC outlines equity goals, it describes environmental hazards, and it (vaguely) states that "barriers" exist for black Detroiters in housing, jobs, education, and transportation. Who or what caused the barriers? The plan avoids blame; it says that it is "talking about love" and that "love of a place, love of a neighborhood, love of a team or a landscape . . . can prompt this city . . . to work and hope for the days of change." When interviewed by reporters, DFC staff emphasized their ecological and economic strategies. The plan does have innovative proposals for managing storm water and improving air quality:

> In the spirit of innovation that has made the city great, Detroit will lead the world in developing landscape as 21st century infrastructure to transform vacant land areas into community assets that remediate contaminated land, manage storm water and highway runoff, and create passive recreational amenities to improve human health and elevate adjacent land values—all without residential displacement, a big change from the urban renewal efforts of the 1960s and 1970s. The iconic boulevards and freeway corridors of the city can be transformed to reinforce a new civic identity through the creation of linear carbon forests that clean air, and storm water management landscapes that collect, treat and recycle water.[17]

And DFC offers interesting ideas about clustering economic, social, and educational activities:

> The commercial corridors map proposes . . . clustering new commercial development in nodes connected along major transit routes and thoroughfares. . . . Clustering commercial and social activities will help to reinforce symbiotic uses and improve walkability within commercial areas. In keeping with aspirations for all neighborhoods in Detroit, schools should function as neighborhood hubs and provide space for both learning and recreational opportunities for the larger community.

The problem is that these ideas have been *marketed to* residents, not deliberated on by them. They sound nice, but there is a need for careful vetting.

The press response was positive. The basic plan had not changed since Bing said that the city would be rightsized, but even left-wing media echoed Detroit Works outreach staff who—denying that *Detroit Future City* is a rightsizing plan—emphasized its green proposals:

> Milestones for progress are charted for . . . an ultimately transformed Detroit that's visualized in the year 2050. That Detroit isn't right-sized, just readjusted. Within those city limits lies room enough for organic farms and high-tech firms alike . . . to support a 21st century city.—Ashley Woods, Detroit editor, *Huffington Post*

The reporter apparently had not yet read the 347-page plan. In the city systems section, the plan mentions rightsizing under the heading "Reform Delivery System:"

1. Use the framework plan to create certainty around residential and employment density in each area of the city.
2. *Right-size* systems so that network capacity matches residential and employment demand for each area in the medium term (*emphasis mine*).
3. Balance investment in areas of greatest need with investment in areas of greatest potential.
4. Address equity: ensure that a good standard of core services are provided to all groups in all areas including high-vacancy areas.

Perhaps the consultants in charge of this section did not know or care that outreach staff were not using the term *rightsizing*. The section details tiered service investments: upgrading services in areas with high growth potential, maintaining and repairing services in moderate vacancy areas, and providing core services in high vacancy areas until the areas transition to being "no longer in residential use," at which point their services are to be "decommissioned." These tiers enable the concentration of scarce funds in areas with market potential by reducing private investments and public utility expenditures in high vacancy areas. Green amenities such as parks are championed to reduce blight in greater downtown, while blue-green infrastructure such as storm-water ponds and urban agriculture are proposed to repurpose land in high vacancy areas.

Neighborhood vignettes begin each section of the plan, but they are not case studies—they are speculative fiction. Here is an excerpt:

> Antonio grew up in the house his grandfather bought in a once-thriving neighborhood. . . .
>   Streetlights that went out stayed out, police calls took longer. . . . Things started to change when the Detroit Strategic Framework was released. The City soon put routine city services and maintenance on a regular schedule . . . and police and fire services have improved.

Nothing in the text marks this story as fiction, but given that it appears in the Detroit Strategic Framework, it cannot be a factual account of what happened after its own release. Each vignette is peppered with ethnic names (Antonio, Bakari, Aisha, Demarco . . .) and heartwarming scenarios:

> Irma, Bill, and Aisha's neighborhood is having its first block party in 30 years today. . . . It hardly seems possible that the pleasant green space where neighborhood kids are playing and grown-ups are cooking out and talking was once a notorious vacant lot that neighbors used to call "The Blob". . . . With a grant for seeds and supplies from a local family foundation, the [community garden] project was underway. "Take Back the Blob," became the neighborhood's rallying cry. . . . Today is the day Aisha lands on the number chosen for the ultimate prize: The Chocolate Blob cake Irma made with her grandson, complete with Blobberry filling (raspberries from the bushes in the garden). The future is bright, all right. But today is pretty sweet, too.

It can be useful to tell a moving story—emotion alerts us to our interests and the needs of others. However, it is problematic to use fiction in a city plan. *Detroit Future City* quotes real people too, but the quotes are cherry-picked. For example, DFC proposes a pilot house-for-house swap to relocate people who volunteer to move from high vacancy areas. Most Detroiters do not live in areas designated as "high vacancy," but the number who do—88,255—is larger than the total residents in Youngstown, Ohio, an early adopter of smart decline that has found it hard to relocate people. The argument for a housing swap is made through images and quotes:

(1) The drawing of a woman in silhouette on a chair, with a quote in speech bubble, "Low density will not work. Sadly for the people who won't or can't leave their homes when they're the last remaining two or three houses on the block, they might just have to. How can the city afford to maintain all that green space?"

(2) The drawing of a man in silhouette striding forward, with a quote in speech bubble, "If the current residents were provided housing swaps into planned and safe communities—it would enable the city to enact some eminent domain and demolish urban blight. Giving the current residents the opportunity to move to better housing, improved services, and a safe environment for their families."

(3) A photo of houses with the caption, "Pilot Project House-for-House Swap Program. A trial house for house swap program would allow residents in High Vacancy areas to move to higher-density, safer areas of the city with better services. This pilot project must be preceded by an in-depth civic engagement program to ensure residents' confidence in the program."

Where are the speech bubbles with quotes from Detroiters who worry about rightsizing? To see if Detroit Works had taken all residents' concerns into account, I asked Dan Kinkead whether Detroit Works had a strategy to counter the risks of rightsizing related to neighborhood stability and public health. He told me that it does not—he said that the focus has been on achieving density. Yet destabilization might influence density; identifying areas as at risk of decommissioning might serve as a kind of redlining that increases disinvestment, which may worsen conditions and increase flight. To its credit, *Detroit Future City* calls for monitoring impacts. However, the call is vague. The plan does not outline rightsizing risks for vulnerable populations—including low-income residents, elders, and people of all ages with disabilities that limit their mobility—and it does not identify a government agency to protect them. Equally disturbing, it does not affirm the right of residents to have the effects of rightsizing monitored and reported by researchers not affiliated with Detroit Works. I attended a community meeting at which a Detroit Works staff person said that the plan follows "best practices." This phrase was misleading: rightsizing a city as large as Detroit is, at best, an experiment—it has not been done before. Given potential risks, full disclosure is critical. You cannot end or amend a harmful experiment if you have not been told that you are a subject. Even some cultural workers who agreed with Detroit Works that rightsizing was the only viable option were worried about growth elites' control of the process. They feared that consultants muddied the waters about what they planned to do, and they worried that rightsizing would be carried out in ways that deepen inequalities.

Detroit Works renamed itself after its plan—Detroit Future City—and then appointed itself to manage redevelopment, arguing that city government lacked the stability and resources for long-term planning. DFC touted the number of people with whom it had talked and the amount of data it had analyzed. Yet conversations and data-crunching do not equal democratic deliberation and decision-making. DFC said that it offered a guide for decisions made by "each of us" in an undefined process that extends into the indefinite future:

> Now—after hundreds of meetings, 30,000 conversations, connecting with people over 163,000 times, over 70,000 survey responses and comments from participants, and countless hours spent dissecting and examining critical data about our city—we are proud to present Detroit Future City. We believe that within this document lies a path forward toward realizing the aspirations of an entire city. Within it lies a guide for decision making that is not exclusively for one entity or one mayor or one generation, but for each of us—and those who come after us—in our roles as citizens, philanthropists, developers, business people, neighborhood champions, parents, and beyond.[18]

DFC reduced representative democracy to fragmented identities (mayor, citizens) among other "roles" (developers, business people). This framing of a Moral We obscured power relations. After *Detroit Future City* was released, some nonprofit leaders were enthusiastic, praising the public outreach and describing the plan as the most realistic strategy for the city's redevelopment.[19] This support enabled DFC to move forward with partnerships to implement the plan.[20] A public forum that I attended, held at the University of Michigan Detroit Center on Woodward Avenue, reflected the range of reactions. On the panel, a black urban farmer said that he was "neither for nor against" the plan.

He feared that his high-vacancy neighborhood might be decommissioned. To avoid this end, he hoped that it could be repurposed with agriculture. A white nonprofit head in an area with less vacancy said that *Detroit Future City* aligned with his group's goals. A white Boggs Center member had good things to say about Pitera but charged that DFC lacked democratic decision-making. Around the city, reactions varied. The Detroit Sierra Club stated that Detroit Works did not adequately address environmental hazards and that its right-sizing plan "contradicts the principles of environmental justice."[21] Some troubled residents told me that DFC staff responded to their concerns by saying that no final decisions had been made, so they should stay involved. This was a continuance—from the town halls and MATF meetings—of residents being urged to participate in a process that was said to be endlessly open. DFC ideas were evolving; the constant was that elites made decisions behind closed doors. Detroit Future City insisted that it did not have a top-down "fix":

> Detroit won't be "fixed" because no city is ever "fixed." Cities are living places that . . . [must] acknowledge changing realities and multiple voices, leading to pragmatic and agreed-on solutions.[22]

How had "multiple voices" been acknowledged? *Who* had agreed to rightsizing? Critics warn that DFC will create two cities: a white, gentrified downtown and black impoverished neighborhoods. This binary frame, useful in the twentieth century, hinders understanding of a twenty-first-century danger. In the DFC rightsizing plan, downtown is *not* the only area targeted for investment. The real danger is that Detroit may split into *three* territories:

- *Wealthy enclaves dominated by white elites in which affluent people of all races reside*: these areas will dominate the city (economically, ideologically) and thus get the greatest investments and the most protection from environmental harm;
- *Middle-class neighborhoods with a racially diverse, precariously fortunate Moral We (including the black middle class)*: these areas with market potential will get positive news coverage ("Detroit is coming back!") and investment to improve living conditions and win their support. The quality of life in these areas will improve, yet the lives of their residents—especially black lives—will be insecure as

government safety nets fray, ecological degradation worsens, and racism persists in the neoliberal order;

- *High poverty neighborhoods with mostly black residents*: these high vacancy areas that have long suffered race-class demonization and neglect will undergo continued disinvestment, sugarcoated with green projects. These projects will have benefits, but they will do little to change disparities. Eventually, the demonized may be driven out of Detroit by (at first) worsening conditions and then escalating rents if the market improves in their areas.

This is the fate of HBURs that are further along in redevelopment.

The central business district is not the only area of investment, but it is the command and control center of the city. DFC and downtown elites support each other. PPS—the placemaking consultants advising Gilbert's downtown plan—notes that DFC speaks of placemaking as a way to further the future city.[23] In 2013, DFC set up its headquarters, chaired by DEGC, the nonprofit that partners with the city to guide development. (DEGC sits on the board of DDP, the downtown business alliance.) George Jackson, the African American who headed DEGC, announced the DFC leads: Dan Kinkead, an architect at Hamilton Anderson, and Heidi Alcock, the former director of a services provider to nonprofits. Kinkead and Alcock are young white professionals. DEGC's control of planning expanded after Governor Snyder chose an emergency manager, Kevyn Orr—a black corporate attorney—to run the city. Orr forced the head of city planning to resign, putting DEGC in charge of her duties. Mike Duggan—the CEO of Detroit Medical Center in Midtown—became the city's first white mayor in four decades, after a 2013 election with low voter turnout: only 25 percent of registered voters in Detroit cast a ballot.[24] Like Michael (the despairing man whom I met by the river), many Detroiters have lost faith in voting and black solidarity. DFC re-organized, appointing Ken Cockrel—a black, moderate, former councilman—as its director. This move made a member of the city's old guard the face of DFC. In 2015, Anika Goss-Foster—a black woman—became head of DFC. She led a mostly white technical team, with black outreach staff. George Jackson left DEGC to start his real estate advisory firm; the revolving door between public and private interests spun.

Side Conversations

"Money Talks"

COMMUNITY ORGANIZERS COULD not focus solely on Detroit Works as it unfolded. They were pulled in many directions by crises—home foreclosures, utility shutoffs, job and pension cuts, school and transit problems. Amid these troubles, the threat of state takeover hung over the city, and rumors about land grabs opened old wounds. People who remembered mid-twentieth-century civil rights battles feared that hard-won voter rights were in jeopardy, and people who recalled Black Bottom worried that redevelopment might become "Negro removal" all over again.

On the evening of January 2, 2012—as the second phase of Detroit Works proceeded elsewhere—hundreds gathered at Tabernacle Missionary Baptist Church to rally against the Emergency Manager Law (Public Act 4). The flyer for the event included a line ("We shall not be moved") from an old civil rights hymn:

> We Shall Not Be Moved
> Rally!
> Black cities in Michigan are under attack by Governor Snyder
> and his Emergency Managers (Local Dictators)!
> What are _you_ going to do about it?
> _You_ need to be at the rally!

As I sat in the pews at the rally, a singer led us in the hymn, "We shall overcome some day." I felt as though I was trapped in a time loop; it was the anthem of my parents' generation—a song that I saw in films—yet this was 2012. The speakers urged us to get our neighbors to sign a petition to put a measure against the emergency manager law on the ballot in Michigan. The petition got enough signatures and the measure succeeded on the state ballot, but the state legislature passed a new emergency manager law that voters could not challenge.

On August 22, 2012—as Detroit Works wrapped up its public outreach—the Detroit Food Policy Council (DFPC) organized and transcribed a public listening session at Gleaners Food Bank to air local concerns about the sale of city-owned land.[1] DFPC monitored land issues because food was grown on some city-owned lots. The organizers counted 240 attendees. I did not see an empty seat; I squeezed against the wall in the crowded room. The panel, which included city planners and urban farmers, discussed challenges to efficiency and fairness in land sales. They suggested that some challenges had to do with organizational and technical capacities (for example, the need to automate city processes), while other challenges had to do with power. Residents told about fighting foreclosures, being exposed to toxic hazards, mowing the grass on lots neglected by land speculators, and hauling water for community gardens. They asked why it was easier and quicker for rich people to get city land. A city planner bluntly stated:

> I hate to say it, but money talks, okay? If we've got a big project and a plant's going to go in, it's going to create jobs; it's going to enhance the community, which gets our attention. It finds its way to the top.

A resident countered:

> The City has kowtowed to corporations for as long as there's been manufacturing in this area. We give them tax breaks. We give them breaks on buying land . . . then when they decide to pick up their marbles and go home, we are standing there whimpering, looking at the empty buildings, looking at the brown fields, and looking at the ways in which they've destroyed neighborhoods. Preferences should be given to the people . . . who live in the neighborhoods, and not to the corporations.

Lila Cabbil, a longtime activist, joined in:

> When we talk about corporations coming in and there's the promise of jobs, we need to be able to have a system of accountability that looks at what really happens in terms of jobs. . . . The [new] jobs are held down by suburbanites, not Detroiters. . . . The other thing that we need to look at is property that came from foreclosure from predatory lending. And we need to really look at how that property is being sold for development.

Because there should be reparations for the people who lost their homes. And we need to hold the banks accountable for that.

Race was not the only divide. A young white newcomer who moved to Corktown to start an urban farm complained about red tape in land sales. An older white woman who described herself as a lifelong Detroiter and urban gardener responded that she "loves" him, but she thought that longtime residents who had cared for the land should get first dibs on it. The harshest criticism was reserved for city government and the banks and rich developers. Some attendees said that the city government should demand that corporations buying city land show the benefits of their development projects. They criticized city officials' negotiations with John Hantz, a developer who wanted to buy over a thousand lots on the lower east side for an urban farm. Hantz said that his enterprise would create jobs and clean up lots, which would improve life for residents and boost urban agriculture in the city. However, skeptics charged that farming was not his ultimate aim; they said that his project cloaked an old land grab scheme to buy cheap land, create scarcity, drive up property values, and then profit by selling the land to gentrifiers, who would drive out longtimers.

On the evening of December 10, 2012—weeks before Detroit Works released Detroit Future City and a few months before the governor appoints an emergency manager over Detroit—the city council held a public hearing at East Lake Baptist Church on the lower east side to discuss the Hantz proposal for a tree farm. The hearing began while I waited in the long line with others shivering outside the church. People stuffed their fists in their pockets and stamped their feet to keep warm. A black man in line said: "They could at least have speakers [audio equipment] out here so we could hear what's going on." An old white man turned to him and said, "Is that a question? Why fascists don't put up speakers?" People chuckled. The people around me spoke against the Hantz proposal. Perhaps people who sided with Hantz were afraid to speak. I do not know how many residents *in the area* of the proposed farm approved or disapproved—the people in line came from all over the city. Hantz had promised local residents that he would clean up the area and create a safer, more attractive neighborhood—something that city government had been unable to do. Some academics supported his vision, including Michael Score—an agricultural educator with Michigan State University's agricultural program, whom Hantz made president of Hantz Farms in 2009. Finally, I got inside and found a seat. I recognized and greeted several folks, including a young black woman, raised in Detroit, who was a top student in the urban studies class that I taught at MSU. I was glad to see young people in the audience—the attendees at public meetings in Detroit were often middle aged or older. The church was large; city council members sat at a table in front. It was hard to hear and see the people who went one by one from the audience to the microphone. I caught bits of sentences that told me this person supported Hantz and that person opposed him, but little else. Then a woman came to the microphone—I heard the passion in the rise and fall of her voice, but I couldn't make out much until the end when her voice rang clear and resonant: "What I see now is a repeat of Black Bottom. . . . A lot of promises were made and nothing was ever done. . . . If you are a second or third or fourth generation of being a black Detroit person. . . . I am going to say to each one of you. . . . Remember Black Bottom! Remember Black Bottom! Remember Black Bottom!" A few people repeated the chant and then it rolled across the church until much of the audience thundered it. Despite protests, the city council eventually approved Hantz's tree farm.

Detroit activists, drawing on ideas from other cities, talked about the need to get community benefits agreements (CBA) from corporations. The activists wanted to have a say in urban design rather than endlessly fighting crises. A year before the 2013 opening of Whole Foods in Midtown, three community organizers—Linda Campbell, Gloria Rivera, and Mary Lou Malone—held discussions with the corporation. The three organizers brought diverse skills and organizational power to the negotiations: Campbell led the Detroit branch of Building Movement, a national organization that worked to build the capacity of local organizations to fight for social change. Rivera, born in Mexico, was a Catholic sister of the Immaculate Heart of Mary order; in the past she had served as the executive director of Freedom House, a refuge for asylum seekers in southwest Detroit. She went on to cofound Great Lakes Bioneers Detroit (GLBD), which promotes ecological and social sustainability in southeast Michigan. Malone co-chaired the MOSES Supermarket Task Force, which strives to eliminate food deserts in Detroit. MOSES is the acronym for

Metropolitan Organizing Strategy Enabling Strength, an interfaith coalition in the Detroit metropolitan area. The organizers struggled for but did not get a promise from Whole Foods to pay a "living wage." Yet Whole Foods did promise to hire local workers, to cultivate and market local vendors, to use local artists to create murals on the store, and to support nutrition education programs. The organizers viewed CBAs as alternatives to "money talks" development. Campbell stated: "The question was how to best represent the concerns of the community with the development of this . . . at the root of it is how decisions are made about development in Detroit and about how to spend resources."[2] Rivera added: "We're really addressing systems, in this case the system around development. Which of course bumps up against other systems—housing, equity. That adds to the complexity, and also adds to creating better, more thought through processes for development."

The Detroit People's Platform (DPP)—a network of social and environmental justice groups—pushed for a citywide CBA ordinance. This push met with resistance from DEGC and from state legislators: in 2014, a state representative introduced House Bill 5977 that would ban cities in Michigan from enacting an ordinance that would require developers to negotiate a CBA. Linda Campbell, representing the DPP, urged the Detroit City Council to oppose the bill. She described the bill as a threat to local democracy:

> Good morning, Council. My name is Linda Campbell, and I am here representing the People's Platform, which is a citywide network of over 2,500 Detroiters. . . . I urge the council today to support the resolution opposing House Bill 5977. House Bill 5977 is a frightful overreach of government that . . . takes away the right of voice from communities. It forces me to question, what is the role then of local government and its residents and citizens if each and every time folks come together to act in a democratic way, we live in fear that someone—some obscure legislator—can go on the floor in Lansing [the state capitol] and strip away the rights that we all believe we're entitled to. We know that this has a far-reaching impact, but we know that it is targeting Detroiters. When will the punitive, small-minded politics cease in Lansing? Again, I urge you to vote in opposition to House Bill 5977 and note that thousands of residents of Detroit across this city stand with you.[3]

Linda Campbell and the DPP succeeded in getting the city council to pass the resolution, and they went on to defeat House Bill 5977. Activists collected signatures to get a CBA proposal on the ballot in Detroit. A city councilman advanced a weaker CBA proposal to compete with it. The activists opposed his proposal because it forbade legally binding agreements and it raised the total project cost that triggered CBA from $15 million to $75 million.[4] They argued that the counter proposal was not strong enough to hold corporations accountable. The weaker CBA proposal passed and went into effect in January 2017. The struggle to pass a strong CBA ordinance in Detroit continued.

V

Consilium Principis

[The emperor] Augustus and his successors . . . consulted their friends and followers . . . before giving judicial decisions in cases of importance. The consilium principis . . . was not . . . a standing body of advisers, but was constituted for each particular occasion.

—Dictionary of Greek and Roman Antiquities (1890)

"Co-Creating the Good" in the "Just City"

THE EXPERTS FLOWN in to redesign cities are here today and gone tomorrow, funded by interests that do not always reside in the city. What can be done to make them accountable to low-income African Americans? To answer this question, we must identify key players and their affiliations, and we must examine the forces that shape their practices. Detroit Works was a reassemblage of architects, engineers, and planners who had, in some cases, collaborated before. A number of them work for international firms that have offices in major cities of the global economy—New York, Los Angeles, Chicago, London, Hong Kong. These cities serve as hubs for a "global intelligence corps" (GIC) of companies that are embedded in design projects around the world.[1] Detroit Works included star GIC players:

- Skidmore, Owings & Merrill (SOM), founded in Chicago in 1936, is one of the largest architectural firms in the world
- AECOM, headquartered in Los Angeles, is an international engineering firm on the Fortune 500 list; it has origins in a Kentucky firm—Ashland Oil and Refining—founded in the 1920s
- Happold Consulting is a division of the professional services firm BuroHappold; founded in 1976 in Bath, Somerset (UK) by Sir Edmund Happold, BuroHappold works on engineering projects worldwide.

The GIC have an enduring presence in important regions of the global economy. SOM, for example, is not new to Detroit; from GM building renovations in the 1990s to recent work on the city's east riverfront, SOM has had a hand in Detroit design. Most firms on the Detroit Works technical team had worked before in Detroit or in other HBURs. For example, Stoss Landscape Urbanism worked on Atlanta's downtown master plan, and AECOM has had projects in New Orleans, Atlanta, and Hartford. However, it is not typical for such a prestigious team to work together on the same HBUR city plan: "GIC's services do not come cheap, and the fact that they are being employed . . . indicates that governments or property developers have enough money to seek out urban planning and design services at the top end of the market."[2] The private foundations that paid for the DFC citywide plan—and the developers and foundations that combined their resources to redesign downtown—recognize the gap between perceptions of Detroit as a place of ruins and its lucrative potential. This gap between the current and potential value of land shape chances to profit from Detroit's geographic location, industrial infrastructure, and cultural and natural resources. In Detroit and other old industrial cities, the GIC are hired not only to help these cities adapt to climate change (a technical fix) but also to rebrand them as green cities (a cultural fix) so that they can compete for capital and gentrifiers.

Design experts are sometimes said to be part of a right-wing cabal. But neither the DFC plan nor Gilbert's downtown plan was the product of a right-wing think tank. Harvard—a stronghold for Ivy League liberals—is a shared link for most of the experts who worked on Detroit Works; the heads of their firms teach at Harvard, donate to its programs, or have ties to its centers. Toni Griffin, the head of the Detroit Works team, is a professor in Harvard's Graduate School of Design (GSD), where she directs the Just City Lab. Chris Reed (Stoss founder) is also a GSD professor. AECOM funds GSD projects. Toni Griffin, Philip Enquist (SOM), and Padraic Kelly (Happold) were members of the Working Group for Sustainable Cities, begun in 2009 at Harvard's Center for the Environment. Maurice Cox—a black architect who is on the DFC board and has been the head of Detroit city planning since 2015—was also a member. The working group hosted conversations with mayors. The founders of two nonprofits on the Detroit Works technical team have Harvard ties beyond GSD: Michael Porter, the founder of the Initiative for a Competitive Inner City (ICIC), is a Harvard business professor. Porter, reportedly the most cited business professor in the world, urges corporations and society to shift from adversarial stances to a realization that they have mutual interests in solving social and ecological problems. Dan Kildee, a Flint-based politician who founded the Center for Community Progress, has led training on repurposing vacant land as part of the Government Innovators Network at Harvard's John F. Kennedy School of Government. Three of the four consulting firms that worked on Gilbert's downtown plan also have Harvard ties.

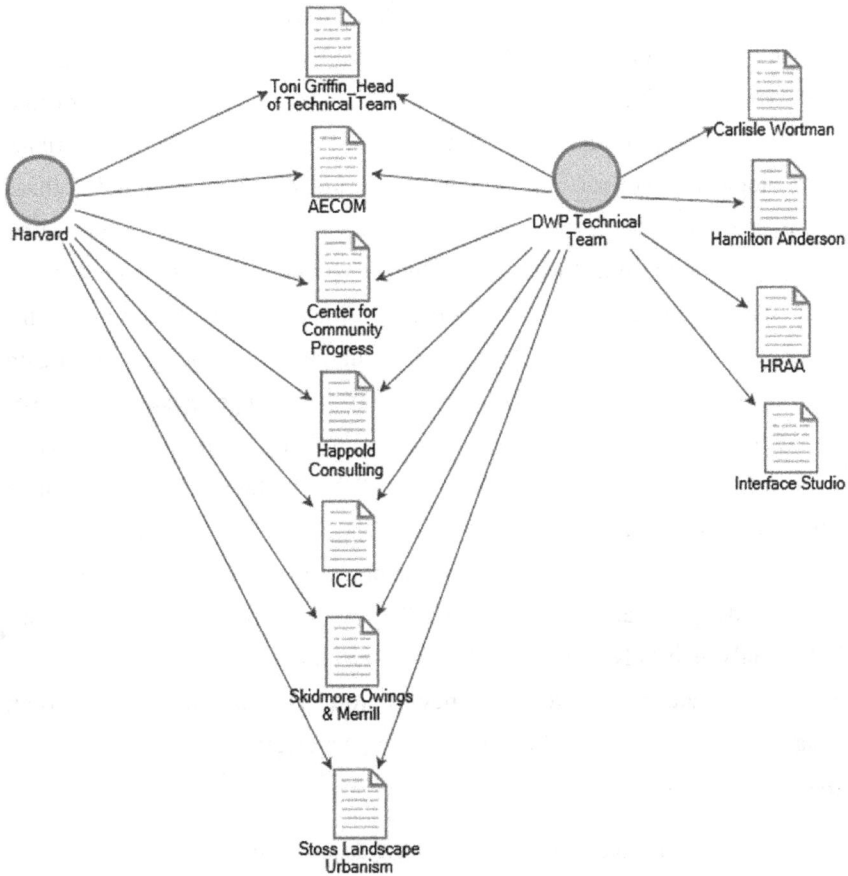

Graphic 3. Harvard Links of Detroit Works Technical Team.

Terry Shook and Kevin Kelley, the cofounders of Shook Kelley, have taught in GSD's executive education program. Robert Gibbs, the president of Gibbs Planning Group, has also taught in the program. PPS has helped Harvard to redesign its public spaces.

Founded in 1936, GSD held a historic conference in 1956 that framed urban design as a field that blends architecture, landscape architecture, and urban planning to advance the public good: "In the United States urban design emerged during the period when every person—including ethnic minorities, the poor, and women—finally gained, in theory, the legal right to occupy and pursue happiness in the shared spaces of the American city."[3] GSD bridges disciplinary silos in ways that, it argues, can be used to build cities that are

inclusive, efficient, and healthy. Mohsen Mostafavi, the GSD dean, popular-
ized the concept of "ecological urbanism." In 2009—before the start of Detroit Works—GSD published an edited volume on ecological urbanism that
combined ecological and social concerns. GSD also had a 2009 conference
on ecological urbanism. The conference included architect Rem Koolhaas
and postcolonial theorist Homi Bhabha in conversation about design. Chris
Reed, whose firm (Stoss) would join Detroit Works, was on the schedule. Yet
GSD also produces critiques of ecological urbanism. Neil Brenner—an internationally recognized GSD professor—charges that ecological urbanism
"normalize[s] contemporary forms of market-oriented governance and associated processes of territorial stigmatization."[4] At Harvard, both advocates and
critics of ecological urbanism talk of justice, but neither side engages much
with black radical thought, judging from their citations.

Yet the civil rights and black power struggles of the 1960s forced the field
of urban design to address its racism. Black activists did not simply criticize
individuals such as New York's Robert Moses—the activists called out professional organizations. In 1968, Whitney M. Young Jr.—the head of the Urban
League—delivered a blistering speech at the American Institute of Architects
(AIA) convention:

> You are not a profession that has distinguished itself by your social and
> civic contributions to the cause of civil rights. . . . You are most distin-
> guished by your thunderous silence and your complete irrelevance. . . .
> [Y]ou are key people in the planning of our cities today. You share the
> responsibility for the mess we are in [in] terms of the white noose around
> the central city. It didn't just happen. We didn't just suddenly get this sit-
> uation. It was carefully planned.[5]

During the 1960s and 1970s, black college students and community organizers disrupted business as usual in urban design, organizing protests (strikes,
sit-ins, boycotts) on campuses and in neighborhoods to demand change. Max
Bond, a black architect and activist, led the Architects' Renewal Committee in
Harlem (ARCH), which advocated on behalf of the grass roots:

> ARCH was often held up as a model for addressing the urban crisis. . . .
> Consulting with community groups . . . staff members raised their clients'

awareness about the deleterious effects of proposed projects, coauthored alternative proposals with them, and then advocated for these alternatives in city government.[6]

Bond had completed his undergraduate and graduate studies in architecture at Harvard. Half a century had passed since W. E. B. Du Bois—a nineteenth-century graduate of Harvard—had faced racial prejudice on its campus, yet Bond found that racism at Harvard had not died:

> Other students burned a cross before the dorm where he [Bond] and . . . other African American freshmen lived in 1952, an event that suggested the racial animosity that pervaded the Ivy League. An architecture professor instructed him to choose a different profession—architecture was not for African Americans, he said.[7]

After leaving Harvard, Bond—facing racial discrimination in the United States—moved to Ghana, where he designed public buildings. The young Bond came from a family of upwardly mobile strivers who fought racism; his cousin was Julian Bond, a civil rights activist who would one day teach at Harvard, among other universities. The opportunity to lead ARCH pulled Max Bond back to the United States. Harlem was a ferment of protests, projects, and blueprints to reshape black urban life. In 1964—while Bond was in Ghana—poet June Jordan (still in her twenties and not yet as famous as she would become) collaborated with the architect Buckminster Fuller on an unlikely plan that reimagined Harlem as conical towers, elevated paths, and green space. In contrast, Max Bond called for rehabilitating the existing architecture of Harlem and preserving its street life. A desire to fight the displacement and degradation of low-income black residents inspired these very different visions for a future Harlem. Bond's down-to-earth vision seemed within reach, yet it is as far from being realized in today's gentrified Harlem as Jordan and Fuller's conical towers.

Pressured by black activists, the GIC and prestigious design schools have increased their hiring of African Americans, but the percentages remain low. Some of these black designers—including Toni Griffin—work to support new generations of black architects and to institutionalize conversations about justice in urban design. Griffin's leadership of Harvard's Just City Lab builds on her past work as the founding director of the J. Max Bond Center on Design for the Just City at the City College of New York. The center was named in honor of the architect after he died in 2009. However, the relationship between black architects and activists has frayed since the 1960s. In Harlem and other cities, the grassroots institutions that were created to ensure community control of planning have become partners with growth elites in market-driven redevelopment. Black architects and activists critique urban design—and clash with each other—in justice-speak. Democratic design is elusive: justice-speak is applauded, but money talks too.

At the 2017 Black in Design conference, organized by the African American Student Union at the Harvard design school, Toni Griffin states: "I was one of two African Americans associate partners at SOM twenty years ago, worldwide. I'm often still the only black girl in the room." Griffin began her career as an architect for SOM, working in Chicago and London. Later, she served as the director of community development in Newark, the deputy director for revitalization in Washington, DC, and vice president for planning and tourism development for the Upper Manhattan Empowerment Zone Development Corporation. Across these places, Griffin has forged ties with leaders in the field of urban design: At the 2012 Openlands luncheon in Chicago—an annual event that brings together conservation groups—Griffin says that "she's had the opportunity now to hire SOM and Phil [Enquist, head of SOM's Urban Design and Planning division]" and that the SOM table includes men who've "hired me and trained me and sat next to me telling jokes while we designed projects at three in the morning in London and drank scotch in Detroit." In 2018, Griffin received the Richard Theodore Greener Academia Award (named after the first black Harvard graduate) from the Harvard Black Graduation Committee. That same year, she won the Chouteau Greenway competition in Saint Louis. Together with a team at Stoss Landscape Urbanism, she proposes to design the greenway in ways that break down racial segregation. A year earlier, a graphic design blogger interviewed Griffin and her colleague—Stoss founder Chris Reed—about how design should respond to social and environmental injustices. Griffin acknowledges the role of design in producing inequalities:

> In my work as an urban planner, the injustices I constantly confront center
> on concentrated poverty, conditions of disinvestment and abandonment,
> and socioeconomic division. . . . The cautionary tale is to acknowledge

that many conditions of injustice have actually been created at the hand of design and policy practices, like federal highway policies and urban renewal that once obliterated black inner-city communities. . . . We designed an elaborate engagement process that was inclusive across all sectors of the Detroit community, identifying what their actual aspirations were going forward.[8]

The Detroit Works engagement process did become inclusive, but it is unclear how resident aspirations informed the rightsizing plan.

In a collection of *Just City* essays—funded by the Ford Foundation—that Griffin edited and made available for free download in 2015, Griffin talks about her childhood and career experiences:

I was born in Chicago the evening before President Lyndon Johnson signed the Civil Rights Act of 1964 into law. Growing up on the south side of Chicago meant that on an average day, I rarely saw or interacted with a person who didn't look like me. . . . My teachers were predominately black, and my classmates were 98 percent black. This environment did not make me feel isolated, segregated or unusual—I just felt normal. . . . While I did not regularly see people who looked like me on TV, this didn't stop me from deciding at the age of 14 that I wanted to be an architect—just like Mike Brady, patriarch of "The Brady Bunch." By the time I entered college at the University of Notre Dame—and the field of architecture—my context became the exact opposite. For the first time in my life, I actually felt like a minority.

Griffin describes her childhood as shaping the values that guide her work. Specifically, she identifies ten principles that should guide urban design:

- Equity
- Choice
- Access
- Connectivity
- Ownership
- Diversity
- Participation
- Inclusion and Belonging

- Beauty
- Creative innovation

These principles are far-reaching: design should craft spaces of beauty for all and enable everyone to participate "in matters affecting social and spatial well-being." Yet (like the DFC plan), this statement of principles does not address power relations. Griffin's justice-speak invokes the Moral We yet remains at the level of an individual striving to follow a self-imposed code:

> I believe I have tried to create places and spaces that promote greater urban justice. Over my career, I have worked on the redevelopment of the Anacostia Waterfront in Washington, where our aim was to direct the city's growth in a manner that would include existing Washingtonians; I have changed land use and zoning regulations to support higher quality infill housing design standards; and I have created . . . [an] integrated citywide framework for new neighborhood typologies and reconfigured infrastructure systems to support shifting demographics of Detroit. I believe my intention was to create a more just city. . . . I feel the pressing need to become more articulate about the specific impacts of my design work on facilitating my vision for the just city. . . . I offer these ten values as my initial metrics for designing for the just city.

Just City includes essays by urban planners and activists (including a Black Lives Matter activist) who condemn social and environmental injustices and call for democratic design in cities across the Americas, Africa, and Asia. However, the essays provide little analysis of the structures that operate in the mind and in places to reproduce unjust planning. *Just City* includes an article by Ben Hecht, the head of a national organization that brings together financial and philanthropic institutions (Kresge is a member) to work on urban projects. In the article, Hecht praises the roles of Dan Gilbert and the Kresge Foundation in Detroit redevelopment. Griffin's essay briefly describes her work in Detroit, but the collection lacks the voices of Detroit activists and any mention of the conflict over DFC. There is a gap between justice-speak and speaking truth to power in the collection. It would be wrong to blame individual planners for injustices that they did not create and cannot solve alone, but this gap must be bridged. It needs to be said that the dependence of urban design on private interests makes it hard for technical experts—no matter how well intentioned—to be accountable to the public, and it is hard for residents to hold them accountable. Griffin's career demonstrates that individuals can make a difference, but the social movements that made her career possible show that only collective struggle can achieve structural transformation. The civil rights and black power movements expanded what black individuals could do by changing laws and institutions. These struggles enabled African Americans to become mayors and architects but did not ensure that black elites would have the resources to protect black lives as they designed the future city. And they did not ensure that black elites would have to answer to low-income black communities.

To understand possibilities for expanding the spatial agency of low-income African Americans, we must go to the grass roots. On a spring day in 2012, I parked near Cass Corridor Commons, a Victorian mansion that housed social and environmental justice groups. I'd come to interview Charity Hicks, the policy director at the East Michigan Environmental Action Council (EMEAC). I ran into Hicks often at public meetings. I saw her in the crowd chanting "Remember Black Bottom!" at the Hantz hearing, and I saw her on MATF telling Detroit Works "Let people have democracy . . . [or] it's going to blow up when it hits the streets." Ever since that meeting, I'd wanted to interview Hicks. She described herself as rooted in Detroit yet branching out to other places. Her work included travel in and beyond the United States, making connections with her counterparts across North America, South America, and Africa who fought for social and environmental justice. For centuries, the African diaspora has woven supportive networks across countries. Hicks followed in the tradition of the abolition movement and the pan-African movement. She said that she was part of a "Generation X" of leaders who, inspired by the history of black Detroit, struggled for a healthier, more powerful relation to community, land, and food.

Hicks, dressed in blue African garments, gave me a tour of the Victorian mansion that housed EMEAC. Built by a well-to-do family in the nineteenth century, the mansion was sold to a church in 1913, during the days when Cass Corridor was Piety Hill. Viola Liuzzo—the white civil rights activist slain in Alabama—attended church here. In 2011, the First Unitarian Universalist Church gave the building to EMEAC, and EMEAC organized a commons with other nonprofits. Hicks showed me the dark, ornate room where wealthy white men once smoked cigars—it was now a meeting room for community workers of all races. The sunny kitchen where servants prepared feasts was used for cooking classes that taught about health and nature. Hicks pointed out the craftsmanship of the ceiling cornices, and she laid her hand on an antique table. She said that whenever she walked through the rooms, she appreciated the workers who built this place and its furnishings, yet she also thought of the indigenous people who loved this place before the mansion was built. Hicks told me that it was important to be conscious of our connections to people and the earth across time. Upstairs, we sat down for our conversation. Her life history informed her work:

> I actually live in Detroit, born, bred and raised, graduated from a Detroit public high school, but at the same time I have some levels of privilege, of degrees. . . . I have to code-switch. So on one side of me, there's this professional: academic, research, technical. But then there's the B side . . . to be multifaceted, you have to have proficiency in all those roles . . . that is part of the profound level of coping because in Detroit, you do have to have some profound coping skills [*laughs*]. I grew up on the east side . . . with five brothers and one sister so there were seven of us. One bathroom. One of the earliest things I learned was consideration of the other. I learned this dancing between my own personal needs and the needs of other people. . . . I became profoundly conscious of the pain of the black community. . . . I tried to heal myself and my community by embodying respect.

The need for respect came up repeatedly in the interview. I asked Hicks about the Detroit Works Project. Hicks was not necessarily opposed to rightsizing, but she argued that Detroit Works had disrespected residents: it had paid more attention to the physical infrastructure than the human infrastructure, and it had not let residents make decisions. The clash between cultural workers (such as Hicks) and Detroit Works was a fight over who should decide the city's future and who and what should be valued in the planning process:

> Detroit Works is top down. . . . You're going to redesign a 140 square mile city, you're gonna create dense little neighborhoods of walkability, but

you abandoned the people. There has to be a co-investment strategy that includes the cultural work that is necessary for the chief asset—the people. The aim is for a more efficient municipal operation, but you haven't retooled the people. How do we invest in those structures, in those operations, that promote investment in people. How do we embody respect for people, not calling them dredges or prostitutes or the illiterate. . . . [We need structures] that will get underneath crime, that will get underneath a carjacking, that will make people feel worthwhile. We have to restore a sense that we are agents of change. . . . Nowhere in 2010 did Bing convene block groups and say, "Look folks, we broke. We can't function. We need permission to develop a plan. . . . Can we enter into some dialogue. . . . Do we have your permission to move forward . . . ?" I'm pretty sure the community would have said, "Yes". . . . There are brilliant, hard-working, thorough, respectable people in Detroit . . . What we got is, "I'm Daddy." What we didn't get, is "how do we co-create the good?"

Hicks's reference to "dense little neighborhoods of walkability" throws shade at green strategies that did not address racial capitalism. She advocated community empowerment and green democracy. She suggested that, to revive Detroit, all Detroiters—including those scorned as "dredges"—must see themselves as change agents who can build the good community. She defined the good community as "levels of relationship based on accountability." Later, reviewing her transcript, I categorized the types of accountability that she mentioned: the ability to (1) share stories about self, other people, and the earth (accounts), (2) ethically and rationally calculate the costs/benefits of action (accounting), and (3) create structures in self and society that keep us "in balance" (accountant):

> The first level is self-to-self . . . the community of the "I". . . . What are our ideals. . . . How do we live our lives so that we're accountable to our own values, upbringing, and personal good? Next, there's a level of accountability of selves to other selves . . . the community of the We. Where's the golden rule?

Hicks's framing of the "I" highlighted self-love. "I" does not simply reason with Self—"I" embraces me. In this embrace, "We" is present in the mind, cherishing and cherished. Hicks stated, "One of the beautiful things we can do as humans is reflect. We can look at stars, we can look at a tree, and that helps to create empathy and sympathy." (I thought about Michael at the river. Without self-love—nurtured by "We"—reflection can be brutal.) Hicks said that love moves the "I" to think about the effects of its actions on here-and-now and distant-and-future, including nature. "I always add into the good community . . . our relationship to the earth, do we honor creation? Or do we waste and destroy and don't really see that we're in relationship with this beauty?" Hicks suggested that the realization of our connections is a necessary precondition for freedom.

In black radical traditions, freedom is variously defined. An important strand equates freedom with group power—most notably, black voting power, which is said to enable control of the land and infrastructure that one needs to live. Another strand of black radical thought frames freedom as the ability to establish a mutuality that enables life and expands the possibilities of what one can do and become:

Nobody's free until everybody's free.

—Fannie Lou Hamer[9]

For to be free is not merely to cast off one's chains, but to live in a way that respects and enhances the freedom of others.

—Nelson Mandela[10]

Mogobe Ramose, a South African philosopher, describes this mutuality as *ubuntu*, a principle that, he argues, is the "fundamental ontological and epistemological category in the African thought of the Bantu-speaking people."[11] For some community organizers in Africa and its diaspora—including Hicks—this mutuality extends to nature. The power of the human and nonhuman world are interdependent; black liberation and environmental protection intertwine. This worldview extends Martin Luther King Jr.'s declaration in his letter from a Birmingham jail to the entire earth: "We are caught in an inescapable network of mutuality, tied in a single garment of destiny. Whatever affects one directly, affects all indirectly."[12]

To realize mutuality, Hicks strove to create spaces in the self and society where dialogue and discourse could occur:

Dialogue is the mythic space. We show our hearts and tell stories—fish stories, stories about the prom and raising children. . . . It conveys a lesson about our morals, our intentions, about how we came to be at this point. . . . It sets the table for us to say "I heard you." . . . Discourse informs the analytical side of us. . . . You get a really great debate, and you think, "Oh! I never thought about it that way."

Applying Hicks's categorization, the narratives of fall and redemption that I collected in Detroit are "dialogue." She told me that dialogue and discourse inspire and inform our protection of the "tangible commons" (roads, schools, rivers) and the "intangible commons" (culture). I-We also needs private space because "if we don't get to inhabit our minds with any sense of this belongs to me only, we turn into caricatures. . . . There is no private contemplation on action. . . . We lose the intimacy of the self, the sanctity of thoughts." The loss of the commons and the private sinks some people into depression. Hicks described being on a research team that interviewed mothers for a health study in a neighborhood with much poverty, crime, and disease. As she asked questions, the women began to weep. They were not used to telling their stories of loss, abuse, and struggle. The research team postponed the study until after they brought in counselors. Hicks said that disconnection sinks some people into depression, while others become "open to criminalization . . . our human spirit requires a certain quality of life that allows us to be who we are. . . . It is our relationships with self and others that will [end] crime."

Hicks stated that destructive behavior was not just a problem of the poor. She said that some people take jobs that harm other people or nature, and some nonprofits bend their mission to get funds from corporations and foundations. These nonprofits claim to involve locals in decision-making, but they do not. She argued that capitalism and racism push people to "dissociate from that basic level of consciousness that informs us about whether our actions are helping or hurting us. . . . You turn into a sociopath." She said that we lose consciousness of "The Good." I asked her what is "The Good." She said, "Normally, in America, we put it to religion. We say, Jesus Christ, he good. If you ain't with Jesus Christ, then you're with the devil. But to me, The Good is Enough." The "I" must recognize when it has enough (food, water, etc.) and leave enough for human and nonhuman others. Rebuilding Detroit should begin with valuing the self and others: "Transformation is . . . the . . . emotional tone before the change . . . the prepping of the space in the mind. . . . It is the creation before creation." Later, I sat in on a meeting that Hicks facilitated, where she demonstrated these practices. The session combined "dialogue" (people sharing stories, singing a song, drawing pictures of their hopes and fears) with "discourse" (policy analysis). Hicks had a talent for explaining and using these organizing strategies, but she did not claim to have invented them. They have developed over centuries in cultures of resistance, which reflect on and deploy them with increasing sophistication as they learn from past struggles.

After I moved from Detroit in 2013, I noted these organizing strategies as I followed news of the struggle to maintain low-income access to water in Detroit. In March 2014, the Detroit Water and Sewerage Department (DWSD) announced that it would shut off water to thousands of residential customers who owed more than $150 or were more than sixty days late. Supporters of DWSD stated that the crackdown was necessary to maintain and upgrade the costly, aging DWSD infrastructure; they argued that people who did not pay their bills make the rates higher for everyone else. They suggested that nonpayers were deadbeats and that there were programs to assist the truly needy. Critics of DWSD argued that these programs lacked adequate funds. Hicks became involved in the water struggle as a founding member of the People's Water Board (PWB), a coalition that advocates for water access and conservation. PWB argues that DWSD should implement a water affordability plan that sets rates based on income. Some critics of DWSD allege that the shutoffs further DFC rightsizing by increasing the hardships that push impoverished people to move from high-vacancy areas. DFC pays lip service to equity, stating that core services such as water should remain in high-vacancy areas until all residents leave. However, it does not offer a plan for maintaining affordable access. To do so would require a strategy for equitably distributing the burden of paying for aging city systems over time. One might argue that this concern was not the mandate of DFC, but devising a frame to maintain access for all to basic services is necessary if the future city is to be a just city.

In community meetings, news interviews, and cross-place networking, PWB combined storytelling about individuals and families suffering from the water shutoffs with a structural analysis of the water crisis ("dialogue and discourse"). In May 2014, Hicks was jailed for confronting the contractor who was cutting off water in her eastside neighborhood. After her release, she helped to coordinate a talk at Wayne State University by Maude Barlow, a Canadian environmentalist who works internationally for water rights. In late May, Hicks went to New York to give a talk at the Left Forum. While she was waiting at a bus stop to go to her talk, she was struck by a hit-and-run driver on May 31 and lapsed into a coma. Detroit activists responded to this tragedy with monetary and emotional support for Hicks and her family, and they intensified their efforts to fight the water shutoffs. In June, the water struggle in Detroit got international news coverage after representatives of the United Nations visited Detroit in response to a petition by local water activists. The UN representatives issued a press release that stated: "Disconnection of water services because of failure to pay due to lack of means constitutes a violation of the human right to water and other international human rights."[13] Amid the water struggle, news reached Detroit that Hicks had died in a New York hospital on July 8, 2014. News of her death spread with accounts about the water crisis. Condolences to Detroiters and vows of support for their struggle came from cultural workers in other cities. They drew parallels to austerity measures and to land and water grabs where they lived. On the day of Hicks's funeral, a hip-hop event at a Midtown park called on youth to become leaders in the struggle, ending its show with a video about Hicks's life and work.[14] The water struggle was joined by progressive groups who had come to Detroit: National Nurses United, the largest union of registered nurses in the United States, and Netroots Nation, a political convention for left-leaning activists who use digital media to influence public debates. The head of the nurses' union declared that the shutoffs had caused a public health emergency, and Netroots Nation attendees blogged and tweeted news of the crisis. Both groups rallied with local water activists. Symbolic deliveries of water to Detroit garnered additional press. The first delivery was a Canadian convoy led by Maude Barlow. The second delivery was driven from West Virginia by Keeper of the Mountains, a group that supplied water to Appalachians after a chemical spill polluted their water.

As international protests against the water shutoffs grew, the federal judge handling Detroit's bankruptcy demanded that DWSD fix the situation because it had "caused a lot of bad publicity for the city it doesn't need right now." On July 21, DWSD announced that it would suspend shutoffs; on July 28, the emergency manager turned over control of the water department to the mayor's office. Mayor Duggan extended the moratorium to "improve" procedures, but the shutoffs resumed at the end of August, after public attention had moved on to other news. The water struggle shows that alliance building—deploying storytelling with analysis—matters. Yet this organizing remains crisis driven. Growth elites dominate the redesign of HBURs because they command the funds to rebuild them. Bolstering government resources might reduce this hold, but racist neoliberal ideologies (manipulating narratives of fall and redemption) are barriers to doing so. A few months before her death, I exchanged emails with Charity Hicks. She wrote:

> Someone told me, how do we bite the hand that is feeding us? This is the deep-seated contradiction of all of us in Detroit and across the nation. The revolution will not be funded. I have been told to shut-up and speak lightly on the Detroit funders because they have significant power nowadays. It is very difficult to have a clear critique of those funders who are attempting the largest urban renewal/social engineering project in current U.S. history when we are all their grantees. I have decided to be on the side of the people and grassroots communities in Detroit.

Much has changed since Whitney Young and other black activists of the 1960s "spoke truth to power." The numbers of black architects and planners have increased, and local groups have become nonprofit partners in development. Yet inclusion in the power constellations that shape urban form has made it hard for individuals to speak out about injustices, even as justice-speak has spread in urban design. If technical experts and cultural workers had a more cohesive front against austerity measures, it would be harder for growth elites to produce neoliberal space. In 2019, Harvard's Kennedy School of Government offered a senior research fellowship to former Michigan governor Rick Snyder, but Snyder was forced to withdraw after opposition from activists because of his role in the Flint water crisis.[15] To prevent future urban crises, it is critical to complete the work of the social movements of the 1960s; cultures of resistance must once again address the *field* of urban design—its firms, its academic institutions, its professional organizations, its partners—and hold the field accountable.

Justice-Speak in City Plans

DFC USES JUSTICE-SPEAK to legitimate smart decline (rightsizing and greening). The scale of DFC's proposed rightsizing is unique, but it is common for the plans of depopulated US cities to include smart decline strategies.[1] The justice-speak in the DFC plan refers only vaguely to the causes of environmental injustices; perhaps planners saw these causes as too controversial to mention. Is the use of justice-speak in *Detroit Future City* similar to the language of other HBUR city plans (especially the language of other severely depopulated HBURs)? Does the language of HBUR city plans differ from the language of non-HBUR city plans? What compels planners to clearly articulate injustices as they write city plans? By "city plans," I mean "comprehensive" or "master" plans (general guides for city development) and "sustainability" or "climate action" plans (frames for aligning cities with their ecosystems). Designs such as *Detroit Future City* should also be considered city plans, if these products of public-private alliances serve those functions. Some city plans drive development, while others sit on the shelf. Regardless of whether they are followed, city plans are part of urban politics; they represent how planners want a city's future to be seen. If a plan does not at least call for reducing social and ecological harms, it indicates that addressing those harms is not deemed politically necessary. Yet justice-speak may be framed in ways that obscure environmental risks and shield political and economic elites from accountability. Comparing the language of city plans provides clues about urban politics that can inform crossplace organizing.

Compared to non-Hispanic whites, African Americans are more likely to express concern about environmental justice, so one might expect that black political power forces the inclusion of environmental and equity goals in city plans. However, studying the fifty-five largest US cities, Portney found no relation between the size of their black populations and the "seriousness" of sustainability policies.[2] Analyzing sustainability initiatives in a survey of US cities with at least 2,500 residents, Opp and Saunders found that cities with higher percentages of African Americans also had higher scores on an index of the "three Es" (environment, economy, and equity goals), but the correlations were not statistically significant.[3] Studying large US cities, Schrock, Bassett, and Green found no relation between the size of the nonwhite population and the inclusion of equity concerns in sustainability plans.[4]

Researchers who study this topic tend to evaluate the goals—not the language—of the plans, giving higher scores to plans that mention larger numbers of goals that are deemed relevant. For example, some researchers count mention of community gardens and fair housing as indicators of social equity. This approach has the virtue of easy quantification, but its operationalization of equity is problematic. These studies do not evaluate whether the equity goals in a plan combine in an effective approach. Also, these studies conflate equity with other principles, obscuring whether a service is framed, for example, as a right or as charity. Thus, these studies have limited value in understanding the politics of sustainability. Perhaps the manner in which goals are framed—not the goals themselves—are crafted to match the views of influential interest groups. Studying a sample of thirty comprehensive plans, Berke and Conroy found that mention of sustainability as a guiding principle did not predict goals.[5] Some case studies suggest that, in conservative cities, planners must frame sustainability in terms of conservative values. Perhaps the converse is also true: in liberal cities, planners must cloak market-driven goals in progressive jargon. Community gardens could be framed as advancing food justice or reducing welfare dependence. Fair housing could be declared a human right or tersely described as a federal mandate. Greenhouse gas reduction could be mentioned with or without a definition of climate change as a global problem caused by human activity—some conservatives admit climate change but deny the extent of the problem and its human causation.

In HBURs, planners contend with opposing trends: the growth of black voting strength and the rise of neoliberal restructuring. In recent years, HBURs have had downtown gentrification, but none have reverted to being majority white cities. The HBURs continue to have grassroots organizing in black neighborhoods, and some HBURs serve as the headquarters for nationally recognized environmental justice organizations such as the Deep South Center for Environmental Justice in New Orleans and Urban Habitat in Oakland. On the one hand, we might assume that HBURs—in particular, those that are severely depopulated—would avoid mention of justice and equity because they fear chasing away corporate investment. On the other hand, we might expect that HBURs—especially if severely depopulated—would signal concern for justice and equity, given that most voters are African Americans. I refer to this signal as justice-speak. Do HBURs include justice-speak in their city plans to a greater degree than do the whitest and most conservative US cities of comparable size? How does severe depopulation influence justice-speak? Are there differences between HBURs and non-HBURs in how social and environmental problems are framed?

To compare whether and how HBURs and non-HBURs articulate just sustainability, I analyze plans for thirty-two cities (for more information about my sample and methods, including a list of cities, see the appendix). My sample includes the recent city plans (combined master plans + sustainability plans, if any) of fifteen HBURs and seventeen non-HBURS that have white majorities or are politically conservative. I developed the Justice-Speak index as an indicator of the degree to which a city plan uses the just sustainability discourse. Agyeman and his colleagues combine climate change and social/environmental justice concerns in their definition of just sustainability.[6] Following their lead, I include climate change and justice-equity measures in the Justice-Speak index.[7] The climate change score gauges the extent to which climate change and its scientific definition are articulated. The justice-equity score indicates the specificity with which plans invoke civil or human rights and identify local violations of those rights. The highest Justice-Speak score—a five—is assigned to cities with scores of "2" for both climate change and justice-equity that bridge these measures by referring to the climate gap—the social disparities in climate change impacts. My comparison cannot be generalized to all US cities, yet it does shed light on whether HBURs—political projects launched by the black masses five decades ago—have produced a distinct planning discourse. If HBURs do engage in more justice-speak, then we should see evidence of it when we compare them with each other and with their polar opposites. My findings should not be used to rank cities as better or worse in advancing social equity. The Justice-Speak index is an indicator of a discursive maneuver, not a measure of the goodness of a plan.

I found that HBURs with population losses over 35 percent tend to have the highest justice-equity scores. HBURs with population losses under

TABLE 5. Justice-Speak index

Score	Description
* CC-0	No mention of climate change, greenhouse gas, or global warming
CC-1	Mentions climate change or its synonyms but does not define climate change
CC-2	States that climate change is a global problem caused by human activity
** JE-0	No mention of justice or equity
JE-1	Mentions justice or equity as a goal but not that local institutions have been unjust
JE-2	States the past or current injustices of local institutions
CC/JE-1	Mentions "climate gap"—disproportionate impacts by race, class, and/or nation

* climate change

** justice-equity

35 percent have similar justice-equity scores to the whitest and most conservative US cities. The severely depopulated non-HBURs have the most zero scores for climate change. Cities with similar scores on the Justice-Speak index do not always legitimate their goals in the same way. A mix of rationales—an ethics of justice, an ethics of care, an ideal of the beautiful, a logic of pragmatism— are used to support goals. The philosopher Carol Gilligan describes justice and care as distinct moral "voices."[8] The voice of justice is heard in declarations of human and animal rights. The voice of care urges concern for the vulnerable and strives to bring humans and the earth into harmony. A third voice, an ideal of the beautiful, inspires the protection and transformation of landscapes. A fourth voice, the logic of pragmatism, argues for maximizing material well-being. Appeals to care, beauty, and pragmatism have political value because they seem apolitical.

Justice-Equity

All severely depopulated HBURs—and one of the nonseverely depopulated HBURs (Washington, DC)—mention historical and/or ongoing race-class

TABLE 6. Sample of US cities with selected attributes by Justice-Speak scores

	* CC 0	CC 1	CC 2		** JE 0	JE 1	JE 2
HBUR (n = 15)	2	5	8		1	6	8
Depopulated (n = 7)	1	2	4		0	0	7
Not Depopulated (n = 8)	1	3	4		1	6	1
Non-HBUR (n = 17)	6	5	6		1	14	2
Whitest (n = 5)	0	2	3		0	4	1
Most Conservative (n = 7) (Includes 2 cities in which whites are not the majority)	2	3	2		0	7	0
White Depopulated (n = 5)	4	0	1		1	3	1

* climate change

** justice-equity

injustices to explain their challenges. They differ in the clarity of their statements. The Birmingham plan is quite detailed in its charges: it outlines the enforcement of racial segregation by Jim Crow laws and deadly bombings, the intentional concentration of industrial pollution and substandard housing in working-class areas, and the adoption of racial zoning that placed African American homes in floodplains. Birmingham states that this history and recent predatory lending have shaped a residential landscape with inequitable distributions of hazards.

Only two non-HBURs frame local race-class injustices: Pittsburgh, Pennsylvania, and Springfield, Missouri. Pittsburgh briefly discusses the impact of metropolitan sprawl on "social equity . . . as job opportunities are distanced from where people live." Springfield devotes much more space to justice-speak. It is known today as a college town that serves as the headquarters of two conservative Christian groups: Assemblies of God and the Baptist Bible Fellowship. However, in 1906 Springfield was infamous for the lynching of three black men and the mass expulsion of black residents. As African Americans fled, they lost their homes and businesses. Springfield is not unique—in the early twentieth century, many US towns terrorized and drove out their black residents.[9] Springfield has had few black residents since this racial cleansing. Citing the persistent racism in the state, the NAACP issued a travel advisory in 2017, which warned African Americans that their civil rights could be violated in Missouri.[10] The Springfield plan, which came out a few years before the NAACP advisory, neither discusses the violent racial past of the city nor details ongoing civil rights violations, but it does admit that the city has been hostile to "diversity":

> Let's face it—our community has what one community member called a "welcoming deficit." There are members of our community that resist the trend of increasing diversity in the Springfield region.

Unlike the plans of the severely depopulated HBURs, the Springfield plan emphasizes individual prejudice more than structural racism, and it attributes some challenges of low-income families to a "culture of poverty"—a term that none of the HBURs use. Nevertheless, the Springfield Plan recommends steps to reduce inequities, and it advises the city government to continue holding "Facing Racism" workshops; no other city in my sample makes such recommendations. Springfield frames diversity as a concern that cuts across all its planning goals, and it emphasizes the need to "act regionally" and to be a "citizen of the region" by addressing the challenges of racially diverse "economically distressed communities" beyond its city borders.

Half of the cities (five of the ten) that score "2" for justice-equity use communitarian language, combining justice-speak with the voices of care, beauty, and pragmatism. I have already detailed the Moral We language of Detroit's plan. Birmingham describes good neighborhoods as places where "people get to know and trust [one] another" so that they can join together to care for one another and the city's "beautiful landscape" of native plants and life-sustaining waterways. Springfield states that it wants to foster a "welcoming" community in which residents collaborate to improve the quality of life for all; it notes that younger generations want to live in diverse cities and that the city may suffer a "brain drain" if it does not become more welcoming. Newark describes tree planting and care as a means not only to protect the environment but also to strengthen social ties. Baltimore—with stronger language than any other city in my sample—frames human and nonhuman life as interconnected; it speaks of cultivating a community where all residents and all species ("no matter how small") are valued and protected as part of the "web of life," sprinkling its plan with quotes from cultural workers around the world who speak of love for nature and humanity. These five cities encourage a sense of community. The other five cities with scores of "2" use terms such as "collaboration" and "engagement" to signify pragmatic means to further equity and to implement their plans, but a sense of community is not celebrated as an end in itself.

Cities with population loss under 35 percent tend to have scores of "1" for justice-equity. They refer to justice or equity as a goal but do not mention that any local injustice has occurred.

Examples:

HBUR: "Atlanta is growing at a tremendous pace. Sustainability serves as the foundation for smart growth in transportation, and preserves and protects our natural resources for business innovation and social equity." (quote from city councilman placed in large type to frame transportation initiatives)

Non-HBUR: "The [Mesa, Arizona] General Plan . . . addresses . . . development and conservation strategies intended to preserve and protect the natural environment while simultaneously considering livability, a strong economy and social equity."

Cities with a justice-equity score of "1" attribute disparities to personal risk factors, individual behaviors, and unforeseen policy consequences, or they do not cite a cause. For example, Atlanta describes its air pollution as disproportionately harming residents with existing health conditions. It explains this problem as a result of its residents being "car-oriented." To help reduce air pollution, Atlanta states that it will educate residents about alternative transportation options. Local officials are characterized as champions of sustainability, now and in the past: "The city's leaders will continue to make progress introducing legislation that encourages smart growth while discouraging sprawl, and redeveloping communities in a sustainable manner." In contrast, local environmental justice activists frame today's environmental problems within decades of racism and classism that have driven sprawl, blocked regional cooperation on transit, and fostered uneven development in the Atlanta metropolitan area. Atlanta's plan is silent about this history. HBURs that score "1" tend to place little or no emphasis on an ethics of care. Atlanta's sustainability plan emphasizes a pragmatic concern with devising strategies that will enhance the prosperity and health of residents and bolster the city's position in the global economic order. Throughout the Atlanta plan, positive business, social, and environmental outcomes are often linked in the same sentence:

> Example #1: There will be many tangible benefits [from investing in sustainability], including a cleaner, healthier city for the next generation, and a city that attracts more attention and investment from global business.

> Example #2: Embedding sustainability into business practices is a proven way to ensure economic vitality and resiliency while also protecting natural resources.

This representation of the world assumes little or no conflict between the demands of the global economy, the needs of local residents, and the requirements of nonhuman nature.

Among *non*-HBURs that score "1," some city plans simply note that fair housing is a federal or state mandate. Disparities, if mentioned, are framed in passive sentences that suggest a causal relation between being in a particular social category and having social problems. For example, the Anaheim comprehensive plan states:

> Certain segments of the population have more difficulty in finding decent, affordable housing due to their special circumstances. . . . Female-headed households are a special needs group due to comparatively low rates of homeownership, lower incomes, and high poverty rates.

Attributing the social problem (difficulty finding affordable housing) to a "special needs" category (female-headed households), the plan does not address how the policies of officials, developers, and employers influence living wage jobs and affordable housing in Anaheim.

The non-HBURs with scores of "1" that express the most concern about disparities frame their concern in an ethic of care. For example, they go beyond the letter of the law to describe fair housing as a means to achieve communitarian aims:

Relatively speaking, housing in Fargo is affordable . . . [but] certain segments of the population do face significant affordability issues. Data show that extremely low income households face the most extreme cost burdens and overall life challenges. . . . *Ensuring access to affordable housing increases equity in Fargo. It ensures everyone has the opportunity to live and work.* It lowers the burden on social services by promoting self sufficiency, boosts the economy by attracting a steady workforce, and contributes to Fargo's future by ensuring families have access to education and services that will help them prosper.

"Equity" does double duty here, referring not only to fairness but also to social investment. Fargo's plan voices care and pragmatism, describing Fargo as a "welcoming city" with an interest in cultivating neighborhoods that have a "sense of community" and "collective efficacy" where residents "watch out for each other." The Fargo plan suggests that, by securing equity and cohesion, Fargo can reduce welfare spending and advance self-sufficiency—goals championed among liberals and conservatives. Fargo has a history of political conservativism, yet its rapidly growing population has swung back and forth in its support for Republican and Democratic presidential candidates in recent elections.

Only two cities have a "0" for justice-equity: Chicago (an HBUR) and Niagara Falls (a non-HBUR). Chicago refers to expanding opportunities for "all," but it does not mention social equity in this expansion (opportunities could expand for all yet inequities could persist). It outlines goals such as the weatherization of low-income homes that other researchers have coded as equity concerns—and it notes that some populations are more vulnerable to climate change impacts—but it does not explicitly frame these environmental realities and policy responses in terms of justice or equity: home weatherization, for instance, is framed in pragmatic terms as making good economic sense. Niagara Falls, a severely depopulated majority white city, seeks to "reposition" itself as "culturally diverse" and "vibrant," but it does not refer to equity.

Climate Change

The HBURs and non-HBURs have similar scores for climate change. With the exception of depopulated non-HBURs, the cities in my sample tend to at least mention climate change. Cities with scores of "1" refer briefly to climate change, often in a paragraph that discusses other topics, or they describe it as real but suggest that its human causation is open to debate:

Examples:

HBUR: "The ecological issues facing the Great Lakes Basin include: land runoff, coastal development & loss of habitat, invasive species, toxic chemicals, climate change, fishing pressure, and water withdrawals."

Non-HBUR: "[To enhance livability . . .] [d]evelop safe, reliable and economical transportation choices to decrease household transportation costs, reduce our nation's dependence on foreign oil, improve air quality, reduce greenhouse gas emissions and promote public health."
 "It is well established by the scientific community that global warming is a real and growing problem. . . . (but) there are varied opinions on the extent of human activity as a cause of this phenomenon."

The climate change statements of HBURs and non-HBURs that score a "2" are more than a paragraph in length, emphasizing scientific agreement about the reality of climate change.

Examples:

HBUR: "A scientific near-consensus has emerged regarding the dangers of increasing concentrations of greenhouse gas (GHG) emissions in the Earth's atmosphere, and the significant role that human activity is playing in increasing those concentrations. . . . The City of Oakland is dedicated to doing its part to reduce GHG emissions and the threat of climate change."

Non-HBUR: "The science is clear—climate change is already occurring and is no longer a distant threat. And the cost of inaction is unacceptable. Globally, the rise in temperatures has profound implications for natural resources, economic prosperity, health and human development. Fort Collins has long committed to reduce community greenhouse gas (GHG) emissions and to increasingly monitor local vulnerability to higher temperatures and actively explore ways to adapt and become more resilient. "

Four of the eight HBURs that score "2" speak about a climate gap, only one of the six non-HBURs that score "2" does so. Among the HBURs, there are differences in the categories of people who are identified as vulnerable, and there are differences in proposals for dealing with climate change. In the introduction of Newark's plan, Mayor Cory Booker expresses concern about the climate gap:

> Climate change is contributing to more severe storms, hotter summers, and other challenges for cities that need affordable energy, clean air, fresh food, and open spaces. These trials disproportionately impact our most vulnerable residents. To be meaningful, sustainability efforts must confront poverty and public health, while strengthening the link between economic development and opportunity for residents, especially our youth.

Throughout the Newark plan, steps are advocated to reduce the impact of climate change and local hazards on "vulnerable receptors," which are identified not only as "schools, daycares, senior centers, [and] public housing" but also as "prisons" and "detention centers"—sites with stigmatized people whose well-being might be ignored in disasters. Similar to Newark, Oakland mentions that climate change will disproportionately harm "vulnerable" groups, but it does not mention the incarcerated. Indeed, it does not explicitly discuss how race or poverty influence risk (even though its identification of areas that are especially vulnerable to climate change include places with high rates of poverty). In this respect, the language of Oakland's plan is not as progressive as Newark's plan. Yet Oakland, to a greater degree than any other city in my sample, merges talk of policy shifts with advocacy of radical lifestyle changes. Many city plans promote public transportation and curbside recycling. In keeping with the Bay Area's counterculture reputation, Oakland's plan goes far beyond these tips, advising residents to consider the possibility that they could become vegetarians, give up their cars, live in cohousing, and consume less to save energy and avoid waste.

It is useful to compare Oakland with Anaheim—its sister city in Orange County, a region that has long been politically conservative. Although they differ in politics, Anaheim and Oakland are comparable in size with large nonwhite populations, and both cities must meet the environmental regulations of California's state government, which is a leader in the fight against climate change. For many years a Republican stronghold, Anaheim has historically championed conservative values: in 1980, Lou Sheldon founded the Traditional Values Coalition in Anaheim; in 2009, Sheldon was one of the endorsers of a widely publicized open letter that denied climate change. Nevertheless, Anaheim (like its sister city, Oakland) scores a "2" in the climate change domain— one of only two politically conservative cities in my sample to do so. Anaheim states that climate change is a global problem caused by human activity, but it does not refer to a climate gap. Rather than urging its residents to consume less, it suggests that they consume differently: shop locally (with an eco-friendly canvas bag), buy a hybrid car, and purchase furniture made from sustainable materials such as bamboo. Perhaps Anaheim's rapidly growing nonwhite population makes a difference (the city is becoming more liberal), but one should note that conservative Arlington, Texas, also has a large nonwhite population; its city plan scores a "0" in the climate change domain. California's greenhouse gas regulations compel city planners in the state to address the topic, but there is not the same degree of statewide pressure on cities to address environmental justice. The city plans of Oakland and Anaheim speak to the middle class, framing consumption practices as lifestyle options. Neither plan frames how race and class shape options, nor do the plans detail the role of public policy in helping the racialized and the impoverished adapt to climate change in their everyday lives. Poverty might force low-income people of color in segregated areas to eat less meat, give up their cars, split the rent with others, and shop locally, but the outcomes of doing so might not be the same as they would be for affluent people in walkable neighborhoods with healthy food shops, the option of telecommuting, and adequate infrastructure (for example, good public transportation or employer-provided shuttles).

Political Power and City Plans

Most cities in my sample see it in their political interest to acknowledge that human activity has caused climate change and to detail concrete steps to address it. There is much less articulation of social injustices. Even when justice is stated as an aim, the definition of justice and the proposed steps to achieve it are often stated vaguely or made to mean less controversial things such as being a good neighbor. Compared to the non-HBURs in my sample, HBURs tend to have higher justice-equity scores. Half of the HBURs that score a "2" for climate change also mention a climate gap, while almost all non-HBURs that score a "2" do not. Among HBURs, cities with population losses over 35 percent generally have higher scores than do the cities with less population loss. Indeed, the framing of equity in HBURs that do not have severe population loss is similar to the language of the whitest and the most politically conservative US cities. Perhaps officials in these HBURs worry that if they confront financial and commercial interests, they will suffer the fate of HBURs that have had massive flights of capital. Even HBURs that use justice-speak are often vague about current injustices.

Federal and state laws make a difference: the civil rights movement's successful fight to pass fair housing laws forces all US cities to at least pay lip service to them, and the environmental movement in California has produced laws that require all of its cities to address climate change. If cross-place organizing pushed federal and state governments to mandate additional local safeguards for racialized and impoverished groups, we would see more justice-speak—articulated with greater clarity—in city plans, even in places with local resistance.

VI

Naming the Baby

The Black Empire Strikes Back

AS I CONCLUDE, six years have passed since I moved from Detroit in 2013. And it has been six years since Dave Bing left office and Mike Duggan was elected the first white mayor since the 1970s. Duggan's election ended the semblance of a black urban regime, but black control of the city was already over. Dan Gilbert and a few other wealthy white businessmen steered Detroit. But then on May 26, 2019, Gilbert suffered a stroke and was hospitalized. The governance of Detroit is unstable, dependent on the health and fortunes of a handful of oligarchs and a fragile downtown recovery. Race further complicates governance. On June 2, 2019, reporter Charlie LeDuff posted a podcast with former mayor Dave Bing. Bing—now 75—speaks frankly. Compared to his State of the City speech in 2010, there is less poetry and more fire.[1]

> **Charlie LeDuff:** Question number one, who runs Detroit, who really controls the levers of power?
>
> **Dave Bing:** I think the business community. I would suggest that you've got the Ford family, you've got the Ilitch family, you now got the Gilbert family. You got Penske, and now Gores is coming in [Tom Gores, founder of a private equity firm, owns the Detroit Pistons. He moved them back to downtown Detroit in 2017]. So you've got five guys who are all billionaires . . . [who] truly run the city. . . . I think that you look traditionally at this city, a lot of the black leadership came from the faith based community and the unions. And I don't see that's the case at all today. The faith based community . . . in a lot of cases has been bought and sold. . . . [they get a check so they] don't say anything.
>
> **Charlie LeDuff:** Okay, so here's the comeback narrative. Um, we've got . . . downtown skyscrapers going up. . . . We got jobs, but is that enough to balance out what we're giving these billionaires [in government incentives]?
>
> **Dave Bing:** No, it's not enough.

Charlie LeDuff: That is damn straight. Okay. You're here. You're here to talk business. Okay. Tell the people.

Dave Bing: Absolutely. . . . At one point in time, you know, we were a manufacturing city and those jobs because of the unions offered people at least enough money to take care of their families. What's available today is not enough for people to live on.

Charlie LeDuff: When the government sticks its beak in the means of production . . . when it's giving money to, let's say Chrysler. . . . Is it socialism or crony capitalism?

Dave Bing: Crony capitalism.

Charlie LeDuff: Damn! Could you, do you feel you couldn't say that when you were running the city?

Dave Bing: I was pretty outspoken.

Charlie LeDuff: You kind of were.

Bing had been *kind of* outspoken. In 2010, he had told the truth that the plan was to rightsize the city—a truth that others sugarcoated with talk of "repurposing." And he had been fearless in denouncing government corruption. But he did not mention in his State of the City that crony capitalism ruled Detroit or that the diminished power of unions had reduced wages or that some black religious leaders had been co-opted. Activists had made these charges long before Bing took office. Why has Bing begun to talk about race and use justice-speak? Now that Detroit's black urban regime has fallen, he sounds a bit like Coleman Young. Bing hints that there are black Detroiters who plan to run against Duggan in the next election.

Had Bing been "naming the baby" in his 2010 speech? My mother heard the Bruh Rabbit story, *Naming the Baby*, in her Alabama childhood, and she told it to me and my brothers. In the tale, Bruh Fox has a deadly plan to trick Bruh Rabbit, but Bruh Rabbit outwits him:

> Bruh Fox promised to give Bruh Rabbit a feast of good cornbread, sweet butter, and cold buttermilk if he weeded his field, but Bruh Rabbit knew that Bruh Fox would skin him and eat him with that cornbread, butter,

and buttermilk as soon as he was done. What could he do? Bruh Rabbit threw down his hoe and began to dance, waving his paws in the air: "I hear my sister calling me! She says, 'Come, name the baby!' Please let me go name the baby, and I'll run back here quick!"

"Naming the baby" is a ruse by Bruh Rabbit to sneak off and eat Bruh Fox's lunch and then escape. The story ends in triumph—its lesson is that there are times in which you must seem to be who you need to be until you can appear as you are. But, as a child, I wondered what happened next: Bruh Rabbit remained in danger. Caroline French—the heroic Detroiter whose deception rescued another black woman from bondage—knew how to "name the baby." However, the toll on previous generations of having to say one thing and think and do another—living constantly at risk—was great. And the dance to survive breeds mistrust. One becomes unsure who is kin—who is the rabbit and who is the fox. Bankole Thompson—the former editor of the *Michigan Chronicle*, a local black newspaper—argues that Bing has come out too late with his critique:

> I had a number of sit-down interviews with Bing when he was leading the city, and . . . I didn't recall any clear-cut anti-poverty policies executed by his administration. . . . [H]is message is a didactic lesson for current black leaders who have chosen to stay silent and safe. It is a reminder for those who have decided not to raise any constructive critique of the missing gaps in the recovery because of foundation grants and pet projects to choose between personal gain and public good. . . . there is [a] dearth of bold leadership . . . to alleviate the sufferings of Detroiters left out of the recovery.[2]

The "Black Empire" is striking back; segments of the black bourgeoisie, minoritized in gentrifying cities, are fighting their subordination by rallying the black vote. This strategy was evident in the 2019 mayoral campaign of Keisha Lance Bottoms in Atlanta, in which her efforts to turn out the black vote resulted in a narrow win against her white opponent. However, the use of justice-speak by old guard black elites does not mean that they reject the neoliberal order. Bing voices support for low-income African Americans, and he volunteers his time to help youth. However, he also continues to praise the austerity measures of emergency manager Kevin Orr. And he still frames black entrepreneurship as the solution to the city's ills, despite the fact that some black business leaders are in fields such as real estate speculation that do not "lift all boats" and at times are predatory. The justice-speak of Bing and others in the old guard may further evolve as they try to get low-income African Americans who have lost faith in black urban regimes to go to the polls.

Listen to the Rain

AS THE TIME drew near for me to leave Detroit, I walked to the river to read one morning. A short distance from my bench, two African American fishermen chatted and sipped coffee. A half hour or so passed. I heard a new voice and looked up: a middle-aged Latino bicyclist was talking with them. Dressed in a cycling jersey, he leaned on his handlebars and asked about their catch and bait. Noticing my gaze, he wheeled over with a grin and introduced himself. As we chatted, he mentioned that he was Puerto Rican. He asked about the book I was reading. I handed it to him. "It's about people in the nineteenth century who tried to create better communities," I told him. He read the cover, "*The Utopian Alternative.* . . . They were socialists?" I nodded, "Kind of socialist." The bicyclist's smile faded a bit. He described himself as a "constitutional conservative." I told him that I was studying the views of Detroiters about the best way to rebuild the city, and I asked his thoughts. He said that Detroit should follow the doctrines of the "founding fathers" who gave US society a "moral compass" and a prosperity engine by merging faith and the market. As I listened, I thought about his Taíno ancestors who saw the ships of Columbus appear in the waters of Borikén, their land claimed for a distant power. And I thought about my African ancestors who came to the Americas in chains (in accord with the moral compass of the Spanish priest, Bartolomé de Las Casas), to do the genocidal labor that the Taínos fled. The historian Vincent Harding, speaking in 2011 at Wayne State University, said that every generation since the "founding fathers"—inspired by new "ideas, concepts, and stories"—has struggled to reinvent democracy. The black urban regime came out of this struggle for freedom. The (economic, political, moral) system of the founders has been open to change, but change has often instituted new forms of violence.

In this book, I have analyzed the (mental | material) structures that shape this struggle as capital and the middle class return to HBURs. My approach makes three breaks with (or rather, *builds bridges to go beyond*) dominant frames for studying the return: First, I bring terms coined by white urban scholars ("neoliberal," "segregation measure," "gentrification," "Anthropocene") into conversation with the much less cited concepts of black scholars ("racial capitalism," "black urban regime," "minoritization," "Man"). I do not suggest that the latter terms should replace the former. Rather, I note that the latter terms are needed to help explain the design of US cities and to frame struggles for black spatial agency within those designs. Second, I study African Americans across income and political spectrums, listening to "folk" accounts as seriously as I read scholarly texts. I do not assume that one is more insightful than the other. Both folk and scholarly accounts are influenced by storytelling traditions—this fact does not detract from their usefulness, but we should be cautious about assuming that either type of account mirrors reality. Third, I recognize that HBURs are complex places; the people who live in and pass through these cities are divided not only by race but also by social class and worldview. These differences are spatially expressed. HBURs require careful observation of the daily rounds and seasonal celebrations that compose the folkways and demographics of their streets in ever-shifting constellations. Long before the residential gentrification of downtown Detroit, redevelopment campaigns drew affluent workers and tourists. Too often, studies of HBURs merely "give voice" to black joys and suffering. This research, emerging from a shallow knowledge of the histories, politics, and cultures of black communities, fails to shed much light on the strategies and outcomes of race-class struggles for spatial agency.

This threefold approach leads me to somewhat different conclusions than other scholars about the politics of the return:

(1) When capital abandons a city, how do people interpret their world?

Views of urban ruin are filtered through folk narratives. The Fall—a moral tale, older than the industrial city—recalls the past of the beloved community as an ideal. Blacks and whites in the United States tell versions of the Fall that support racial solidarities. In its valuing of the past, the Fall is inherently conservative. Neoliberal elites mine and manipulate this narrative, but they cannot completely control it. Reactionary and radical movements invoke the narrative of the Fall. As capital reinvests in central cities, versions of the Fall that warn of monsters do not always serve business and real estate interests. The tale of the Fall is common, but it is not told by everyone: there is also, for example, the chilling story of The One.

(2) How and why is green redevelopment on the agendas of growth elites, technical experts, and cultural workers in HBURs?

Nature, an agent in urban politics, has pushed cities to put greening on redevelopment agendas by threatening disasters. The ecology exerts force, but perceptions of and responses to nature are not a direct reaction to its qualities:

- Growth elites' green agenda is influenced by federal and state regulations. Beyond this requirement, they find use in the Garden—it helps them to rebrand cities and increase land values. The Garden is not the only cult of nature that is deployed in the Return: growth elites also reharness ancient seasonal rituals. Growth elites command the resources but lack the skills for greening cities, so they harness technical experts and cultural workers.
- Technical experts—driven by their conflicting allegiances to their professional ethics and their funding sources—address ecological degradations in ways that make possible (but do not determine) uneven development. Inequitable outcomes are made more likely as democratic deliberation is stifled.
- Cultural workers' vision of the Garden is ancient; fear of climate change heightens the appeal of this vision. Cultural workers frame the Garden as a moral order that is not controlled by money, but they rely on growth elites for funding. Black cultural workers who advocate the Garden must contend with ambivalence in black neighborhoods. African Americans often cherish the values and the pleasures of the Garden, yet our history of exploited, stigmatized agricultural labor makes some of us wary of green projects.

(3) How do growth elites, technical experts, and cultural workers mobilize (symbolic, social, material) resources for shaping perceptions and agendas in HBURs?

They mobilize resources by joining together in power constellations. Growth elites do not so much disempower technical and cultural workers as *mine their intelligence* (in the words of Trudell)—growth elites need their power to operate. This power constellation, which has internal contradictions, generates conflicts as it interacts with residents of different races and classes. These contradictions and conflicts are spatially expressed: the artist enclaves in greater downtown clash with the central business district. Nevertheless, the central business district, operating as a magnet, pulls all that is profitable in the artist enclaves into its domain (geographically and financially). This pull is exemplified by the popular natural food shop in the Corridor that became a tenant in one of Gilbert's buildings in the financial core. All of greater downtown is a beachhead for citywide minoritization. Across the city, race-class fractions adopt placemaking, and they deploy the forum, the tour, the mission, and the parade/march to shape how the public (including residents, tourists, journalists, and scholars) see the city in order to advance their agendas. Detroit Works' forum used cultural workers to engage residents, but it did not let residents decide the plan. As HBURs rebuild, planners use justice-speak. Their justice-speak is often framed as love, and love is reduced to accord. They avoid discord by not mentioning structural racism and classism. The claims in their public outreach get little fact-checking: local news media, suffering cuts in staff and resources, often just report what they say.

(4) How can the frames and agendas of green redevelopment be made to support the spatial agency and the freedom of low-income African Americans?

The first step is to get woke. In the words of Sylvia Wynter, we must fight for our "full cognitive and behavioral autonomy . . . from Man." As John Trudell taught, "This is about taking the power of our intelligence and using it clearly and coherently, rather than chaotically and distortedly. Because every time we do that, we're cooperating with them. No matter how good our intentions." Getting woke requires stirring the self, yet it cannot be done simply through lifestyle changes. Throughout this book, I have used the colloquialism, "speak truth to power." However, the problem is not so much that technical and cultural workers do not speak truth to power, but rather that they give away their power when they speak.

The second step is to surveil the power constellations that shape urban form and to organize on multiple spatial scales to force their accountability to communities. The water struggle in Detroit and the protests against Snyder's Harvard fellowship suggests that strategic, coordinated pressure on vulnerable interests in the global network that shapes urban form can stir public support, fracture elite alliances, unsettle social order, and win (at least temporary) concessions. It remains to be seen whether the struggle can move beyond concessions to an expansion of freedom. To do so, we would have to remove the harness that binds technical and cultural work to growth elites.

There are signs of resistance; the recalled past, memorialized on streets, ignites rebellion. In July 2013, a few weeks after I moved from Detroit, Dan Gilbert's Rock Ventures hired Complex Movements—an artist and organizing collective that incorporates Detroit hip-hop and techno—to host an event at Capitol Park. Rock Ventures booked the collective to enliven the park for gentrifiers, but the collective designed the event to celebrate Capitol Park's transgressive legacy. Dan Gilbert's placemaking plan promoted the "architecturally significant" buildings and "gracious" past of the Capitol Park area, yet the area also can be read as a social tinderbox.[1] The first governor, Stevens Mason—who tried to get Canada to return black people fleeing slavery and who advocated the removal of Michigan's indigenous population—is buried in a vault on the plaza. A few steps from his tomb, a plaque in the park commemorates a barn that once stood nearby, used by Seymour Finney, a white hotel owner, to hide fugitives on the Underground Railroad. The July 2013 event revived this subversive spirit. A member of the artists' collective described the event to me, and I saw some of it online. Complex Movements invited elders who were being evicted from the Section 8 building across the street from Capitol Park. Gilbert did not own the building, but the market-rate conversion of the building fit with his plan for transforming the Capitol Park area into a gentrified art enclave. The Capitol Park event began and ended with ritual saging and Anishinaabe drumming, the event bringing together black, white, Arab, Latinx, and Ojibwe Detroiters who are deejays, dancers, poets, performers, and visual artists. The artists spoke and performed about Capitol Park's past, including its indigenous history, the Underground Railroad, and the more recent history of the area as an incubator of Detroit techno and house music. The artists shared the microphone with Section 8 residents who spoke out about the evictions. They told me that Gilbert's representative watched them in shock and anger. When I heard about their handling of Gilbert's hiring of them, I smiled and thought to myself: "That's 'naming the baby'!" The Capitol Park event shows that cultural workers can outwit growth elites and show up in solidarities that go beyond race. But it jeopardized the musicians' ability to pay their bills. They said that Gilbert's representative threatened not to pay them. They were paid, but they recognized that this kind of subversion is something "you can only do once, before they catch on to you." Ultimately, the event did not stop the evictions of the elders. Perhaps if the organizing of Capitol Park residents had begun earlier—through events in the park that affirmed their solidarity, built bridges to other areas of the city, and mobilized them to struggle for housing policies that would secure their future—it would have been harder to dislodge them. But it is difficult to sustain solidarity; racial capitalism—in its most recent incarnation, the neoliberal order—undermines ethical codes and allegiances. Like everyone else, cultural workers need to put food on the table, and they need resources (money, technology, land) for their projects. To meet these needs, they compete for jobs, loans, and grants against Detroiters who differ in race, class, education, family wealth, and length of residency in the city. As they compete, the system of rewards perpetuates inequalities, which leads to mistrust and resentment. Perhaps the most contentious divide is differences in the ability to buy land and buildings. Some cultural workers who advocate the Garden have become landowners and real estate speculators in Detroit and other cities. Like the utopian socialists of the past, cultural workers charge each other with hypocrisy and beat their chests in contrition. To prevent the movement ossifying into *performances of movement* that have the sound but not the substance of radical action, there is a need to pour rage and contrition into an organized struggle to change housing policies and to transform land ownership and use.

The Detroit Future City plan—echoing cultural workers—speaks of love. Is there a place for love in this struggle? I think of Michael's warning that the Moral We is a deception. I also think back on my conversation with the bicyclist at the river: he cited Hayek and Friedman as influences on his thought. "What about Ayn Rand?" I asked. He shook his head. "Godless capitalism is as bad as godless communism," he said. The bicyclist told me that, without God, capitalism has no moral compass. He stated that the US founding fathers created a system that merged faith and the market. If one follows God's law, one can succeed in this system, and there can be good communities. We chatted for an hour or so. I was struck by the similarities between his philosophy and that of the green anarchists with whom I had chatted in the Corridor—not in the specifics, but in their belief that the city's material circumstances would improve if it had a spiritual rebirth. The bicyclist suggested that I read Francis Schaeffer, a conservative theologian who influenced the rise of the Christian Right. Schaeffer's long hair, eccentric attire, and years of living in a quasi-commune would have helped him to fit into the street culture of the enclave that was once Piety Hill. Perhaps one day cultural workers on the right and the left will join forces in a Moral We. This outcome would not necessarily be virtuous. Time shuffles clothing and skin color and ideas into startling new constellations, but the racial capitalism of the founders survives. What type of governance—and what types of selves—will emerge as cultural workers on the left and right interact with each other, with growth elites, and with non-human agents (technology, nature) in the evolving racial capitalism? As I sit by the river and listen to the bicyclist, I find myself enjoying his melodious voice going on and on under a beautiful blue sky as the fishermen sip coffee and seagulls land on the rail. But I have no faith in a love for humanity that seeks refuge in a civil "middle ground." True love fights for right relations between self and other. It is a pleasure, for the moment, to sit and listen by the river: it speaks to the connection of all life on earth. But I will get up from here and write field notes about my chat with the bicyclist that will be used in a book that attacks his position. Maybe the bicyclist has his own book in the works. We are on opposite sides of the struggle of our time. Where it will end is an open question. In place of civility, we must strive to speak and hear the truth. Those of us who consider ourselves on the right side of history must not become so mesmerized with our own rhetoric that we lose sight of how the struggle impacts the possibilities for life on earth as it unfolds. I recall the poet Avotcja with her rain stick, *"Listen listen listen Boricua, listen to the rain."*

Appendix: Methods

Case Study

AT THE TURN of the twentieth century, W. E. B. Du Bois criticized scholars who framed the "Negro problem" in terms of pathology. This frame persists. Whether ethnographers blame uncaring whites or the black underclass for this pathology, their storytelling is predictable: they submit low-income black neighborhoods to the gaze of middle-class readers for diagnosis and treatment. Yet most people in these neighborhoods—even the supposed monsters— would prefer these places to be spaces of peace and well-being. Why can't they decide urban futures?

Case studies of the teenager who sells drugs or the mother who gets welfare provide insights into their worlds, but by themselves these studies shed little light on the processes that placed their subjects in danger—processes that began before they were born. And these case studies obscure the class structure of African Americans within central cities—from the homeless person to the store clerk to the professional to the millionaire. To be clear, I am not demanding laudatory accounts of "decent" black people. On the contrary, I argue that there is a need for interrogation of the decent and the normal, for nonobvious lines of research that ask whether decent people shape dangerous futures. The social and environmental crises that we face today in the United States go much deeper than the problem of the teen drug dealer. Compared to street crime, city planning is seemingly more open to view, given state and local "sunshine laws" and the federal Freedom of Information Act (FOIA). However, if one were to assume that city planning is more easily observed than drug deals on the corner, one would be wrong. Privatized governance cloaks city planning. Yet there are moments when privatized governance surfaces to gather information and win support. These moments enable a view of the decent folks of all races who shape urban futures. My case study captures one such moment. My aim is not so much to spotlight urban problems for expert treatment as to uncover how and why racialized and impoverished people are thwarted when they try to solve their own problems.

I moved to Detroit in 2010 to study whether and how various race-class groups would have decision-making power in the Detroit Works Project. Public meetings were about to begin. My study was not "hypothesis testing": my questions evolved in response to what I saw. In 2010, I thought that I was observing a process that would end in a formal master plan; I was wrong. I had no way of knowing that the Bing administration and the Kresge Foundation would have a falling out that would split the project into short-term and long-term teams, and I could not imagine that a billionaire developer (who moved his headquarters downtown the same year that I arrived) would develop a downtown plan that would transform the central business district and merge with citywide planning. A strength of ethnographic research is that it can shift its focus and tactics as the observed engage in moves and countermoves.

For my case study, I used mixed qualitative methods that enabled a triangulation or (more aptly) a "crystallization" of findings. I talked with activists, residents, and Detroit Works staff; analyzed government, business, and foundation materials; and observed planning meetings, political rallies, city tours, land uses, and everyday life.[1] I prioritized harvesting the *naturally occurring speech* (chats, tweets, blogs, ephemera, public meetings, street performances) deployed to shape views and practices. I am more interested in observing how people actually use symbolic, social, and material resources in social struggles than with recording how they frame these struggles to me as a researcher. Even in formal interviews, I often let the conversations meander to find where people wanted to take me and how they used language as a vehicle. Increasingly, we ethnographers recognize the need to explain our methods for representing speech, especially our practices for dealing with stigmatized languages such as African American Vernacular English (AAVE).[2] I recorded and transcribed formal interviews, USSF speeches, public meetings led by city officials, and some street events (for example, the block party in the Corridor and the Allied Media tour of Manistique Garden). For casual conversations, I repeated phrases in my head until I could write them down in my field notes. I strive to convey cultural worlds (and differences of race and class within those worlds) by replicating the grammatical structure and figurative language

of speakers. However, neither my transcripts nor my field notes fully reproduce the sound of speakers—I do not attempt to indicate their pronunciations.
AAVE is a complex soundscape of cadence and rhythm that shifts across contexts to convey meaning, but ethnographers typically convey AAVE in their
field notes through simple notations—for example, dropping the final g's on
words. I find this practice problematic, especially when the representation is
based on memory. It is easier for me to recall the structure and content of a
sentence than the sound of syllables. Hybrid speech increases the difficulty of
recall. Middle-class African Americans (including myself) who learned AAVE
as children often retain its flavor—even when we use Standard English grammar, the style switching in sound and figuration is not complete. Beyond this
challenge, there are myriad ethnic, regional, and idiosyncratic differences in
speech that ethnographers often do not capture. For example, some English
speakers—black and white, working class and middle class—pronounce tr-
and dr- blends as chr- and jr- (trees become chrees and drive becomes jrive).
Why should I note that this person is dropping g's, when I do not note that
this other person is saying chrees? When and why do we hear and record lin-
guistic difference? Are our ears tuned to hear only those features of AAVE that
reproduce stock characters? Linguists use intricate notations to capture the
complexities of speech. For the most part, I did not need that level of detail to
answer my research questions. However, perhaps I should have represented
the soundscape of Detroit Works outreach in more detail. The accents changed
as spokespersons changed from black city officials to white consultants to cultural workers of diverse races and classes. A weakness of my study is that while
I paid close attention to shifts in the discursive frames and the visuals of public
outreach (the color of faces, types of tools), I did not analyze changes in the
"music" of voices. Perhaps the "music" influenced reception.

For my observations, I selected two areas of greater downtown into which
whites and Asians were moving (downtown and Midtown/Cass Corridor),
and I chose three areas outside greater downtown with residents of different
demographics (a high-income, majority black area in northwest Detroit; a
low-income, majority black area on the lower east side; and a low-income,
majority Latinx area in southwest Detroit). Sometimes my observations took
place outside Detroit. For example, I attended the 2010 Growing Power Farm

Conference in Milwaukee at which Detroit farmers interacted with urban farmers from other cities. I used qualitative and mapping software to help analyze cross-place relations. Traditionally, urban ethnography has been rooted in a place—a street, a store, a park. But to understand how that place functions, one must trace the circulation of people, goods, and ideas within and beyond it. Competing groups travel across neighborhoods and cities to advance their goals. I describe my approach as *cross-place ethnography*. It has parallels with the "global ethnography" approach, but I do not assume the scales of time and space that shape an event.[3] Before moving to Detroit, I had spent a few years conducting oral histories with three research assistants, driving from Michigan State University in East Lansing, where I taught. I also read about Detroit's social and natural histories. This historical immersion helped me to trace the effects of the neoliberal order and older (human | natural) systems. Across time and space, I attended to material, social, and symbolic relations. Links across blocks and links across oceans may be equally important, and the networks that are activated across days may reflect allegiances forged across centuries. To capture cross-place activity, I set up Google Alerts to track when planners and developers gave speeches or reports about Detroit within and beyond the city. I moved from Detroit in 2013, but I tracked developments until 2019.

For the ethnographer, writing style is not merely a method to engage the reader—it can advance or hinder the analysis. I faced a challenge: how do I make green redevelopment come alive for the reader in a way that serves my analytical frame? The style of most urban ethnographies, focused on a small cast of neighborhood characters, is a brew of literary realism, the sentimental novel, and noir fiction—techniques that suit exposition of small group dynamics in the here-and-now. This style can be powerful, but it does not work for my subject, which delves into how urban imaginaries—evolving over centuries—interact with the global order and the built-and-natural environment to shape urban futures. The magical realism of Africa and the Americas—the work of Butler, Borges, Allende, Ellison, Morrison, Okri, Thiongo—informs my technique. I do not mimic the *content* of magical realists; rather, I am a student of their *craft*: how they frame epic scales / how they do transitions / how they unearth imaginaries. I did not accept any story as real simply because it was compelling, yet I found it of interest that some stories dominated. The techniques of magical realism are useful for the exposition of "social facts" when combined with analysis of evidence.

What should be the relation of the ethnographer to the community that she studies? As an African American who has benefited from movements against racism and poverty, I felt obliged and moved to help certain Detroit groups. My most in-depth involvement was with a small group whose leader asked for help. For a year, I drove a couple of members without cars to Detroit Works meetings, found requested data, and framed their questions to Detroit Works staff. The group got their information; I got to observe their interactions with Detroit Works. However, I chose not to join any group. I distanced myself not to maintain "scholarly detachment" (a fiction) but because it does not make sense to align with a group before one knows its aims, ethics, and impact. I checked people out, and I'm sure that they checked me out too. If I had been a native Detroiter already familiar with folks, I might have used a more engaged style.

What should be the relation of the urban ethnographer to the academy? In Detroit, I crossed paths with an administrator from Michigan State University, where I was an assistant professor. We were both at a community event. He asked me who was the senior researcher in charge of my team. I told him that I was doing independent research. His smile faded and his eyes opened wide: "You've got to get with somebody!" It was a good tip. I would have liked to "get with somebody." Teamwork would have meant less work for me, it would have been good for my career, and it would have let me do useful work—MSU teams were studying the health and well-being outcomes of urban greening. However, I was not aware of any MSU team that focused on power relations, and I thought it was important to study power. Some community organizers told me that they had mixed feelings about the collaborations of university researchers, private foundations, and local developers. The academy is not a neutral observer of green redevelopment. I wanted to analyze and critique power constellations that included academics, so I chose independence over collaboration. Or rather, I chose to form my own team. At the start of my ethnography, I got help from three research assistants who had grown up in Detroit, knew its streets, and cared about its people. Eventually, however, limited funds drove me to work alone.

What should be the relation of the urban ethnographer to nature? In urban studies (including my own work), nature tends to be merely a backdrop. I have made steps toward integrating nature into my analysis, but I have not gone far enough. My father no longer hunted for food and chopped wood for warmth after he left the pine forests of East Texas, yet he was no less connected to nature in California. When I was around ten, he got a job for the water department in Antelope Valley—the high desert above Los Angeles. Sometimes I rode with him as he checked dials at far-flung wells and water pumping stations. He loved the desert, and he taught me to love it too: its blue skies and starry nights that stretch forever, its silences so deep that you can hear each breath, heartbeat, and footstep, its flowers that appear after spring rains. In the desert you see clearly that life exists because of the miracle of water. My father cared for the infrastructure that carried water across cities and towns. I strive for my work to reflect that caring and connection.

Qualitative Analysis of City Plans

Complementing my case study of Detroit, I compared "justice-speak"—talk of environmental and social justice—in the city plans of fifteen HBURs and seventeen non-HBURs. My analysis integrates auto-coding with substantive interpretation, using computer-assisted qualitative data analysis software (CAQDAS). The literature on critical discourse analysis informs my approach. CAQDAS can be useful in critical discourse analysis when the sample size is relatively large, but its tools for automatic codes and cross-tabs should not replace in-depth readings and contextualizations to discern meanings.

Sample Selection

My purposive sample consists of the city plans for fifteen HBURs and seventeen non-HBURS in the United States that have white majorities and/ or are politically conservative (for lists of cities and their demographics, see Tables 7, 8, 9, and 10 at the end of this appendix). I selected the top five whitest large cities from the US Census brief, the *White Population 2010*. I chose five severely depopulated, majority white cities from a list in a federal policy brief. To identify seven conservative cities, I chose the "most conservative" large cities (population over 250,000) from a much-cited study that ranked US cities based on the policy preferences of residents. I recognize that conservatism is subjective and thus rankings may vary; my aim was simply to identify cities that most people would agree tend to be politically conservative. Across the categories, I chose cities with populations over 50,000—large enough to be recognized as an urbanized area by the US Census and to have local agencies with the capacity for sustainability planning.

The HBUR median population is 390,724. Chicago and Philadelphia are outliers, with over one million residents. Seven of the fifteen HBURs had lost 35 percent or more of their population by 2010 since their peak. Compared to the other cities, these depopulated HBURs have the highest percentages of African Americans and the most poverty. The non-HBUR median population is 208,916. The cities include fifteen majority white/non-Hispanic cities: (1) the five US cities over 100,000 that have the largest percentage (> 70 percent) of white/non-Hispanic residents, (2) five US cities over 250,000 that are among the most politically conservative, and (3) five US cities that had lost 35 percent or more of their residents by 2010 since their peak.[4]

The non-HBURs also include two politically conservative cities—Anaheim and Arlington—in which no racial-ethnic group has a majority. These two cities have notable Asian and Latino populations. I included these two cities to help distinguish the influence of white majorities from political conservatism. Most HBURs and non-HBURs in my sample are comparable in size. However, on average, the severely depopulated HBURs are much larger than the severely depopulated non-HBURs in my sample, because white majority shrinking cities in the United States tend to be relatively small.

Data Collection

Between 2016 and 2017, I searched the local government website of each city to find (1) the city's most recent comprehensive plan since 2000, and (2) its most recent sustainability plan since 2000. City councils approved most of the plans. In two cases—Detroit and Springfield—public-private partnerships developed city plans, with the support of their city governments. Technically, these frameworks are neither comprehensive plans nor sustainability plans, but they serve some of their functions. Springfield's plan was approved by its city council; Detroit's plan was unveiled by its mayor but has not been formally approved (as of the date of this writing). I uploaded comprehensive plans and sustainability plans into CAQDAS. Some cities only had one of these plans. When both types of plans were available for a city, I classified the two plans as one case. Springfield had a recent master plan and a public-private plan, which I treated as one case. My website provides links to the plans (alesiamontgomery.com).

Data Analysis

The just sustainability paradigm combines the NEP and the EJP, merging a scientifically informed discourse with a social and environmental justice agenda. I developed the Justice-Speak index, which has climate change and justice-equity dimensions, as an indicator of the degree to which a city plan is framed within this paradigm. The climate change score gauges the extent to which climate change and its scientific definition are articulated. The justice-equity score indicates the specificity with which plans invoke civil or human rights and identify local violations of those rights (in the past or currently). It is not derived from a count of goals, and it is not based on a mere mention of "disparities," which could be framed as having causes other than structural injustices and thus do not assert rights.

I used auto-coding to help assign scores. For justice-equity, I searched for "justice" and "equity," their roots (-just-) (-equit-), and their synonyms ("fair," "equal," "rights"). For climate change, I searched for "climate change," "global warming," and "greenhouse gas." To eliminate unrelated usages, I checked context. After assigning scores, I carefully read each plan, discovering and coding rationales other than justice for addressing social and environmental problems. I also examined whether the plans linked social and environmental concerns (for example, mention of the climate gap).

My aim is to identify meaningful discursive differences among city plans; I make no claims about statistical significance. I use narrow category ranges (0–2) to increase the accuracy of my coding and to ease secondary analyses by other researchers. If the categories of my index were more complex, my interpretations would be more precise, but it would be harder to systematically identify differences across a sample that is relatively large for a qualitative study. I undertook two rounds of coding, separated by three months, to check and reflect on the accuracy of my categorizations. Other researchers may have different interpretations of the fine-grained analyses that I provide of specific quotations, but there should be close agreement on the sorting of city plans into the broad categories of the index. Appendixes to city plans (for instance, appended documents from state or federal agencies) are not included in my analysis. However, I do code mention of state or federal documents *in the body* of city plans (for example, one city states, "The Fair Housing Act not only prohibits discrimination, but in conjunction with other statutes, directs HUD and its program participants to take proactive steps to overcome historic patterns of segregation.").

For the climate change score, the plan receives a "1" if it mentions the term "climate change" or its synonyms; the plan gets a "2" if it goes beyond this mention to affirmatively articulate the scientific definition of climate change (i.e., climate change is a global problem caused by human activity). For the justice-equity score, if the plan mentions legal requirements or states ideals but does not identify local injustices, then the plan receives a "1" for justice-equity. If the plan goes beyond reference to the law or ideals by identifying local injustices, then the plan receives a "2." I assigned an extra point to plans that refer to a climate gap. Thus, the highest Justice-Speak score—a five—is assigned to cities with scores of "2" for both climate change and justice-equity that refer to the climate gap.

TABLE 7. HBUR demographics, population loss < 35%

	1950 Population	Peak Year Population	2010	% Change Since Peak	Black	White (non-Hispanic)	Asian	Native American	Hispanic (Any Race)	Median Household Income	% Persons in Poverty
Atlanta	331,314	496,973 (1970)	420,003	-15	54.0%	36.3%	3.1%	0.2%	5.2%	$46,631	25.0
Chicago	3,620,962	3,620,962 (1950)	2,695,598	-26	32.9%	31.7%	5.5%	0.5%	28.9%	$47,270	22.6
Hartford	177,397	177,397 (1950)	124,775	-30	38.7%	15.8%	2.8%	0.6%	43.4%	$29,430	33.6
Oakland	384,575	399,484 (2000)	390,724	-2	28.0%	25.9%	16.8%	0.8%	25.4%	$52,583	20.5
Philadelphia	2,071,605	2,071,605 (1950)	1,526,006	-26	43.4%	36.9%	6.3%	0.5%	12.3%	$37,192	26.5
Portsmouth	80,039	114,773 (1960)	95,535	-17	53.30%	40.3%	1.1%	0.4%	3.1%	$43,674	18.1
Richmond	230,310	249,621 (1970)	204,214	-18	50.6%	39.1%	2.3%	0.3%	6.3%	$40,496	25.6
Wash., DC	802,178	802,178 (1950)	601,723	-25	50.7%	34.8%	3.5%	0.3%	9.1%	$65,830	18.6
Average ($\bar{x}$)					44.0%	32.6%	5.2%	0.5%	16.7%	$45,388	23.8

TABLE 8. HBUR demographics, population loss > 35%

	1950 Population	Peak Year Population	2010	% Change Since Peak	Black	White (non-Hispanic)	Asian	Native American	Hispanic (Any Race)	Median Household Income	% Persons in Poverty
Baltimore	949,708	949,708 (1950)	620,961	-35	63.7%	28.0%	2.3%	0.4%	4.2%	$41,385	23.8
Birmingham	326,037	340,887 (1960)	212,237	-38	73.4%	21.1%	1.0%	0.2%	3.6%	$31,445	30.2
Cleveland	914,808	914,808 (1950)	396,697	-57	53.3%	33.4%	1.8%	0.3%	10.0%	$25,977	34.0
Detroit	1,849,568	1,849,568 (1950)	713,777	-61	82.7%	7.8%	1.1%	0.4%	6.8%	$26,325	39.3
Gary	133,911	178,320 (1960)	80,294	-55	84.8%	8.9%	0.2%	0.3%	5.1%	$26,885	38.1
New Orleans	570,445	627,525 (1960)	343,829	-45	60.2%	30.5%	2.9%	0.3%	5.2%	$37,146	27.3
Newark	438,776	442,337 (1930)	277,140	-37	52.4%	11.6%	1.6%	0.6%	33.8%	$33,960	29.1
Average (x̄)					67.2%	20.2%	1.6%	0.4%	9.8%	$31,875	31.7

TABLE 9. Non-HBUR demographics, population loss < 35%

	1950 Population	Peak Year Population	2010 Population	% Change Since Peak	Black	White (non-Hispanic)	Asian	Native American	Hispanic (Any Race)	Median Household Income	% Persons in Poverty
Conservative US Cities											
Anaheim, CA	14,556	336,265 (2010)	336,265	0	2.8%	27.5%	14.8%	0.8%	52.8%	$59,165	16.1
Arlington, TX	7,692	365,438 (2010)	365,438	0	18.8%	44.9%	6.8%	0.7%	27.4%	$52,933	16.6
Colorado Springs	45,472	416,427 (2010)	416,427	0	6.3%	70.7%	3.0%	1.0%	16.1%	$53,962	13.7
Jacksonville, FL	204, 517	821,784 (2010)	821,784	0	30.7%	55.1%	4.3%	0.4%	7.7%	$47,557	17.3
Mesa. AZ	16,790	439,041 (2010)	439,041	0	3.5%	64.3%	1.9%	2.4%	26.4%	$48,547	15.7
Oklahoma City	243,504	579,999 (2010)	579,999	0	15.1%	56.7%	4.0%	3.5%	17.2%	$45,824	18.2
Virginia Beach	5,390	437,994 (2010)	437,994	0	19.6%	64.5%	6.1%	0.4%	6.6%	$65,219	7.9

Whitest US Cities

Boise, ID	34,393	205,671 (2010)	205,671	0		1.5%	85.2%	3.2%	0.7%	7.1%	$48,524	15.6
Fargo, ND	38,256	105,549 (2010)	105,549	0		2.7%	89.0%	3.0%	1.4%	2.2%	$45,458	16.3
Fort Collins, CO	14,937	143,986 (2010)	143,986	0		1.2%	83.1%	2.9%	0.6%	10.1%	$53,780	18.6
Spokane, WA	161,721	208,916 (2010)	208,916	0		2.3%	84.0%	2.6%	2.0%	5.0%	$40,367	18.7
Springfield, MO	66,731	159,498 (2010)	159,498	0		4.1%	86.8%	1.9%	0.8%	3.7%	$32,333	25.6
Average ($\bar{x}$)						9.5%	67.7%	4.5%	1.2%	15.2%	$49,472	16.7

TABLE 10. Non-HBUR demographics, population loss > 35%

	1950 Population	Peak Year Population	2010 Population	% Change Since Peak	Black	White (non-Hispanic)	Asian	Native American	Hispanic (Any Race)	Median Household Income	% Persons in Poverty
Canton, OH	116,912	116,912 (1950)	73,007	-38	24.2%	67.9%	0.3%	0.5%	2.6%	$30,209	31.7
Niagara Falls, NY	90,872	102,394 (1960)	50,193	-51	21.6%	69.1%	1.2%	1.9%	3.0%	$31,452	21.8
Pittsburgh, PA	676,806	676,806 (1950)	305,704	-55	26.1%	64.8%	4.4%	0.2%	2.3%	$39,195	22.6
Scranton, PA	125,536	143,433 (1930)	76,089	-47	5.5%	80.1%	3.0%	0.2%	9.9%	$38,463	20.5
Utica, NY	101,531	101,740 (1930)	62,235	-39	15.3%	64.5%	7.4%	0.3%	10.5%	$30,942	29.6
Average (x̄)					18.5%	69.3%	3.3%	0.6%	5.7%	*$34,052*	25.2

Notes

Why Doesn't Black Political Power Save Black Lives?

1. Christine MacDonald and Jennifer Chambers, "Detroiters' Income Rises for Second Year but Poverty Rate Doesn't Improve," *Detroit News*, September 13, 2018, www.detroitnews.com/story/news/local/detroit-city/2018/09/13/ census-detroiters-income-rise/1268641002/.

2. Throughout this book, I use the construction (mental | material). By separating "mental" from "material" with a vertical bar then enclosing both terms in round vertical brackets, I signify a divide that is a function of the language and concerns of specific classes, cultures, and vocations—it has no fixed position. In the language of science, the divide usually disappears—neurologists frame thoughts as brain processes that have materiality. In contrast, cultural workers in Detroit often frame the (mental | material) as a dynamic system in which our thoughts are moral (or immoral) forces that shape our built-and-natural environment—we bring into being what we dream.

3. Charity Hicks, Transcript of Charity Hicks, interviewed by Kate Levy, in online archive, I Do Mind Dying, interview by Kate Levy, 2015, www .detroitmindsdying.org/full-length-interviews/.

4. Larry Gabriel, "The Future of Climate Change," *Detroit Metro Times*, accessed July 27, 2018, www.metrotimes.com/detroit/the-future-of-climate -change/Content?oid=2202205.

5. "Charity Hicks Speaks about 'Visionary Organizing in an Age of Climate Crisis' in Montreal," 2013, www.youtube.com/watch?time_continue=252&v =wG1I4eThoAA.

6. Bill Wylie-Kellerman, "The Detroit Water Struggle: A Story," *Critical Moment* (blog), September 30, 2014, https://critical-moment.org/2014/09/30/ the-detroit-water-struggle-a-story/.

7. Rachel Morello-Frosch, Manel Pastor, Jim Sadd, and Seth Shonkoff, *The Climate Gap: Inequalities in How Climate Change Hurts Americans and How*

to Close the Gap (Berkeley: University of California; Los Angeles: University of Southern California, 2009).

8. Natalie Sampson et al., "Planning for Climate Change in Legacy Cities: The Case of Detroit, Michigan," *Michigan Journal of Sustainability* 2 (Fall 2014), http://dx.doi.org/10.3998/mjs.12333712.0002.004.

9. Nicole Rupersburg, "The Long and Successful Journey to Erase Detroit's Food Desert Narrative," Thrillist, August 28, 2017, www.thrillist.com/eat/nation/erasing-detroits-food-desert-narrative. Jay Walljasper, "Grassroots Movement Shatters Myth That Detroit Is 'Food Desert,'" *Model D*, August 14, 2012, accessed September 3, 2018, www.modeldmedia.com/features/fooddesertmyth812.aspx. Jay Walljasper, "A City Lover's Guide to America's Most Underrated City," *Model D*, November 6, 2012, accessed September 3, 2018, www.modeldmedia.com/features/jaywalljasper1112.aspx.

10. Ken Harney, "Detroit Real Estate: Comeback Kid?" *Forbes*, accessed September 3, 2018, https://www.forbes.com/sites/realtorcom/2012/06/14/detroit-real-estate-comeback-kid/.

11. Reif Larsen, "Detroit: The Most Exciting City in America?" *New York Times*, November 20, 2017, sec. Travel, www.nytimes.com/2017/11/20/travel/detroit-michigan-downtown.html.

12. John O'Connor, "Destination: Detroit Restaurant Review," *Saveur*, April 20, 2015, accessed May 26, 2018, www.saveur.com/article/travels/where-to-eat-in-detroit-michigan.

13. Lisa Baertlein, "Motown Hopes Food Will Spur Rebirth, Growth," Reuters, April 4, 2012, www.reuters.com/article/us-usa-detroit-food/motown-hopes-food-will-spur-rebirth-growth-idUSBRE83306420120404.

14. Patricia Montemurri, "Meals on Bicycle Wheels," *Detroit Free Press*, March 28, 2011, sec. Metro, https://search-proquest-com.stanford.idm.oclc.org/docview/858788946/abstract/73535621F0EB482CPQ/1. Al Mascia, "Homeless Lady Dies in Detroit Discovered by Franciscan Friar," accessed March 7, 2018, www.youtube.com/watch?v=EgWrM30RYVk&feature=youtu.be.

15. Tom Di Liberto, "December Wildfires Scorch Southern California in 2017," NOAA Climate.gov, December 15, 2017, www.climate.gov/news-features/event-tracker/december-wildfires-scorch-southern-california-2017. Annie Lowrey, "The Most Expensive Weather Year Ever," *The Atlantic*, December 20, 2017,

www.theatlantic.com/business/archive/2017/12/expensive-weather-storms/ 548579/. Robin Respaut and Dave Graham, "Battered Puerto Rico Hospitals on Life Support after Hurricane Maria," Reuters, September 25, 2017, www .reuters.com/article/us-storm-maria-puertorico-hospitals/battered-puerto -rico-hospitals-on-life-support-after-hurricane-maria-idUSKCN1BZ13S.

16. "Billion-Dollar Weather and Climate Disasters: Table of Events, National Centers for Environmental Information (NCEI)," accessed February 2, 2018, www.ncdc.noaa.gov/billions/events/US/1980-2017.

17. Congressional Budget Office, "Trends in the Distribution of Household Income between 1979 and 2007" (Washington, DC: CBO, 2011).

18. Devah Pager, "The Mark of a Criminal Record," *American Journal of Sociology* 108, no. 5 (March 1, 2003): 937–75, https://doi.org/10.1086/ 374403. Devah Pager, Bart Bonikowski, and Bruce Western, "Discrimination in a Low-Wage Labor Market: A Field Experiment," *American Sociological Review* 74, no. 5 (October 1, 2009): 777–99, https://doi.org/10.1177/ 000312240907400505.

19. Pew Research Center, "Income Inequality in the U.S. Is Rising Most Rapidly among Asians," July 12, 2018, www.pewsocialtrends.org/2018/07/12/income -inequality-in-the-u-s-is-rising-most-rapidly-among-asians/.

20. Edward N. Wolff, *A Century of Wealth in America* (Cambridge, MA: Harvard University Press, 2017).

21. Melvin L. Oliver and Thomas M. Shapiro, *Black Wealth, White Wealth: A New Perspective on Racial Inequality* (New York: Routledge, 2006).

22. US Census Bureau, "Table 3: Summary Statistics for Black- or African American–Owned Firms in the 50 Most Populous Cities: 2007," in Survey of Business Owners (Washington, DC, 2011), www.census.gov/content/dam/ Census/library/publications/2007/econ/black_table3.pdf.

23. Thomas Shapiro, Tatjana Meschede, and Sam Osoro, "The Roots of the Widening Racial Wealth Gap: Explaining the Black-White Economic Divide," Institute on Assets and Social Policy, Brandeis University, 2013. Yunji Kim and Mildred E. Warner, "Geographies of Local Government Stress after the Great Recession," *Social Policy an Administration* 52, no. 1 (January 2018): 365–86, https://doi.org/10.1111/spol.12307.

24. Jamie Peck and Heather Whiteside, "Financializing Detroit," *Economic Geography* 92, no. 3 (July 2, 2016): 235–68, https://doi.org/10.1080/00130095 .2015.1116369.

25. USGCRP, "Fourth National Climate Assessment," 2018, https://nca2018 .globalchange.gov.

26. Breana Noble, "Snyder Calls for Civility, Teamwork during 'Exit Interview,'" *Detroit News*, November 11, 2018, www.detroitnews.com/story/news/local/ detroit-city/2018/11/09/snyder-exit-interview-detroit-economic-club/ 1933672002/.

27. Pearl Cleage, Pearl Cleage describes the sights, sounds, and smells of her childhood in Detroit, Michigan, interview by Jodi Merriday, September 23, 2004, the *HistoryMakers*, https://stanford-thehistorymakers-org.stanford .idm.oclc.org/story/227942.

28. Maureen Taylor and Marian Kramer, Transcript of Maureen Taylor and Marian Kramer, interview by Jennifer Lyle, March 5, 2004, Global Femi- nisms Comparative Case Studies of Women's Activism and Scholarship, In- stitute for Research on Women and Gender, University of Michigan, https:// globalfeminisms.umich.edu/sites/default/files//TaylorKramer_U_E_102806 %20%281%29.pdf.

29. Monica M. White, "Sisters of the Soil: Urban Gardening as Resistance in Detroit," *Race/Ethnicity: Multidisciplinary Global Contexts* 5, no. 1 (2011): 13–28, https://doi.org/10.2979/racethmulglocon.5.1.13.

30. Robert Maniscalco, *Gilda Snowden, a Memorial Tribute, 1954–2014*, Detroit, 2014, https://www.youtube.com/watch?v=gxWBOC2y558.

31. Halima Cassells, On the Free Market of Detroit and processes in the neigh- borhood, interview by urbanNext, undated, accessed June 29, 2019, https:// www.youtube.com/watch?v=eaa6D_CxQRE.

32. dream hampton, *Treasure: From Tragedy to Trans Justice, Mapping a Detroit Story (TRAILER)*, Detroit, 2015, https://vimeo.com/126086558.

33. Tawana Petty, "Petty Propolis Bio," Mother/Organizer/Author/Poet, accessed February 14, 2019, http://honeycombthepoet.org/music.html.

34. Maya Stovall, *Liquor Store Theatre: Ethnography and Contemporary Art in De- troit* (Detroit: Department of Anthropology, Wayne State University, 2018).

35. Adolph L Reed, *Stirrings in the Jug: Black Politics in the Post-Segregation Era* (Minneapolis: University of Minnesota Press, 1999).

36. Thomas Macias, "Environmental Risk Perception among Race and Ethnic Groups in the United States," *Ethnicities* 16, no. 1 (February 1, 2016): 111–29, https://doi.org/10.1177/1468796815575382. Paul Mohai and Bunyan Bryant, "Is There a 'Race' Effect on Concern for Environmental Quality?" *Public Opinion Quarterly* 62, no. 4 (1998): 475–505, www.jstor.org/stable/2749675. Xinsheng Liu, Arnold Vedlitz, and Liu Shi, "Examining the Determinants of Public Environmental Concern: Evidence from National Public Surveys," *Environmental Science and Policy* 39 (May 1, 2014): 77–94, https://doi.org/10.1016/j.envsci.2014.02.006. Aaron M. McCright and Riley E. Dunlap, "Cool Dudes: The Denial of Climate Change among Conservative White Males in the United States," *Global Environmental Change* 21, no. 4 (October 1, 2011): 1163–72, https://doi.org/10.1016/j.gloenvcha.2011.06.003.

37. Kent E. Portney, *Taking Sustainable Cities Seriously* (Cambridge, MA: MIT Press, 2016). Greg Schrock, Ellen M. Bassett, and Jamaal Green, "Pursuing Equity and Justice in a Changing Climate: Assessing Equity in Local Climate and Sustainability Plans in U.S. Cities," *Journal of Planning Education and Research* 35, no. 3 (2015): 282–95.

38. Reed, *Stirrings in the Jug*, 38, 79.

39. Milton D. Friedman, "Capitalism and the Jews" (1972), https://fee.org/articles/capitalism-and-the-jews/.

40. Roger Scruton, *How to Think Seriously about the Planet: The Case for an Environmental Conservatism* (New York: Oxford University Press, 2012).

41. Gary S. Becker, *The Economics of Discrimination* (Chicago: University of Chicago Press, 2010).

42. Milton Friedman and Rose Friedman, *Free to Choose: A Personal Statement* (San Diego: Harcourt Brace Jovanovich, 1990), 140.

43. Jamie Peck, Nik Theodore, and Neil Brenner, "Neoliberal Urbanism: Models, Moments, Mutations," *SAIS Review of International Affairs* 29, no. 1 (June 26, 2009): 49–66, https://doi.org/10.1353/sais.0.0028.

44. Brian L. Dunnigan, "Charting the Shape of Early Detroit: 1701–1838," in *Mapping Detroit: Land, Community, and Shaping a City*, ed. June Manning Thomas (Detroit: Wayne State University Press, 2015), 1701–838.

45. Carl C. Anthony, *The Earth, the City, and the Hidden Narrative of Race* (New York: New York University Press, 2017), 105.

46. Roxanne Dunbar-Ortiz, *An Indigenous Peoples' History of the United States* (Boston: Beacon Press, 2014).

47. Cedric J Robinson, *Black Marxism: The Making of the Black Radical Tradition* (Chapel Hill: University of North Carolina Press, 2000), 2.

48. In response to charges that capitalism has historically thrived on racism, Friedman describes slavery and colonialism as aberrant forms of capitalism that melt in the face of competitive markets (see www.youtube.com/watch?v=4xeebU8VhmY). For counterarguments, see Sven Beckert, *Empire of Cotton* (New York: Alfred Knopf, 2014). Also, see Edward E. Baptist, *The Half Has Never Been Told: Slavery and the Making of American Capitalism* (New York: Basic Books, 2016).

49. Marcus Rediker, *The Slave Ship: A Human History* (New York: Penguin, 2007).

50. Anita Rupprecht, "Excessive Memories: Slavery, Insurance, and Resistance," *History Workshop Journal*, no. 64 (2007): 6–28, www.jstor.org/stable/25472933.

51. Nikki Jones and Christina Jackson, "'You Just Don't Go down There': Learning to Avoid the Ghetto in San Francisco," in *The Ghetto: Contemporary Global Issues and Controversies*, ed. Ray Hutchison and Bruce Haynes (Boulder, CO: Westview Press, 2012), 83–110.

52. Susan M. Opp and Kyle L. Saunders, "Pillar Talk: Local Sustainability Initiatives and Policies in the United States—Finding Evidence of the 'Three E's': Economic Development, Environmental Protection, and Social Equity," *Urban Affairs Review* 49, no. 5 (September 1, 2013): 678–717, https://doi.org/10.1177/1078087412469344. James Svara, Tanya Watt, and Katherine Takai, "Advancing Social Equity as an Integral Dimension of Sustainability in Local Communities," *Cityscape* 17, no. 2 (2015): 139–66. Schrock, Bassett, and Green, "Pursuing Equity and Justice in a Changing Climate," 282–95.

53. Raoul S. Liévanos, "Impaired Water Hazard Zones: Mapping Intersecting Environmental Health Vulnerabilities and Polluter Disproportionality," *ISPRS International Journal of Geo-Information* 7, no. 11 (November 2018): 433, https://doi.org/10.3390/ijgi7110433. Nathan McClintock, "A Critical

Physical Geography of Urban Soil Contamination," *Geoforum* 65 (October 1, 2015): 69–85, https://doi.org/10.1016/j.geoforum.2015.07.010. Tara Duggan, "The Bay Area's Hidden Problem: Hunger and Food Insecurity," *San Francisco Chronicle*, November 18, 2018, www.sfchronicle.com/food/article/The -hidden-hungryA-Bay-Area-paradox-13379274.php.

54. Applied Survey Research, "City of Oakland 2017 Homeless Census & Survey," San Jose, CA, 2017. Otis R. Taylor Jr., "Oakland Homeless Camps Point to Racial Bias," *San Francisco Chronicle*, July 1, 2017, www.sfchronicle.com/ news/article/Oakland-homeless-camps-point-to-racial-bias-11260015.php.

55. Christina Zdanowicz and Holly Yan, "This Is Why the Oakland Teachers' Strike Will Be Different from All the Others—CNN," *CNN*, February 21, 2019, www.cnn.com/2019/02/20/us/oakland-teachers-strike-walkup/index .html?no-st=1550772293.

56. Alison Hope Alkon and Josh Cadji, "Sowing Seeds of Displacement: Gentrification and Food Justice in Oakland, CA," *International Journal of Urban and Regional Research*, accessed September 27, 2018, https://doi.org/10 .1111/1468-2427.12684.

57. Paul Mohai and Bunyan Bryant, "Is There a 'Race' Effect on Concern for Environmental Quality?" *Public Opinion Quarterly* 62, no. 4 (1998): 475–505, http://www.jstor.org/stable/2749675.

58. Anna Clark, "Opinion: Going without Water in Detroit," *New York Times*, December 20, 2017, sec. Opinion, www.nytimes.com/2014/07/04/opinion/ going-without-water-in-detroit.html.

59. Peter J. Hammer, "The Flint Water Crisis, the Karegnondi Water Authority, and Strategic-Structural Racism," *Critical Sociology*, October 6, 2017, 0896920517729193, https://doi.org/10.1177/0896920517729193.

60. "In Detroit, City-Backed Water Shut-Offs 'Contrary to Human Rights,' Say UN Experts," *UN News*, October 20, 2014, https://news.un.org/en/story/ 2014/10/481542-detroit-city-backed-water-shut-offs-contrary-human-rights -say-un-experts. "Groups Discuss Detroit Water Shutoffs with UN Experts," *Detroit Free Press*, accessed September 23, 2018, www.freep.com/story/news/ local/michigan/detroit/2014/10/19/detroit-water-shutoffs-united-nations/ 17585855/. Rebecca Burns, "Now the UN Is Intervening in Detroit's Water Conflict: Could Thirsty Cities Riot?" *The Guardian*, October 17, 2014,

sec. Cities, www.theguardian.com/cities/2014/oct/17/united-nations-detroit
-water-cities-riot-protests. "UN Human Rights Experts Urge US to Increase
Efforts to Address Water Contamination," *UN News*, March 3, 2016, https://
news.un.org/en/story/2016/03/523562-un-human-rights-experts-urge-us
-increase-efforts-address-water-contamination.

61. Kevin Morgan, "Nourishing the City: The Rise of the Urban Food Question
in the Global North," *Urban Studies* 52, no. 8 (June 2015): 1379–94, https://
doi.org/10.1177/0042098014534902.

62. Laura A. Reese, "Economic versus Natural Disasters: If Detroit Had a
Hurricane . . . ," *Economic Development Quarterly* 20, no. 3 (August 1, 2006):
219–31, https://doi.org/10.1177/0891242406289344.

63. Henry A. Giroux, "Reading Hurricane Katrina: Race, Class, and the Biopol-
itics of Disposability," *College Literature* 33, no. 3 (2006): 171–96, www.jstor
.org/stable/25115372.

64. Rebecca J. Kinney, *Beautiful Wasteland: The Rise of Detroit as America's
Postindustrial Frontier* (Minneapolis: University of Minnesota Press, 2016).

65. John Arena, *Driven from New Orleans: How Nonprofits Betray Public Housing and Promote Privatization* (Minneapolis: University of Minnesota Press,
2012).

66. Darwin BondGraham, "Building the *New* New Orleans: Foundation and
NGO Power," *Review of Black Political Economy* 38, no. 4 (January 2011):
279–309, https://doi.org/10.1007/s12114-010-9081-z.

67. David Levy and Rasmus Kleis Nielsen, eds., *The Changing Business of Journalism and Its Implications for Democracy* (Oxford: Reuters Institute for the
Study of Journalism, 2010).

68. Simon L. Lewis and Mark A. Maslin, "Defining the Anthropocene," *Nature*
519, no. 7542 (March 2015): 171–80, https://doi.org/10.1038/nature14258.

69. Sylvia Wynter, "Unsettling the Coloniality of Being/Power/Truth/Freedom:
Towards the Human, After Man, Its Overrepresentation—An Argument,"
CR: The New Centennial Review 3, no. 3 (2003): 257–337.

70. Keeanga-Yamahtta Taylor, ed., *How We Get Free: Black Feminism and the
Combahee River Collective* (Chicago: Haymarket Books, 2017).

71. Janell Ross and Wesley Lowery, "Looting Rumors and Fear of Crime Often
Exaggerated after Natural Disasters," *Washington Post*, September 1, 2017,

www.washingtonpost.com/national/looting-rumors-and-fear-of-crime-often
-exaggerated-after-natural-disasters/2017/09/01/14fc6546-8f57-11e7-a2b0
-e68cbf0b1f19_story.html?utm_term=.22bba471857c. Kristin Askelson and
Claire Taylor, "Away from Their Flooded Homes, Harvey Evacuees Fret about
Looters," *USA Today*, August 30, 2017, https://www.usatoday.com/story/news/
nation/2017/08/30/harvey-evacuees-worry-about-looters/617218001/.

72. Jayne Cortez, "Talking About New Orleans," in *On the Imperial Highway:
New and Selected Poems* (Brooklyn, NY: Hanging Loose Press, 2009), https://
www.poets.org/poetsorg/poem/talking-about-new-orleans.

73. Bonnie Elizabeth Haskell, "Sexuality and Natural Disaster: Challenges of
LGBT Communities Facing Hurricane Katrina," *SSRN Electronic Journal*,
2014, https://doi.org/10.2139/ssrn.2513650. Brandon L. Garrett and Tania
Tetlow, "Criminal Justice Collapse: The Constitution after Hurricane Katrina," *Duke Law Journal* 56 (2006): 52.

74. Francis Desiderio, "'A Catalyst for Downtown': Detroit's Renaissance Center,"
Michigan Historical Review 35, no. 1 (2009): 83–112, www.jstor.org/stable/
25652152.

75. Derek S. Hyra, *The New Urban Renewal: The Economic Transformation of
Harlem and Bronzeville* (Chicago: University of Chicago Press, 2008).

76. John R. Logan and Brian J. Stultz, "The Persistence of Segregation in the
Metropolis: New Findings from the 2010 Census Logan Stultz," Census
Brief Prepared for Project US2010, 2011, https://s4.ad.brown.edu/Projects/
Diversity/Data/Report/report2.pdf.

77. US Census Bureau, "Longitudinal Employer-Household Dynamics," 2010,
http://onthemap.ces.census.gov.

78. Max Wallace, *The American Axis: Henry Ford, Charles Lindbergh, and the
Rise of the Third Reich* (New York: St. Martin's Press, 2004).

79. Kenneth T. Jackson, *The Ku Klux Klan in the City, 1915–1930* (Chicago:
Ivan R. Dee, 1992).

80. Alex Baskin, "The Ford Hunger March—1932," *Labor History* 13, no. 3
(June 1, 1972): 331–60, https://doi.org/10.1080/00236567208584211.

81. Beth Tompkins Bates, *The Making of Black Detroit in the Age of Henry Ford*
(Chapel Hill: University of North Carolina Press, 2012).

82. Peter H. Amann, "Vigilante Fascism: The Black Legion as an American Hybrid," *Comparative Studies in Society and History* 25, no. 3 (1983): 490–524, www.jstor.org/stable/178625. Allie Gross, "Michigan Has Long Been Fertile Ground for the Far Right," *Detroit Free Press*, August 17, 2017, www.freep .com/story/news/local/michigan/2017/08/17/michigan-far-right-ku-klux -klan-black-legion/564650001/.

83. Eric Larson, "Real Estate Value and Quality of Life Impacts of a Downtown Park" (2014), www.youtube.com/watch?v=OR6fxWTIMqU.

84. Karolyn Frost, *I've Got a Home in Glory Land: A Lost Tale of the Underground Railroad* (New York: Farrar, Straus and Giroux, 2008).

85. Winona LaDuke, interview by Kirk Heinze, *Greening of the Great Lakes*, WJR, March 7, 2017, audio, 25:21, http://spartanpodcast.com/?p=4662.

86. Tyler Abrahams, "Black Lives Matter: From a Facebook Post to an Activist Movement," *Cougar Chronicle* (blog), accessed February 1, 2018, https:// csusmchronicle.com/17421/news/black-lives-matter-from-a-facebook-post -to-an-activist-movement/.

Defining "Sustainability" and "Just Sustainability"

1. Thomas R. Anderson, Ed Hawkins, and Philip D. Jones, "CO2, the Greenhouse Effect, and Global Warming: From the Pioneering Work of Arrhenius and Callendar to Today's Earth System Models," *Endeavour* 40, no. 3 (September 1, 2016): 178–87, https://doi.org/10.1016/j.endeavour.2016.07.002.

2. Scott Campbell, "Green Cities, Growing Cities, Just Cities?" *Journal of the American Planning Association* 62, no. 3 (Summer 1996): 296, https:// stanford.idm.oclc.org/login?url=https://search.ebscohost.com/login.aspx ?direct=true&db=aph&AN=9607210569&site=ehost-live&scope=site. Riley E. Dunlap and Kent D. Van Liere, "The 'New Environmental Paradigm,'" *Journal of Environmental Education* 9, no. 4 (July 1, 1978): 10–19, https://doi.org/10.1080/00958964.1978.10801875.

3. World Commission on Environment and Development, *Our Common Future ("Brundtland Report")* (New York: Oxford University Press, 1987), www.bne-portal.de/fileadmin/unesco/de/Downloads/Hintergrundmaterial _international/Brundtlandbericht.File.pdf?linklisted=2812.

4. First National People of Color Environmental Leadership Conference, "Principles of Environmental Justice," October 1991, www.ejnet.org/ej/principles .html.

5. 1992 Rio de Janeiro Conference on Environment and Development and United Nations, eds., *Agenda 21: Programme of Action for Sustainable Development; Rio Declaration on Environment and Development* (New York: United Nations Department of Public Information, 1993).

6. Congress for the New Urbanism, "The Charter of the New Urbanism," 1993, www.cnu.org/who-we-are/charter-new-urbanism.

7. Friedrich Engels, "Conditions of the Working-Class in England," 1845, www .marxists.org/archive/marx/works/1845/condition-working-class/index.htm.

8. Ebenezer Howard, *Garden Cities of Tomorrow* (London: Swan Sonnenschein, 1902), http://archive.org/details/gardencitiestom00howagoog.

9. June Manning Thomas, *Redevelopment and Race: Planning a Finer City in Postwar Detroit* (Baltimore: Johns Hopkins University Press, 1997).

10. Bernice Johnson Reagon, *"Had, Took, Misled," Give Your Hands to the Struggle (Liner Notes)* (Smithsonian Folkways, 1997), https://folkways-media.si .edu/liner_notes/smithsonian_folkways/SFW40049.pdf.

11. Nathan Hare, "Black Ecology," *Black Scholar* 1, no. 6 (April 1, 1970): 2–8, https://doi.org/10.1080/00064246.1970.11728700.

12. Dorceta E. Taylor, "The Rise of the Environmental Justice Paradigm: Injustice Framing and the Social Construction of Environmental Discourses," *American Behavioral Scientist* 43, no. 4 (January 1, 2000): 508–80, https://doi .org/10.1177/0002764200043004003.

13. Julian Agyeman, *Sustainable Communities and the Challenge of Environmental Justice* (New York: New York University Press, 2005).

14. Julian Agyeman and Bob Evans, "'Just Sustainability': The Emerging Discourse of Environmental Justice in Britain?" *Geographical Journal* 170, no. 2 (2004): 155–64, www.jstor.org/stable/3451592.

15. Department of Economic and Social Affairs, United Nations, "World Economic and Social Survey 2013: Sustainable Development Challenges," 2013, www.scribd.com/document/208308756/2843WESS2013.

16. XiaoHu Wang et al., "Capacity to Sustain Sustainability: A Study of U.S. Cities," *Public Administration Review* 72, no. 6 (November 1, 2012): 841–53, https://doi.org/10.1111/j.1540-6210.2012.02566.x.

17. "Noam Chomsky Debates with Michel Foucault (1971)—Classroom—Art and Education," accessed December 8, 2018, www.artandeducation.net/classroom/video/66054/noam-chomsky-debates-with-michel-foucault-1971.

Power Constellations, Practice Theory, and "Getting Woke"

1. Ruth Wilson Gilmore, "Beyond the Prison Industrial Complex" (2011), www.youtube.com/watch?v=sTPjC-7EDkc.

2. Robert A. Dahl, *Who Governs?: Democracy and Power in an American City* (New Haven, CT: Yale University Press, 2005).

3. G. William Domhoff, *Who Really Rules?: New Haven and Community Power Reexamined* (Santa Monica, CA: Goodyear, 1978).

4. John R. Logan and Harvey L. Molotch, *Urban Fortunes: The Political Economy of Place* (Berkeley: University of California Press, 2007).

5. Clarence N. Stone, *Regime Politics: Governing Atlanta, 1946–1988* (Lawrence: University Press of Kansas, 1989).

6. Joichi Ito, "Emergent Democracy," *ArXiv:1807.06953 [Physics]*, July 14, 2018, http://arxiv.org/abs/1807.06953.

7. Vandana Shiva, *Earth Democracy: Justice, Sustainability, and Peace* (London: Zed Books, 2006).

8. Diana Coole and Samantha Frost, eds., *New Materialisms: Ontology, Agency, and Politics* (Durham, NC: Duke University Press, 2010).

9. Abel Wolman, "The Metabolism of Cities," *Scientific American* 213 (1965): 179–90, https://metabolismofcities.org/publication/138.

10. Theodore R. Schatzki, Karin Knorr Cetina, and Eike von Savigny, eds., *The Practice Turn in Contemporary Theory* (New York: Routledge, 2001).

11. Ann Swidler, "Culture in Action: Symbols and Strategies," *American Sociological Review* 51, no. 2 (1986): 273–86, https://doi.org/10.2307/2095521.

12. Ntozake Shange, *Sassafrass, Cypress, and Indigo* (New York: St. Martin's Press, 1982).

13. F. Max Müller, trans., *The Upanishads* (Delhi: M. Banarsidass, 1975).

14. Farid ud-Din Attar, *Conference of the Birds* (1177).

15. Teresa of Avila, "The Interior Castle," Sacred Texts, 1577, www.sacred-texts .com/chr/tic/index.htm.

16. Frank Uekötter, *The Green and the Brown: A History of Conservation in Nazi Germany* (New York: Cambridge University Press, 2006).

17. Marja Spierenburg and Harry Wels, "Conservative Philanthropists, Royalty and Business Elites in Nature Conservation in Southern Africa," *Antipode* 42, no. 3 (June 1, 2010): 647–70, https://doi.org/10.1111/j.1467-8330.2010.00767.x.

18. W. M Adams and Martin Mulligan, eds., *Decolonizing Nature: Strategies for Conservation in a Post-colonial Era* (New York: Routledge, 2002).

19. Thomas Hobbes, "Leviathan," 1651, www.gutenberg.org/files/3207/3207-h/ 3207-h.htm.

20. Michael Hardt and Antonio Negri, *Empire* (Cambridge, MA: Harvard University Press, 2001), www.hup.harvard.edu/catalog.php?isbn= 9780674006713&content=reviews.

21. Loïc Wacquant, "Crafting the Neoliberal State: Workfare, Prisonfare, and Social Insecurity," *Sociological Forum* 25, no. 2 (2010): 197–220.

22. Henri Lefebvre, *The Production of Space* (Oxford: Wiley-Blackwell, 1992).

23. David Harvey, *Spaces of Hope* (Berkeley: University of California Press, 2000).

24. Andrew Herscher, *Unreal Estate Guide to Detroit* (Ann Arbor: University of Michigan Press, 2014).

25. Katherine McKittrick, *Demonic Grounds: Black Women and the Cartographies of Struggle* (Minneapolis: University of Minnesota Press, 2006).

26. Basil Johnston, *Ojibway Heritage* (Toronto: McClelland and Stewart, 2011).

27. Antoine Laumet de Lamothe Cadillac, *Historical Collections, Document 45, Papers of Cadillac, 25th. Sept. 1702*, vol. 33 (Lansing: Michigan Pioneer and Historical Society, 1702).

28. Kyle T. Mays, "Pontiac's Ghost in the Motor City: Indigeneity and the Discursive Construction of Modern Detroit," *Middle West Review* 2, no. 2 (June 24, 2016): 115–42.

29. Carroll P. Kakel, *The American West and the Nazi East: A Comparative and Interpretive Perspective* (New York: Palgrave Macmillan, 2014).

30. Grace Lee Boggs, *The Next American Revolution: Sustainable Activism for the Twenty-First Century* (Berkeley: University of California Press, 2012).

31. "Yes We Can—Barack Obama Music Video," 2008, www.youtube.com/watch?v=jjXyqcx-mYY.

32. Kathryn E. Holland Braund, "The Creek Indians, Blacks, and Slavery," *Journal of Southern History* 57, no. 4 (1991): 601–36, https://doi.org/10.2307/2210598. David M. Katzman, "Black Slavery in Michigan," *Midcontinent American Studies Journal* 11, no. 2 (1970): 56–66, www.jstor.org/stable/40640913. Karolyn Smardz Frost, *A Fluid Frontier: Slavery, Resistance, and the Underground Railroad in the Detroit River Borderland* (Detroit: Wayne State University Press, 2016).

33. Lester K. Spence, *Knocking the Hustle: Against the Neoliberal Turn in Black Politics* (Brooklyn, NY: Punctum Books, 2015).

34. Andrew Feenberg, *The Philosophy of Praxis: Marx, Lukács, and the Frankfurt School*, rev. ed. (Brooklyn, NY: Verso, 2014).

About Me and the Study

1. Countee Cullen, *The Medea and Some Poems* (New York: Harper and Brothers, 1935).

Sankofa and the Angel of History

1. Jason Stanley, *How Fascism Works: The Politics of Us and Them* (New York: Random House, 2018).

2. Kim Crawford, *The Daring Trader: Jacob Smith in the Michigan Territory, 1802–1825* (East Lansing: Michigan State University Press, 2012). Sean P. Harvey, "'Must Not Their Languages Be Savage and Barbarous Like Them?' Philology, Indian Removal, and Race Science," *Journal of the Early Republic* 30, no. 4 (2010): 505–32, www.jstor.org/stable/40926063.

3. Walter Benjamin, *The Arcades Project*, trans. Howard Eiland and Kevin McLaughlin, 3rd ed. (Cambridge, MA: Belknap Press of Harvard University Press, 2002), 3.

4. Walter Benjamin, *Illuminations: Essays and Reflections* (New York: Mariner Books, 2019), 201.

5. Michigan Childhood Lead Poisoning Prevention Program, Michigan Department of Health and Human Services Division of Environmental Health, "2016 Data Report on Childhood Lead Testing and Elevated Levels: Michigan," 2018, www.michigan.gov/documents/lead/2016_CLPPP_Annual _Report_5-1-18_621989_7.pdf.

6. R. Rabin, "Warnings Unheeded: A History of Child Lead Poisoning," *American Journal of Public Health* 79, no. 12 (December 1989): 1668–74, https:// doi.org/10.2105/AJPH.79.12.1668.

7. Robert Bullard et al., "Toxic Wastes and Race at Twenty: 1987–2007," Cleveland, Ohio, 2007, www.nrdc.org/sites/default/files/toxic-wastes-and-race-at -twenty-1987-2007.pdf.

8. Paula Chakravartty and Denise Ferreira da Silva, "Accumulation, Dispossession, and Debt: The Racial Logic of Global Capitalism—An Introduction," *American Quarterly* 64, no. 3 (2012): 361–85.

9. Nathan Bomey, *Detroit Resurrected: To Bankruptcy and Back* (New York: Norton, 2017).

10. Drew Sharp, *Dave Bing: A Life of Challenge* (Champaign, IL: Human Kinetics, 2013).

11. Gallup, "Is Detroit the Least Safe City?" Gallup.com, 2007, http://news.gallup .com/poll/102853/Detroit-Least-Safe-City.aspx.

12. "Sankofa," performed by Cassandra Wilson, accessed July 7, 2019, www .youtube.com/watch?v=7CEauXcBPgo.

Interior Architecture of Minoritized Space

1. Thomas J. Sugrue, *The Origins of the Urban Crisis: Race and Inequality in Postwar Detroit* (Princeton, NJ: Princeton University Press, 2014). Loïc Wacquant, "Scrutinizing the Street: Poverty, Morality, and the Pitfalls of Urban Ethnography," *American Journal of Sociology* 107, no. 6 (May 1, 2002): 1468–532, https://doi.org/10.1086/340461.

2. Neil Smith, *The New Urban Frontier: Gentrification and the Revanchist City* (New York: Routledge, 1996).

3. Neil Smith, "Gentrification and the Rent Gap," *Annals of the Association of American Geographers* 77, no. 3 (1987): 462–65, www.jstor.org/stable/2563279.

4. Ernest W. Burgess, "Residential Segregation in American Cities," *The ANNALS of the American Academy of Political and Social Science* 140, no. 1 (November 1928): 105–15, https://doi.org/10.1177/000271622814000115.

5. Mike Maciag, "Gentrification in America Report," *Governing*, February 2015, www.governing.com/gov-data/census/gentrification-in-cities-governing -report.html.

6. Michel S. Laguerre, *Minoritized Space: An Inquiry into the Spatial Order of Things* (Berkeley: University of California Institute of Governmental Studies Press, 1999).

7. Mitchell Ojmarrh and Michael S. Caudy, "Race Differences in Drug Of- fending and Drug Distribution Arrests," *Crime and Delinquency* 63, no. 2 (February 2017): 91–112. M. S. Shiels et al., "Trends in U.S. Drug Overdose Deaths in Non-Hispanic Black, Hispanic, and Non-Hispanic White Persons, 2000–2015," *Annals of Internal Medicine* 168, no. 6 (March 20, 2018): 453– 55. US Department of Health and Human Services, "Results from the 2013 National Survey on Drug Use and Health: Summary of National Findings," Rockville, MD, 2014, https://www.samhsa.gov/data/sites/default/files/ NSDUHresultsPDFWHTML2013/Web/NSDUHresults2013.pdf.

8. James Forman, *Locking Up Our Own: Crime and Punishment in Black Amer- ica* (New York: Farrar, Straus and Giroux, 2017).

9. George Jackson, *Soledad Brother: The Prison Letters of George Jackson* (Chi- cago: Chicago Review Press, 1994), 255.

10. Steve Farkas et al., *Aggravating Circumstances: A Status Report on Rudeness in America* (New York: Public Agenda, 2002).

11. Public Religion Research Institute, "The Divide over America's Future: 1950 or 2050? Findings from the 2016 American Values Survey," PRRI, 2016, www.prri.org/research/poll-1950s-2050-divided-nations-direction -post-election/.

12. Philip Kasinitz and David Hillyard, "The Old-Timers' Tale: The Politics of Nostalgia on the Waterfront," *Journal of Contemporary Ethnography* 24, no. 2 (July 1, 1995): 139–64, https://doi.org/10.1177/089124195024002001.

13. Timothy A. Gibson, "'I Don't Want Them Living around Here': Ideologies of Race and Neighborhood Decay," *Rethinking Marxism* 10, no. 4 (December 1, 1998): 141–55.

14. Arlie Russell Hochschild, *Strangers in Their Own Land: Anger and Mourning on the American Right* (New York: New Press, 2018).

15. Cathy J. Cohen, Matthew Fowler, Vladimir E. Medenica, and Jon C. Rogowski, "The 'Woke' Generation? Millennial Attitudes on Race in the US," GenForward report, University of Chicago, 2017.

16. Elijah Anderson, *Streetwise: Race, Class, and Change in an Urban Community* (Chicago: University of Chicago Press, 2013), 2.

17. Mary Pattillo, *Black on the Block: The Politics of Race and Class in the City* (Chicago: University of Chicago Press, 2008), 53.

18. Mitchell Duneier, *Slim's Table: Race, Respectability, and Masculinity* (Chicago: University of Chicago Press, 2015), 65.

19. Wacquant, "Scrutinizing the Street," 1468–532.

20. Clifford Geertz, *The Interpretation of Cultures* (New York: Basic Books, 1973), 209.

21. Adam Serwer, "Bill Cosby's Famous 'Pound Cake' Speech, Annotated," Buzz-Feed, 2015, www.buzzfeed.com/adamserwer/bill-cosby-pound-for-pound.

22. Robert Young, "Reflection on Dr. Martin Luther King Jr.," *Michigan Chronicle*, January 20, 2010.

23. Ron Scott, *How to End Police Brutality: An Organizer's Manual* (Detroit: Ron Scott, 2015), loc. 404 of 640, Kindle.

Narrative of the Fall

1. Leslie K. Pielack, *The Saginaw Trail: From Native American Path to Woodward Avenue* (Charleston, SC: History Press, 2018).

2. Joe Darden, *Detroit: Race and Uneven Development* (Philadelphia: Temple University Press, 2010), 67.

3. "Racism at Hudson's," *Michigan Now*, 2013, www.michigannow.org/2013/02/13/racism-at-hudsons/.

4. Matthew Fowler, Vladimir E. Medenica, and Cathy J. Cohen, "Why 41 Percent of White Millennials Voted for Trump," *Washington Post*, December 5, 2017. Robin Kelley, *Race Rebels: Culture, Politics, and the Black Working Class* (New York: Simon and Schuster, 1996).

5. Tomás Jiménez, "Other Side of Assimilation, Stanford SSDS Social Science Data Collection," accessed February 4, 2018, https://data.stanford.edu/osa.

6. Robert Salonga, "How East Palo Alto Shed Its 'Murder Capital' Status and Found Peace," *Mercury News* (blog), January 4, 2018, www.mercurynews.com/2018/01/02/how-east-palo-alto-shed-its-crime-rep-and-built-a-new-path-forward/.

7. William Bunge, *Fitzgerald; Geography of a Revolution* (Cambridge, MA: Schenkman, 1971).

8. Reynolds Farley, Sheldon Danziger, and Harry J. Holzer, *Detroit Divided* (New York: Russell Sage Foundation, 2000).

9. Mark Puls, "Jeffries Towers Tumble: Implosion Makes Way for New Housing," *Detroit News*, April 30, 2001.

10. Corey Williams, "New Latino Wave Helps Revitalize Detroit," *USA Today*, February 28, 2008, https://usatoday30.usatoday.com/news/nation/2008-02-28-2962316916_x.htm.

11. Elena Herrada and J. C. Guerrero, "Detroit Latino March," *Inside Southwest Detroit*, 2008, http://insidesouthwest.com/?p=53.

12. Robert H. Zieger and Gilbert J. Gall, *American Workers, American Unions: The Twentieth Century* (Baltimore: Johns Hopkins University Press, 2002), 50, 52.

13. James Boudouris, "A Classification of Homicides," *Criminology* 11 (1974): 525–40, https://heinonline.org/HOL/P?h=hein.journals/crim11&i=525.

14. Dorceta E. Taylor, "Black Farmers in the USA and Michigan: Longevity, Empowerment, and Food Sovereignty," *Journal of African American Studies* 22, no. 1 (March 1, 2018): 49–76, https://doi.org/10.1007/s12111-018-9394-8.

15. Arlie Russell Hochschild, *Strangers in Their Own Land: Anger and Mourning on the American Right* (New York: New Press, 2018).

16. Martin Luther King Jr., "The World House," in *Where Do We Go from Here: Chaos or Community?* (Boston: Beacon Press, 1968), 177–202.

17. "James Baldwin and Nikki Giovanni, a Conversation," *Soul!* (London, 1971), www.youtube.com/watch?v=eZmBy7C9gHQ.

18. Frantz Fanon, *The Wretched of the Earth* (New York: Grove/Atlantic, 2007).

The One

1. Derek S. Hyra, *The New Urban Renewal: The Economic Transformation of Harlem and Bronzeville* (Chicago: University of Chicago Press, 2008).

2. Michael T. Taussig, *The Devil and Commodity Fetishism in South America* (Chapel Hill: University of North Carolina Press, 1980).

3. Calvin L. Warren, *Ontological Terror: Blackness, Nihilism, and Emancipation* (Durham, NC: Duke University Press, 2018).

4. J. A. Mbembé, "Necropolitics," trans. Libby Meintjes, *Public Culture* 15, no. 1 (March 25, 2003): 11–40, https://muse.jhu.edu/article/39984.

5. George Jackson, *Soledad Brother: The Prison Letters of George Jackson* (Chicago: Chicago Review Press, 1994), 4, 100.

6. Zora Neale Hurston, *Dust Tracks on a Road: An Autobiography* (New York: Harper Perennial, 2010), 146–147, Kindle.

State of the City

1. "Detroit's Unemployment Rate Is Nearly 50%, According to the Detroit News," *Huffington Post*, March 18, 2010, www.huffpost.com/entry/detroits-unemployment-rat_n_394559.

2. Christine MacDonald, "Bing: I'll Move Some Residents," *Detroit News*, February 25, 2010, 1-dot edition, https://infoweb.newsbank.com/resources/doc/nb/news/12E1AC38E839A350?p=AWNB.

3. "Motor City Fights against Fulfilling a Death Wish: David Usborne On," *The Independent*, May 31, 1993, www.independent.co.uk/news/world/motor-city-fights-against-fulfilling-a-death-wish-david-usborne-on-the-battle-to-salvage-detroit-2316297.html.

4. Abayomi Azikiwe, "Demonstrate at Mayor Bing's State of the City Address," *Pan-African News Wire*, March 19, 2010, http://panafricannews.blogspot.com/2010/03/detroit-demonstration-today-against-war.html.

5. J. Woodford Howard, *Mr. Justice Murphy: A Political Biography* (Princeton, NJ: Princeton University Press, 1968).

6. Steven Malanga, "The Next Wave of Urban Reform," *City Journal*, December 23, 2015, www.city-journal.org/html/next-wave-urban-reform-13322.html.

7. Charlie LeDuff, "What Killed Aiyana Stanley-Jones?" *Mother Jones*, November 2010.

8. "New Spirit in Detroit," *The Nation*, January 19, 1974, 66–67.

9. Executive Office of the President, "Building and Restoring Civic Capacity: The Obama Administration's Federal-Local Partnership with Detroit (2011–2016)," 2016, https://obamawhitehouse.archives.gov/sites/obamawhitehouse.archives.gov/files/documents/DFWG_Report_Final_120216.pdf.

10. Russ White, "Mayor Dave Bing Hopes Golden Opportunities Will Help Grow Detroit Green," MLive.com, 2010, www.mlive.com/environment/index.ssf/2010/07/detroit_mayor_dave_bing_hopes.html.

Downtown

1. Alysa Zavala, "2nd Annual Christmas Wonderfest: Traditional Treats and Convivial Commerce," *Real Detroit Weekly*, November 14, 2012, www.realdetroitweekly.com/detroit/ 2nd-annual-christmas-wonderfest/Content?oid= 1556746.

2. Gil White and Brad Garmon, "Walkable, Vibrant Cities Are Key to Michigan's Economic Recovery," *Michigan Complete Streets Coalition* (blog), June 25, 2009, https://michigancompletestreets.wordpress.com/2009/06/25/walkable-vibrant-cities-are-key-to-economic-recovery/.

3. Soji Adelaja, *Regional Strategies to Attract Industries: Coopetition for Innovation and Prosperity* (East Lansing, MI: Michigan State University, 2010).

4. Statement on Detroit Friends potato chip package. www.detroitchips.com.

5. Matt Burns, "An Interview with Dan Gilbert, Self-Made Hometown Billionaire and the Leader of the Detroit Renaissance," *TechCrunch* (blog), December 3, 2012, http://social.techcrunch.com/2012/12/03/an-interview-with-dan-gilbert-self-made-hometown-billionaire-and-the-leader-of-a-detroit-renaissance/.

6. Opportunity Detroit, "A Plan for Our Time," Detroit, 2013.

7. Kirk Pinho, "High Returns Bring Foreign Investors to Detroit Real Estate Market," *Crain's Detroit Business*, November 29, 2015, www.crainsdetroit .com/article/20151129/NEWS/311299980/high-returns-bring-foreign -investors-to-detroit-real-estate-market.

8. "2018 BE 100s," *Black Enterprise*, 2019, https://www.blackenterprise.com/ 2018-be-100s/.

9. Nancy Derringer, "Once a Gem of West Michigan, African-American Resort Community Idlewild Seeks New Identity," *Bridge Magazine*, July 18, 2013, www.mlive.com/business/2013/07/once_a_gem_african-american_re.html.

10. Dorothy Weddell, "Profile: Howard F. Sims, President, Sims-Varner & Associates Inc.," *Detroit Free Press*, accessed December 8, 2018, http://freep .newspapers.com/image/97684748/?terms=sims%2Barchitect.

11. *Detroit Future City: Design for Rapid Change* (Seattle: University of Washington, College of Built Environments, 2015), https://vimeo.com/118193552.

12. Lawrence Lessig, "Corrupt and Unequal, Both: Fighting Corruption in America and Abroad," *Fordham Law Review* 84 (2016): 445–52.

13. Brett Callwood, "Detroit's Campus Martius park wins Urban Land Institute award," *Crain's Detroit Business*, April 16, 2010, http://www.crainsdetroit .com/article/20100416/free/100419907/detroit-scampus-martius-park-wins -urban-land-institute-award (accessed 1 July 2013).

14. CSL International, "Economic Impact Study: Detroit Riverfront 2013," Plano, TX, 2013.

15. Donna Terek, *2011 Second Annual Diner En Blanc Detroit*, accessed December 26, 2018, https://vimeo.com/176992852.

16. Linda McIntire, "Miracle on Woodward Avenue," December 31, 2008, www .pps.org/article/mcintyrelanov2006.

17. Lynn Staeheli and Donald Mitchell, *The People's Property?: Power, Politics, and the Public* (New York: Routledge, 2016).

18. The Renaissance Center promotional film is available at www.youtube.com/ watch?v=h6RlUsi_-ZA, accessed February 15, 2016.

19. The Opportunity Detroit advertisement was aired during the televised World Series, www.youtube.com/watch?v=qOR3X0IU8_U, accessed February 15, 2016.

20. Louis Aguilar, "Gilbert Seals $618M Tax Incentive Package for 4 Detroit Projects," *Detroit News*, May 22, 2018, www.detroitnews.com/story/news/local/detroit-city/2018/05/22/tax-breaks-dan-gilbert-downtown-detroit-hudson-book-monroe-development/629505002/. Massachusetts Institute of Technology Planning Department of Urban Studies "Leveraging Development Incentives in Detroit," 2016, https://ocw.mit.edu/courses/urban-studies-and-planning/11-437-financing-economic-development-fall-2016/assignments/MIT_11437_DEGCReport_UpdatedJuly2017.pdf.

21. Nezar Alsayyad and Ananya Roy, "Medieval Modernity: On Citizenship and Urbanism in a Global Era," *Space and Polity* 10, no. 1 (April 2006): 1–20, https://doi.org/10.1080/13562570600796747.

22. Eric Larson, "Real Estate Value and Quality of Life Impacts of a Downtown Park," presentation at the Downtown Development District (DDD) Leading Minds Breakfast, New Orleans, LA, October 30, 2014, www.youtube.com/watch?v=OR6fxWTIMqU.

23. "Bryant Park," accessed January 5, 2019, https://bryantpark.org/index.php/about-us.

24. "Hudson-Webber Foundation," NEIdeas, accessed October 16, 2019, https://neideasdetroit.org/funders/hudson-webber-foundation-detroit/.

25. "New Economy Initiative for Southeast Michigan Announces More Than $3 Million in Grants," November 11, 2009, https://neweconomyinitiative.org/new-economy-initiative-for-southeast-michigan-announces-more-than-3-million-in-grants/.

26. Sugar Law Center, "Protesters' Rights: Detroit Michigan," Detroit, 2010.

27. City of Detroit Law Department, "Opinion of the Corporation Counsel Regarding First Amendment Rights and Regulations in City of Detroit Parks," March 26, 2015, www.aclumich.org/sites/default/files/file/CampusMartiusInterimRules.pdf.

28. Joe Guillen, "In Downtown Detroit's Campus Martius Park, Someone Will Always Be Watching You," *Detroit Free Press*, September 24, 2017, www.freep.com/story/news/local/michigan/detroit/2017/09/24/campus-martius-security-cameras-privacy-concerns/688829001/.

29. Ethan Kent, "Place Capital: The Shared Wealth That Drives Thriving Communities," 2011, www.pps.org/article/place-capital-the-shared-wealth-that-drives-thriving-communities.

30. Opportunity Detroit, "A Placemaking Vision for Downtown Detroit" (Detroit: Opportunity Detroit, 2013), http://opportunitydetroit. com/wp-content/themes/Opportunity_Detroit/assets/.

31. Complex Movements video-recorded Vanessa Hicks and other Griswold tenants in 2013 at Capitol Park; the Hicks quote is from their interview. For more information about the collective, see https://emergencemedia.org/pages/complex-movements (accessed 15 February 2016)

32. http://midtowndetroitinc.org/about-midtown-detroit-inc/who-we-are.

33. Jennifer Chen, "World's Most Underrated Cities," msnbc.com, April 7, 2011, www.nbcnews.com/id/41978106/ns/travel-destination_travel/t/worlds-most-underrated-cities/.

34. Darrell Dawsey, "Tensions Heighten in Corktown as New Arrivals Clash with the Community's Homeless Population," MLive.com, January 3, 2011, www.mlive.com/news/detroit/index.ssf/2011/01/tensions_heighten_in_corktown.html.

The Corridor

1. "Detroit Artist Market—Willis Remembered," www.youtube.com/watch?v=CROLEYysfRk.

2. Gilda Snowden, Oral history interview with Gilda Snowden, interview by Sean Marshall, April 13, 2011.

3. Gerhardus Schultink, "Land Use Planning and Open Space Preservation: Economic Impacts of Low-Density Urbanization and Urban Sprawl," *Journal of Civil, Environmental, and Architectural Engineering* 3, no. 1 (2009): 25, www.canr.msu.edu/csus/uploads/files/schultin/Economic_Impact_Farmland_Conversion.pdf.

4. Armando Delicato and Elias Khalil, *Detroit's Cass Corridor* (Charleston, SC: Arcadia Publishing, 2012).

5. George Hunter, "Revival of Detroit's Cass Corridor Crowds Out Criminals," *Detroit News*, July 12, 2016, www.detroitnews.com/story/news/local/detroit -city/2016/07/12/detroit-evolving-cass-corridor-criminals/87010800/.

6. Stephen Goodfellow, "Intervening Years between Early and Late Willis Galleries: Bastard Gallery No.1, 1978," Tribes of the Cass Corridor—Bastard Gallery, Detroit Book of the Dead 1980, accessed December 1, 2018, http:// corridortribe.com/tribes/willis_tribe/bastard_gallery_1978.htm.

7. Adrienne Maree Brown, *Emergent Strategy: Shaping Change, Changing Worlds* (Chico, CA: AK Press, 2017).

8. Benjamin Shepard, *Play, Creativity, and Social Movements: If I Can't Dance, It's Not My Revolution* (New York: Routledge, 2011).

9. Gary A. Donaldson, "A Window on Slave Culture: Dances at Congo Square in New Orleans, 1800–1862," *Journal of Negro History* 69, no. 2 (April 1, 1984): 63–72, https://doi.org/10.2307/2717598.

10. Louis Aguilar, "Detroit's Midtown District Is Booming," *Detroit News*, January 25, 2010, http://detnews.com/article/20100125/METRO/1250372.

11. Data Driven Detroit (D3) notes that the National Establishment Time-Series (NETS) may include some establishments that are no longer in operation. I paid D3 to perform the analysis.

12. Luc Boltanski and Eve Chiapello, *The New Spirit of Capitalism* (New York: Verso, 2005).

13. US Census Bureau, "Profile of General Demographic Characteristics: 2000," 2000, http://factfinder2.census.gov. US Census Bureau, "Profile of General Population and Housing Characteristics: 2010," 2010, http://factfinder2 .census.gov.

14. "Remembering Grace Lee Boggs (1915–2015): 'We Have to Change Ourselves in Order to Change the World,'" *Democracy Now!*, October 5, 2015, www .democracynow.org/2015/10/6/remembering_grace_lee_boggs_1915_2015.

15. Grace Lee Boggs, "Our Organic Intellectuals," *Boggs Center* (blog), March 14, 2010, http://boggscenter.org/our-organic-intellectuals/.

16. Grace Lee Boggs and James Boggs, "The City Is the Black Man's Land," *Monthly Review* 17, no. 11 (April 4, 1966): 35–46, https://doi.org/10.14452/ MR-017-11-1966-04_4.

17. Lisa M. Collins, "On a Roll," *Detroit Metro Times*, September 4, 2002, www .metrotimes.com/detroit/on-a-roll/Content?oid=2174436.

18. Elijah Anderson, *The Cosmopolitan Canopy: Race and Civility in Everyday Life* (New York: W. W. Norton, 2011).

The Neighborhoods

1. Ali Dirul, "Inspiring Possibilities through the Power of Solar," TedX Detroit, 2018, www.youtube.com/watch?v=jcqt9MgkWbA.

2. Mic Write, *H.O.M.E.S.—Mic Write Ft. Doss the Artist*, 2015, www.youtube .com/watch?v=kmq9M9om7oM.

3. Michael Winter, "In Detroit, Jesse Jackson Calls Urban Farming 'Cute but Foolish,'" *City Farmer News*, September 7, 2010, http://cityfarmer.info/in -detroit-jesse-jackson-calls-urban-farming-cute-but-foolish/.

4. Detroit Food Policy Council, "Public Land Sale Process in Detroit," 2012.

5. Christine E. Carmichael and Maureen H. McDonough, "Community Stories: Explaining Resistance to Street Tree-Planting Programs in Detroit, Michigan, USA," *Society and Natural Resources*, January 7, 2019, 1–18, https://doi .org/10.1080/08941920.2018.1550229.

6. Joshua Akers, Vincent Béal, and Max Rousseau, "Redefining the City and Demolishing the Rest: The Techno-Green Fix in Postcrash Cleveland, Ohio," *Environment and Planning E: Nature and Space*, June 2, 2019, https://doi.org/ 10.1177/2514848619854371.

7. Lisa M. Collins, "School of Life," *Detroit Metro Times*, November 24, 2004.

8. FoodTalksDC, "Detroit Food Stories," Storytelling, Washington, DC, FoodTalksDC, accessed December 29, 2018, www.foodtalksdc.com/ detroitfoodstories.

9. Ann R. Markusen, "City Spatial Structure, Women's Household Work, and National Urban Policy," *Signs* 5, no. 3 (1980): S23–44, www.jstor.org/stable/ 3173805.

10. Darlene Clark Hine, *Hine Sight: Black Women and the Re-construction of American History* (Bloomington: Indiana University Press, 1997).

11. Dorceta E. Taylor, *The State of Diversity in Environmental Organizations* (Ann Arbor: University of Michigan, School of Natural Resources and Environment, 2014).

12. "Behind the Rise and Fall of Growing Power," Civil Eats, March 13, 2018, https://civileats.com/2018/03/13/behind-the-rise-and-fall-of-growing-power/.

The Transnational

1. "Program Book—US Social Forum 2010," *Issuu*, accessed July 7, 2018, https://issuu.com/ussocialforum/docs/ussf2010-program.

2. John Trudell, "I'm Crazy?," accessed December 1, 2018, Detroit, 2010, Speech at USSF 2010, www.youtube.com/watch?v=ctUecTdPEO0.

3. Sacramento Knoxx, *Sacramento Knoxx Featuring John Trudell—"Our Fantastic World*," accessed December 1, 2018, Remix of John Trudell speech at USSF 2010, Detroit, 2010, www.youtube.com/watch?v=b_HMlo6f-O8.

Detroit Works Begins

1. Joseph Nevadomsky, Natalie Lawson, and Ken Hazlett, "An Ethnographic and Space Syntax Analysis of Benin Kingdom Nobility Architecture," *African Archaeological Review* 31, no. 1 (March 2014): 59–85, https://doi.org/10.1007/s10437-014-9151-x.

2. Hubert Massey, "Charles H. Wright Museum of African-American History—Hubert Massey Murals," September 6, 2016, https://hubertmasseymurals.net/2016/09/charles-h-wright-museum-of-african-american-history/.

3. Nancy Kaffer, "Detroit Mayor Dave Bing urged to keep land-use plan process open," *Crain's Detroit Business*, May 19, 2010. Retrieved from http://www.crainsdetroit.com/article/20100519C03/305199993/detroit-mayor-dave-bing-urged-to-keep-land-use-plan-processopen.

4. Sherrie Welch, "Kresge to Begin Making Grants to Fuel Future City Changes by Summer," *Crain's Detroit Business*, January 14, 2013, www.crainsdetroit.com/assets/PDF/CD84987111.PDF. "Ford Foundation Awards $1.5 Million to University of Detroit Mercy to Design Civic Engagement Process," *Philanthropy News Digest* (PND), accessed August 18, 2018, http://philanthropynewsdigest.org/news/ford-foundation-awards-1.5-million-to-university-of-detroit-mercy-to-design-civic-engagement-process.

5. S'bu Zikode, "We Are the Third Force," *Abahlali BaseMjondolo* (blog), accessed January 5, 2019, http://abahlali.org/node/17/.

6. D. K. Kim and J. L. Jackson, "Democracy's Anxious Returns," *ANNALS of the American Academy of Political and Social Science* 637, no. 1 (2011): 6–16, www.academia.edu/4315668/Introduction_Democracy_s_Anxious _Returns.

Phase One

1. Christine MacDonald, "Secrecy an Issue in Plan to Reshape Detroit: Meeting, Contract Openness Are Questioned as Effort Proceeds," *Detroit News*, January 21, 2011, sec. Metro.

2. Mark Purcell, *Recapturing Democracy: Neoliberalization and the Struggle for Alternative Urban Futures* (New York: Routledge, 2008), 27.

3. Detroit Works Project, "Close-Ended Feedback Summary: Cluster-Based Meetings, January 2011–March 2011." Detroit, 2011.

4. Detroit Works Project, "Cluster-Based Meetings Verbatim Comments, January 2011–March 2011." Detroit, 2011.

5. Mark Guarino, "Retooling the Motor City: Can Detroit Save Itself?" *Christian Science Monitor*, July 23, 2011, www.csmonitor.com/Business/2011/0723/Retooling-the-Motor-City-Can-Detroit-save-itself.

6. People's Movement Assembly, *People's Response to Detroit Works Project*, accessed December 1, 2018, Detroit, 2010, www.youtube.com/watch?time _continue=8&v=Y0E7lJut3e0&feature=emb_logo.

Phase Two

1. Matthew Dolan, "Revival Bid Pits Detroit vs. Donor," *Wall Street Journal*, July 2, 2011, sec. US, www.wsj.com/articles/SB10001424052702304887904576397760319014524.

2. "Architecture Program Report" (Detroit: University of Detroit Mercy, School of Architecture, August 2013), http://architecture.udmercy.edu/programs/files/Architecture-Program-Report-2013.pdf.

3. Grace Lee Boggs, "These Are the Times That Grow Our Souls," *Animating Democracy*, 2003, 11.

4. Kyong Park, "Adamah," Vimeo, accessed January 22, 2019, https://vimeo.com/9609433.

5. Kresge Foundation, "Kresge Annual Report," 2009, https://kresge.org/library/2009-kresge-annual-report. Nancy Kaffer, "Foundations, City at Brink of Plan to Shrink Detroit," *Crain's Detroit Business*, January 24, 2010, www.crainsdetroit.com/article/20100124/SUB01/301249965/foundations-city-at-brink-of-plan-to-shrink-detroit.

6. Dan Kinkead, "HAA Research: Consolidating Detroit," December 5, 2009, www.roguehaa.com/haa-research-consolidating-detroit/.

7. Deborah Popper and Frank J. Popper, "Small Can Be Beautiful," *Journal of Planning Literature* 17, no. 2 (2002): 262–331.

8. John Gallagher, *Reimagining Detroit: Opportunities for Redefining an American City* (Detroit: Wayne State University Press, 2010).

9. Roger Starr, "Making New York Smaller," *New York Times*, November 14, 1976, sec. Archives, www.nytimes.com/1976/11/14/archives/making-new-york-smaller-the-citys-economic-outlook-remains-grim.html.

10. Joseph P. Fried, "City's Housing Administrator Proposes 'Planned Shrinkage' of Some Slums," *New York Times*, 1976.

11. Mary Breasted, "Congress Passes a Bill to Aid Urban Gardens," *New York Times*, July 7, 1976, sec. Archives, www.nytimes.com/1976/07/07/archives/congress-passes-a-bill-to-aid-urban-gardens.html.

12. Detroit Works Project, *Who Is Detroit?* Detroit, 2012, www.youtube.com/watch?v=3tF-InoBb8k.

13. Jonathan Oosting, "Past mistakes, future hopes: Detroit Works looks to win over residents, reimagine city," *M-Live*, December 19, 2011. Retrieved from http://www.mlive.com/news/detroit/index.ssf/2011/12/past_mistakes_future_hopes_det.html.

14. Toni Griffin, "Detroit Works Project," presentation at Michigan State University, East Lansing, MI, October 21, 2013.

15. *Detroit Future City: Design for Rapid Change* (Seattle: University of Washington, College of Built Environments, 2015), https://vimeo.com/118193552. [Note: An architect on the Detroit Works team mentions the plan to "right-size" between 34:00 and 35:00 on the video.]

16. M. Dittmer and A. G. Deines, "Civic Engagement: Multiple Scales of Public Exchange," *Dichotomy: School of Architecture Student Journal* 17 (2011): 10–27.

17. DFC, "Detroit Future City," Detroit, 2012.

18. DFC, "Detroit Future City."

19. Heaster Wheeler and Alice Thompson, "No Debate, Detroit Future City Is the People's Plan," April 3, 2013, www.mlive.com/news/detroit/index.ssf/2014/04/commentary_no_debate_detroit_f.html.

20. Barbara Brown Wilson, *Resilience for All: Striving for Equity through Community-Driven Design* (Washington, DC: Island Press, 2018).

21. Sierra Club, "The State of Detroit`s Environment," 2013, https://studyres.com/doc/23404868/the-state-of-detroit-s-environment.

22. DFC, "Detroit Future City."

23. Project for Public Spaces, "Detroiters Work: The Lighter, Quicker, Cheaper Regeneration of a Great American City," 2013, www.pps.org/article/detroiters-work-the-lighter-quicker-cheaper-regeneration-of-a-great-american-city.

24. Wayne County Clerk's Office, "November 5, 2013 General Election Results," Detroit, 2013, www.waynecounty.com/elected/clerk/november-5-2013-general.aspx. Khalil Alhajal, "Detroit's 25-Percent Voter Turnout Was Higher Than New York, Miami and Other Major Cities," mlive.com, November 7, 2013, www.mlive.com/news/detroit/2013/11/detroits_25-percent_voter_turn.html.

Side Conversations

1. Detroit Food Policy Council, "Public Land Sale Process in Detroit," 2012.

2. Adrienne Maree Brown, "How Is Whole Foods Thriving in Detroit?" *Salon*, August 29, 2013, www.salon.com/2013/08/29/how_is_whole_foods_thriving_in_detroit/.

3. "Detroit People's Platform: Updated HB5977 ACTION," December 8, 2014, http://detroitpeoplesplatform.org/2014/12/08/.

4. "One Year Later, How Is Detroit's Community Benefits Ordinance Working Out?" *Detroit Today*, Detroit, WDET, January 18, 2018, https://wdet.org/posts/2018/01/18/86280-one-year-later-how-is-detroits-community-benefits-ordinance-working-out/.

"Co-Creating the Good" in the "Just City"

1. Elizabeth Rapoport, "Globalising Sustainable Urbanism: The Role of International Masterplanners," *Area* 47, no. 2 (June 2015): 110–15, https://doi.org/10.1111/area.12079. Stephen Ward, "A Pioneer 'Global Intelligence Corps'?: The Internationalisation of Planning Practice, 1890–1939," *Town Planning Review* 76, no. 2 (June 1, 2005): 119–41, https://doi.org/10.3828/tpr.76.2.2.

2. Elizabeth Rapoport and Anna Hult, "The Travelling Business of Sustainable Urbanism: International Consultants as Norm-Setters," *Environment and Planning A: Economy and Space* 49, no. 8 (August 2017): 1779–96, https://doi.org/10.1177/0308518X16686069.

3. Richard Sommer, "Beyond Centers, Fabrics, and Cultures of Congestion: Urban Design as a Metropolitan Enterprise," in *Urban Design*, ed. Alex Krieger and William S. Saunders (Minneapolis: University of Minnesota Press, 2009).

4. Neil Brenner and Christian Schmid, "Towards a New Epistemology of the Urban?" *City* 19, no. 2–3 (May 4, 2015): 151–82, https://doi.org/10.1080/13604813.2015.1014712.

5. Mimi Zeiger, "Remembering Whitney M. Young Jr.'s Landmark Speech," *Architect*, 2018, www.architectmagazine.com/practice/remembering-whitney-m-young-jrs-landmark-speech_o.

6. Sharon E. Sutton, *When Ivory Towers Were Black: A Story about Race in America's Cities and Universities* (New York: Oxford University Press, 2017).

7. Brian D. Goldstein, *The Roots of Urban Renaissance* (Cambridge, MA: Harvard University Press, 2017), 62.

8. Cynthia Smith, "Planning and Designing Beyond Equity in Cities Across America," *Cooper Hewitt*, February 20, 2017, https://www.cooperhewitt.org/2017/02/20/22454/

9. Fannie Lou Hamer, *The Speeches of Fannie Lou Hamer: To Tell It like It Is* (Jackson: University Press of Mississippi, 2011).

10. Nelson Mandela, *Long Walk to Freedom: The Autobiography of Nelson Mandela* (Boston: Little, Brown, 2008).

11. Mogobe B. Ramose, "An African Perspective on Justice and Race," *Polylog*, 2001, https://them.polylog.org/3/frm-en.htm.

12. Martin Luther King Jr., "Letter from Birmingham Jail," The Martin Luther King Jr. Research and Education Institute, May 17, 2017, https://kinginstitute .stanford.edu/encyclopedia/letter-birmingham-jail.

13. Office of the High Commissioner for Human Rights, United Nations, "Detroit: Disconnecting Water from People Who Cannot Pay—an Affront to Human Rights, Say UN Experts," June 25, 2014, www.ohchr.org/EN/ NewsEvents/Pages/DisplayNews.aspx?NewsID=14777.

14. Emergence Media, *Charity Hicks: Wage Love*, 2014, https://vimeo.com/ 101035835.

15. Will Jarvis, "Controversial Ex-Governor Is Out as Harvard Fellow, Days after He Was Appointed," *Chronicle of Higher Education*, July 3, 2019, www.chronicle.com/article/Controversial-Ex-Governor-Is/246611.

Justice-Speak in City Plans

1. Megan E. Heim LaFrombois, Yunmi Park, and Daniel Yurcaba, "How U.S. Shrinking Cities Plan for Change: Comparing Population Projections and Planning Strategies in Depopulating U.S. Cities," *Journal of Planning Education and Research*, June 23, 2019, https://doi.org/10.1177/ 0739456X19854121.

2. Kent E. Portney, *Taking Sustainable Cities Seriously* (Cambridge, MA: MIT Press, 2016).

3. Susan M. Opp and Kyle L. Saunders, "Pillar Talk: Local Sustainability Initiatives and Policies in the United States—Finding Evidence of the 'Three E's': Economic Development, Environmental Protection, and Social Equity," *Urban Affairs Review* 49, no. 5 (September 1, 2013): 678–717, https://doi.org/ 10.1177/1078087412469344.

4. Greg Schrock, Ellen M. Bassett, and Jamaal Green, "Pursuing Equity and Justice in a Changing Climate: Assessing Equity in Local Climate and Sustainability Plans in U.S. Cities," *Journal of Planning Education and Research* 35, no. 3 (September 1, 2015): 282–95, https://doi.org/10.1177/ 0739456X15580022.

5. Philip R. Berke and Maria Manta Conroy, "Are We Planning for Sustainable Development?" *Journal of the American Planning Association* 66, no. 1

(Winter 2000): 21–33, https://stanford.idm.oclc.org/login?url=https://search
.ebscohost.com/login.aspx?direct=true&db=aph&AN=2989497&site=ehost
-live&scope=site.

6. Julian Agyeman, *Sustainable Communities and the Challenge of Environmental Justice* (New York: New York University Press, 2005).

7. Julian Agyeman and Bob Evans, "'Just Sustainability': The Emerging Discourse of Environmental Justice in Britain?" *Geographical Journal* 170, no. 2 (2004): 155–64, www.jstor.org/stable/3451592.

8. Carol Gilligan, "Mapping the Moral Domain: New Images of Self in Relationship," *CrossCurrents* 39, no. 1 (1989): 50–63, www.jstor.org/stable/24459760.

9. Elliot Jaspin, *Buried in the Bitter Waters: The Hidden History of Racial Cleansing in America* (New York: Basic Books, 2008).

10. NAACP, "Travel Advisory for the State of Missouri," August 2, 2017, www.naacp.org/latest/travel-advisory-state-missouri/.

The Black Empire Strikes Back

1. "Interview with Dave Bing," No BS News Hour with Charlie LeDuff, June 2, 2019, https://www.nobsnewshour.com/no-bs-news-hour-june-2nd-2019/.

2. Bankole Thompson, "Ex-Mayor Bing's Black Leadership Message Fails," *Detroit News*, June 5, 2019, www.detroitnews.com/story/opinion/columnists/bankole-thompson/2019/06/06/bankole-ex-mayor-bings-black-leadership-message-fails/1351032001/.

Listen to the Rain

1. Opportunity Detroit, *A Placemaking Vision for Downtown Detroit* (Detroit: Opportunity Detroit, 2013), http://opportunitydetroit.com/wp-content/themes/Opportunity_Detroit/assets/.

Appendix: Methods

1. Laura L. Ellingson, *Engaging Crystallization in Qualitative Research: An Introduction* (Los Angeles: Sage, 2009).

2. Tamara Mose Brown and Erynn Masi de Casanova, "Representing the Language of the 'Other': African American Vernacular English in Ethnography,"

Ethnography 15, no. 2 (June 1, 2014): 208–31, https://doi.org/10.1177/1466138112471110.

3. Michael Burawoy et al., *Global Ethnography: Forces, Connections, and Imaginations in a Postmodern World* (Berkeley: University of California Press, 2000).

4. I selected the top five whitest large cities from the US Census brief, *The White Population 2010*; I used a study that ranked large cities based on the policy preferences of residents to identify the seven most conservative cities (Chris Tausanovitch and Christopher Warshaw, "Representation in Municipal Government," *American Political Science Review* 108, no. 3 [2014]); I chose severely depopulated, majority white cities with at least 50,000 residents from a list in a federal policy brief (Alan Mallach, *Facing the Urban Challenge: The Federal Government and America's Older Distressed Cities*, Brookings Institution Metropolitan Policy Program, 2010).

Index

Page numbers in *italics* refer to images.

www.ingramcontent.com/pod-product-compliance
Lightning Source LLC
Chambersburg PA
CBHW050334270326
41926CB00016B/3456